TRIUMPHS AND TRAGEDIES . . .

Susan Hayward, Hollywood's Divine Bitch and a feminist before the fashion, lived a life to pale even her great screen roles.

The fiery redhead started her drive to achieve early, fixing hazel eyes on a motion-picture career but filling in with jobs as diverse as modeling and delivering newspapers. She was brought to the film capital to test for Scarlett O'Hara in *Gone With the Wind,* lost the part but stayed on to win five Academy Award nominations and finally the Oscar itself.

In the interim there were two marriages—one unhappy, one blissful—and twin sons—one blonde, one redheaded—and a constantly surfacing strife that persisted to her last day.

The triumphs and tragedies, the many facets of her complicated personality—all are here in this first book ever on one of the first ladies of movies' Golden Age: Susan Hayward.

The Complete Life Story of Susan Hayward

...Immortal Screen Star

by Doug McClelland

PINNACLE BOOKS • NEW YORK CITY

For my parents, Elna and Dick

SUSAN HAYWARD:
ACTRESS OF INFINITE VARIETY

Copyright © 1973, 1975 by Doug McClelland

An original Pinnacle Books edition, formerly titled
SUSAN HAYWARD: THE DIVINE BITCH,
published for the first time anywhere.

ISBN: 0-523-00706-X

First printing, November 1973
Second printing, August 1975

Printed in the United States of America

PINNACLE BOOKS, INC.
275 Madison Avenue
New York, N. Y. 10016

CONTENTS

PROLOGUE

SUSAN HAYWARD, ONE OF THE BEST
By George Marshall*

My first thoughts about Susan Hayward, of course, are about her ability as an actress. To me, she is one of the best, because her emotions stem from the inside and are not just the mouthings of an inadequate actress who reads lines without the slightest idea of what they mean. Susan knows her craft. She also has sincerity and courage, and at times can be a bit stubborn, but not to the point of being disagreeable.

Her courage turned up on *The Forest Rangers,* which I directed early in her career.

If you saw it, you remember the part where she and Paulette Goddard had to run through some fire. Paulette got scared, and in spite of our showing her all the safety factors and how impossible it was for her to be injured or burned, she still backed off and started to cry. I really think that she had a date and wanted to get off early. Susan came up to me and whispered, "Get the cameras going." Then she went over to Paulette, as though to comfort her. When I gave her the signal, she grabbed Paulette by the hand and said "For God's sake, stop being such a baby!" and pulled her through the scene. Iron-

*In films since 1913, and still active, George Marshall estimates that he has directed over four hundred pictures, including Susan Hayward's *The Forest Rangers, Star Spangled Rhythm,* and *Tap Roots.*

ically, in the story it was Susan who was supposed to become frightened.

Several years later on another film, *Tap Roots*, some of that stubbornness came to life.

The scene, in a way, was rather clichéd, but it played an important part in the plot. Susan was in a wheelchair, since she was not supposed to be able to walk. The character played by Van Heflin thought that she could and was intent upon proving it. He felt that if he could make her mad enough, she would get up.

The first take was a real dud. She played it almost apathetically, and here is where our wills clashed for the first time. She felt that she should play the scene in this deadened form, while I knew that it had to be explosive to be in contrast to everything she had done before. I explained this to her and told her to get loosened up. She could do better than she had shown. The next take was a little better, but not much. This time I just said, "Shall we try again?"

I don't know, maybe it was because she was tired. These stars do have to get up pretty early in the morning to get ready for the day—sometimes around four-thirty or five A.M. Or perhaps it was just that she was determined to play the thing without emotion.

Van was quite a help, and on the next take his needling had more fire than before. It helped a little, but she still had not reached the peak I needed. So, after a couple more attempts, I tried the sarcastic approach. I turned to Van and said, "Well, it's the old story—some people have it and some don't. But let's try again." Well, I can tell you that all the fire under that red head came ablaze on the next take and it ended almost in a scream, which was exactly what I wanted. When the camera was cut she shouted at me, "I suppose you are going to tell me that is what you wanted!" I added insult to injury by saying, "Fine, Susie, just fine. I really didn't think you could do it."

She burst into tears, called me a miserable # @ * % & ¢,

and ran to her dressing room. She was back in a little while after she had fixed her face, to give me a big kiss and say, "I'm sorry. I knew in my heart what you wanted. I just didn't want to give in. But I still think you are a miserable #@*%&¢!"

Susan has always been one of my favorite people. Some of the other reasons follow.

FOREWORD

In 1958 Robert Wise, director of *I Want to Live!* starring Susan Hayward, said: "In motion pictures, Susan Hayward is as important a figure as Sarah Bernhardt was to the stage. Somewhere within her is a chemical combination that can excite and hold audiences as surely as Garbo and very few other greats of the screen. Susan is one of two or three actresses who can hold up a picture all by myself."

This is not a biography of Susan Hayward, whom I have met only from my enchanted seat on the aisle. It is a critical study of her long career—most particularly her many films—and that "chemical combination" that sets her apart. Call it a "critography." Biography enters only when it has a bearing on Susan Hayward's art. En route, this is also a look at a period in Hollywood movie history when there was only one way to be "relevant"— be entertaining.

For their help, thanks to: Bernie Bennett; Bruco Enterprises; Loraine Burdick; Caesar's Palace; Cinemabilia; Collectors Book Store; John Cocchi; Donald Darroch; Homer Dickens; Donald Dickstein; Charlie Earle; David Finkle; Bob Freund; Esther Katz; Larry Edmunds Bookshop; Tony Lawrence; Candy Leigh; Leonard Maltin; Alvin H. Marill; Clifford McCarty; Dion McGregor; Memory Shop; the Miami *Herald;* the Miami *News;* Movie Poster Service; Movie Star News; James Robert Parish; Bill Pratt; Bea Smith; Malcolm G. Smith; the staff and Theater Collection, Library and Museum of Performing Arts, Lincoln Center; Lou Valentino; and Lois Wilson.

Particular thanks to George Marshall for his prologue, written especially for this book; and to Bill O'Connell for his satirical epilogue, reprinted with the permission of the author and the Pace College *Push,* where it first appeared in 1970. Plus, those who have provided the new quotes and information for the text and who are named there.

The most thanks, though, to Jim Meyer, whose great and very special help made this book possible.

D. McC.,
New York City

I

THE BATTLE

Millie Pickens: Say, if I had a wad of folding dough like that I'd go right out and buy an outfit that would knock this neighborhood cockeyed!

—*Among the Living*

1.   UP THROUGH THE CEMENT

The film *Ada,* released in the early 1960s, was, despite its faults, quintessential Susan Hayward that contained the following exchange:

Dean Martin: "I'll bet you were a tough little girl."

Hayward (playing a not altogether fictional prostitute-turned-governor): "I'm a tough *big* one!"

In a career that has spanned almost four decades, including many of the most popular pictures of all time, actress Hayward—"whose perfect profile," Hedda Hopper once reported, "goes clear down to the ankles"—received virtually every major award for film acting. She scored especially in tempestuous real-life reel lives with a blowtorch technique that seared the memory. She was equally unstinting in her portrayal of Susan Hayward.

An ex-press agent of hers opined that the imp-faced veteran of almost seventy film appearances went through life "with her fists up." In a 1959 *Variety* notice, a writer said that Hayward was one of the few actresses left whose eyes could still flash. Sometimes, as several years later in that paean to pill-popping, *Valley of the Dolls,* it is hard to tell where Hayward leaves off and the role begins: "Miss Hayward epitomizes the indestructible star whose razor-sharp tongue and stainless steel claws preclude the need for capsulated crutches. She is memorable," wrote the *Hollywood Reporter*'s man.

"The Divine Bitch" as another reviewer alluding to her demiheroine screen persona divined her, was born Edythe Marrener in a Church Avenue and East Thirty-fifth Street tenement in Brooklyn, New York, on June 30, 1918 (also given, variously, as 1917, 1919 and 1920), the third child of Walter and Ellen Marrener. Florence was the eldest, and frail Walter, Jr., was next. Hayward's glib, personable, but ultimately disabled father worked mostly as a subway guard, but he is said to have also worked in vaudeville and as a barker at nearby Coney Island in his youth. Hayward inherited his hazel eyes, red hair, and theatrical bent. She was her father's favorite because she resembled his mother, Kate Harrigan, who had been an actress in Ireland. Susan's own mother was of Swedish descent, a stern woman with a highly volatile nature that she passed on to her youngest. According to astrology (which Hayward has long followed, says Hollywood astrologer Carroll Righter), Susan was a "moon child"—one of those born between June 22 and July 22 and charted as emotional and creative, outwardly tough, inwardly sensitive, and old in their youth but young when they mature.

One critic put it all another way: "Susan combines the hard-headedness of the Swedes, the witchery and recalcitrance of the Irish, and the boisterousness of Brooklyn."

Her mother, by then a tired-looking woman little resembling her coruscating daughter, died in the late 1950s. In bitter revelations a couple of years later, onetime model and Broadway chorus girl Florence, with whom Hayward had not been friendly for years, announced that her second husband had left her and she was on relief, fighting alone to keep her son and baby girl from being taken away from her. Furthermore, Florence asserted, her mother's ashes were still in a cardboard box with a vault number attached to them, and it was a pity that Hayward wouldn't have them put in a proper urn and sent back home to New York. Hayward's feelings on all this remain unknown. There is no public record of any resolution of the matter, but sister Florence's own publicly venomous story suggested she herself was no lily.

While Hayward's brother Walter (Wally), who is married and was once a theater and sports arena usher, is scarcely known to his movie star sister's crowd, he was much closer to her than Florence was. In later years they were seen out dining together and Hayward talked of their plans to travel together.

Her strife began early, as did the creative urge, fanned by necessity. When she had just started school she was struck by a car that fractured both her legs and dislocated a hip, immobilizing the child in casts for some time. For months her mother had to pull her in a little wagon to P.S. 181, where she hobbled from room to room on crutches. Drawing came naturally to her and became an important pastime, as painting did in later years. The gritty tyke's recovery was so complete that many years later she sang and danced one of the contemporary theater's most exhausting musical comedy roles, *Mame*.

While not a churchgoer, Hayward professed in a mid-1950s *Photoplay* interview called "Brooklyn's Child is Full of Faith" that faith had seen her through many difficult times:

"Ever since I was a little girl, I have always believed what my father told me. 'Edie,' he would say, 'as long as you believe, an angel sits on your shoulder and looks after you.' As I grew older, that angel became less real, it became more of a symbol of God, of a beneficent power, whatever you want to call it. As long as I believed in it, no problem seemed too big for me to meet, no day seemed without hope. Only when I forgot to believe, when I failed to trust, did I despair and permit the problems of career, of maintaining a home for my two children, of personal frustrations to overcome.

"My father taught me from childhood to fight for whatever I believed in. He was always saying, 'You must be like a rubber ball. The harder they hit, the higher you'll bounce. That is, if you're a good ball to start with. And if you're not, you might as well give up anyway.'

"And mother—it was she who believed I could do

7

anything I set my mind to. It was she, too, who always fought our inclinations as youngsters to say, 'I can't do this, or I can't do that,' by telling us not to say we can't do a thing, because of course we could do anything anyone else could.

"My grandmother came from County Cork, and she once told me she had actually dreamed about the man she was going to marry. She just knew it was he. Well, she met him and married him—that's how much faith *she* had. I remember, too, the stories my mother used to tell me about my brother Wally's illness. As an infant he had a serious abdominal condition—an obstruction that made it all but impossible for him to retain food. My mother took care of him herself, virtually breathed life into him again. At two he weighed only seven pounds. The illness had left his legs weak and he had to wear braces. One day it was time to get new braces so she took Wally in her arms and got on a streetcar to go downtown. On the streetcar mother noticed a woman in the seat opposite glancing over sympathetically. 'You look troubled,' said the woman to my mother. 'I am indeed,' said my mother, and poured out her heart about Wally's illness.

"Then the stranger said, 'Take off the braces; he will be all right.' And you know something? My mother knew then that Wally would live and be strong and well. Do you see now why we have always felt that for us the omens were right?"

At twelve, around the time the Marreners moved to Bedford Avenue, Hayward had the distinction of being the first female newsboy hired by the Brooklyn *Eagle*. Jealous boy competitors tied tin cans to her borrowed bike, among other methods devised to discourage her. But nothing stopped her from getting those newspapers through.

In the early 1950s she apprised: "I was brought up on the installment plan, which is one reason why I can't go one cent into debt for anything now. Back in Brooklyn, we'd have a nice new icebox for a few months, and then someone would come and take it away. Or we'd have a beautiful new stove until those same men came back and we'd have to go down to the corner and buy a second-hand one for three dollars.

"We were always poor. If I got my dress dirty, we didn't have enough money to get it cleaned. If my shoes were worn out, I had to stuff cardboard in them. I played near the Gowanus Canal. There was a wonderful odor of gas tanks and fish—sometimes, I have to admit, I get homesick for it. We were like the Nolan family in *A Tree Grows in Brooklyn*. In fact, we *were* the Nolans, and I was the adolescent, dreamy Francie Nolan—who, like the lone tree outside her fire escape window, Francie's adored, n'er-do-well father promised, couldn't be stopped from 'bustin' right through the cement and growin'.'

"My kids will never know the games I played in my pigtail days in Brooklyn," continued Hayward. "Calendars were for the birds. We didn't tell seasons by them. There was the 'immy' season when you played marbles —we called them 'immies.' And the bottletop season when we traded bottletops, and the steal-the-ice-from-the-iceman season. We had the baseball card season, when we collected pictures of baseball players, and the kite-flying season—my father was wonderful at this; he loved to build all kinds of kites.

"But my favorite was the selling-old-newspapers-to-the-junkman season. You slipped as many flat rocks as you could in between the layers of papers to make them weigh more. And if a rock slipped out, the junkman got mad, called you terrible names and chased you out of his yard. Oh, there was the Thanksgiving-singing season, when we'd dress up in old clothes and sing beneath the windows. The grown-ups were supposed to throw pennies down. Sometimes, old witches would throw down heated pennies and when we ran to pick them up, they'd burn our fingers.

9

"We played games, but we also learned to fight. In my neighborhood, it was the survival of the fightingest. We learned to land on our feet."

More recently, she called Brooklyn "one of the places that's great to have been born in and just as great to leave. Being born in Brooklyn is some kind of common denominator with stars. I guess it represents a sense of struggle and, when you leave it, a sense of achievement. Yet, when you come from there you feel you have roots."

2. "I WANTED OUT!"

In her book, *A Life on Film*, Mary Astor wrote of Hollywood at work during the Depression: "We were the hope peddlers—we pushed it in all sorts of brightly colored capsules . . . People didn't kick the habit for years."

Edie Marrener got hooked early. She enjoyed "escaping" at the movies and hoped desperately to be an actress—"I wanted out!" The older brother of a childhood girlfriend remembers her as "the neighborhood sweetheart." The dainty youngster performed in living room productions and school plays, specializing in witches and old ladies "because," she has said, "they were challenging parts." Inspired by Miss Florence O'Grady, her English teacher at Girls Commercial High (now called Prospect Heights High), "and all the others who drummed 'Achieve. Achieve!' " she also entered local talent contests. Her high school yearbook called her "The Class Actress." According to an old biographical sketch that had a faint sheen of movie studio refinish, as well as sounding like one of Hayward's own later scripts: "Ever practical, she had studied dress designing and stenography at school. Once she was preparing a design for a commercial art competition there when a friend

10

carelessly splattered water on it. With quick courage, Susan embellished the pattern of the water marks so cleverly she won the prize—seventy-five dollars. Upon graduation she was employed by a dress designing firm [another source called it a handkerchief factory] and within four months worked up to the position of head designer. But it didn't last long. The designs by Hayward were considered too unconventional by her boss."

She had been trying to crash the theater all the while, anyway.

More than a few mornings she arrived in the city for a day's job-hunting with nothing but subway fare home in her purse. "When the stuck-up secretaries in the theatrical agencies asked me what experience I'd had, I didn't even have to answer. All they had to do was look at my cheap camel's hair coat, the beanie I'd made myself, and my face without make-up. Naturally, I never got beyond the reception room," Hayward had admitted. She had done some modeling in early adolescence, though, and these jobs came more easily. Never losing sight of her original goal, she attended Manhattan's Feagan Drama School on a one-term scholarship. Her first time before movie cameras was for a 1936 Vitaphone "Pictorial Short" in which she was seen as—a New York model.

Before long, the family moved to the other side of Flatbush, Avenue D—"where they had trees."

Commercial artist Jon Whitcomb was around then. "Susan had a kind of self-confidence that made you remember her"—his affection for her, legend has it, caused all his popular "Whitcomb girls" to resemble Hayward. "The first time I saw her, she swept into the studio as if she owned the place. Soon after she was in demand, modeling through Walter Thornton's agency. Long before such catchphrases as 'positive thinking' were in vogue, she was using it to propel herself to fame." Thornton himself knew her as "a real lone wolf, a girl with no time for friends or social life."

In 1953, Associated Press correspondent Bob Thomas

11

noted: "When actresses win awards they usually thank everyone from their producers to their prop men. If Susan Hayward ever wins an Academy Award—and her adherents say that's a certainty—it would be fitting and proper for her to thank only a Brooklyn girl named Edythe Marrener. That's Miss Hayward's real name. The flame-haired actress has achieved film stardom mainly through her own efforts, and she probably would be the first to admit it. She is volcanic, realistic, and, above all, frank."

Even after she had attained stardom Hayward liked her privacy, especially after working the six-day week of pre-Screen Actors Guild days. One Hollywood couple she and her first husband, actor Jess Barker, knew paid two surprise visits to their home, but on the third Sunday Hayward spouted, "Didn't you see the 'no admittance' sign?" The pair never called again.

Barker himself has called her an enigma. As did Eddie Albert, who convincingly played some very intimate scenes with Hayward in probably her two best films, *Smash-Up, The Story of a Woman* and *I'll Cry Tomorrow*. "While it is true I made two pictures with Susan Hayward, I can't help you at all with your book. She was a very private person and, outside of an occasional 'Good morning,' I had no contact with her whatever," he wrote me—although photos were published showing Albert, his wife Margo, who was also in *Tomorrow,* and Hayward absorbed in conversation on the set between scenes.

Michael Gordon, director of her archetypal *I Can Get It for You Wholesale* in 1951, concurs with Albert. "To say that Susan was a highly talented and able actress would be merely to state the obvious," he began in a letter to me. "She prepared conscientiously and worked with exemplary concentration not only when the cameras were rolling but during rehearsals as well. In a word, she was thoroughly professional in the best sense of the word. While I have reason to believe she enjoyed working with

12

me as much as I did her, our relationship remained pretty much on that level. One of the characteristics of Susan that I remember very distinctly was her strong sense of personal reserve that discouraged any probing into her private life or feelings—past or present—that didn't have a direct bearing on the business at hand. As a consequence, I knew her less intimately than almost any actress I've ever worked with for that length of time. I don't recall that this impeded the work to any appreciable degree, but our collaboration remained precisely that; it never developed into what could be accurately described as a friendship."

A more total conservatism was indicated recently by Jim Backus, who was featured in her 1957 comedy, *Top Secret Affair*. "Most of my scenes were with Kirk Douglas," he prefaced. "We shot the picture at Warner Brothers and Susan, of course, was a top star by then. She's an extremely beautiful girl. It was, as they say, a very pleasant engagement. She didn't do any unnecessary screaming. The only thing she insisted on was stopping work one day when President Eisenhower landed at Burbank Airport so she could go and watch him. So I guess she is a card-carrying Republican. I *know* she was one of our better actresses. She had great intensity."

She tended to look at a stranger with head slightly lowered and eyes blazing straight ahead, much like a welterweight looking for an opening through which to spring.

"When I am vacationing, I want to vacation. When I am working, I want to work," an early '50s Hayward told a reporter. "I don't like a picture on which I work a couple of days and then am off for a couple. I want to work every day. I'm jealous of the other actors. Some day I'll do a picture in which I play all the roles."

Twenty years later, she confessed to the Los Angeles *Herald-Examiner:* "I never much thought of myself as an 'artiste.' I'm a working actress, and, I think, a good one; but what I'm really interested in is the chance to get

13

out there and make-believe. Actors are like children, you know; we still like to dress up and play house. I never really cared for any of the star trappings—not the big premieres, the fancy parties, or the fame.* I don't even like doing interviews.

"There used to be a lady columnist** in this town— I won't tell you who it was because she's still alive— who sent me up the wall every time she visited my set. She'd ask a question and there was nothing to do but belt her in the mouth. But I learned how to deal with her. I'd just tell her the most outlandish lies about myself and she'd print them."

In a '56 *Redbook* Cameron Shipp put down that she "brightens when audiences applaud, and she enjoys dining in expensive showplaces. She makes grand entrances, but poor exits. There are no trailing scarves for Susan, no radiant smiles as she leaves a night club or a restaurant. She hurries out, almost furtively. . . . Although she is one of the hardest workers on the screen today, she will sleep until noon every day, if she can. She combines enormous energy with a touch of laziness. No sentiment, no nonsense is apparent; if it is there, Susan hides it. In marked contrast to stars like Joan Crawford (who thinks she invented Christmas), Susan does not shower friends with expensive gifts. She does not even send Christmas cards.

"She is cautious. Once Susan had savings accounts in nine Los Angeles banks."

There was a time while studying at Feagan's when the very young Hayward let down her guard and set out to elope by subway with her equally callow boyfriend. "The elopement fizzled when we reached Times Square and he wired his father in Pennsylvania for money, mean-

---

*Even though her footprints embedded in cement in the courtyard of Hollywood's Grauman's Chinese Theater are unique even for the biggest of stars—they're etched in gold dust.

**Probably Sheilah Graham.

while depositing me at the YWCA," she recalled in an atypical personal flashback. "The next morning his father arrived. 'Do you love this girl?' he asked his son. 'Well,' my hero stammered, looking at the ground. That did it. I took my suitcase and went home to make some explanations to my sizzling parents. And then I found out the boy was trying to win *my* scholarship for the following term! I was through with men after that for some time."

3. SUSAN AND SCARLETT SQUARE OFF

Certain Hayward records of this early period are vague when not downright contradictory, as Hayward dates in general somehow have a way of being. Some list her as a 1938, some a 1939 arrival in the movie capital, then ruled gloriously by ex-junkmen, pool hustlers, furriers, etc. But facts show it was in 1937 that— against the wishes of her father who didn't think she was ready to handle the "brutal, vulgar, grasping" *Hollywood in the Thirties* of John Baxter's recent book—she went West to try for the bitch role of all time, Scarlett O'Hara in *Gone with the Wind,* accompanied by her sister Florence. It is less certain just whose idea it was. One story had director George Cukor spotting her on the cover of a *Saturday Evening Post* and bringing her to the attention of producer David O. Selznick. Another had the latter's wife, Irene Mayer Selznick, the daughter of MGM chief Louis B. Mayer, spying her in a millinery show she was working. Hayward's father, plagued by heart trouble, died before he could learn she had flunked her test.

"I looked like a snub-nosed teen-ager in it. What did I know about Southern belles?" she has said of her grab for the part that won stardom for Britain's Vivien Leigh, as well as the Oscar, and immortality.

Early in '69 Hayward's test was shown with several

other hoop-skirted hopefuls in *Hollywood: The Selznick Years,* a TV documentary special written, produced, and directed by Marshall Flaum. This segment provided that hour's most amusing as well as historically interesting moments. "Scarletts" Jean Arthur, Joan Bennett, Frances Dee, Paulette Goddard, and Lana Turner were girlishly present in various shades of hair and drawl. Hayward tested with Alan Marshal, an all-purpose Ashley Wilkes serving in many of the other gals' tests, too. For her love scene she managed the required slapping of the indefatigable Marshal believably; but, then fiercely independent (externally, anyway), she seemed to be choking on the words that had her throwing herself at the vacillating Wilkes character. After director Cukor yelled "Cut!" a delightfully unaffected Hayward could be seen in singular spontaneous footage, doubling up with laughter at, evidently, the way it had gone.

Susan and Scarlett, who also triumphed over deprivation, were not to be separated that easily. Almost eerily, the specter of the belle of Tara has from time to time through the years influenced the actress who, a few seasons after the test, would have been able to play all facets of Miss O'Hara superlatively. As late as 1972, when Harold Rome's stage musical version of *Gone with the Wind* opened in London, American reviewer Joe Fleischman wrote for *Record World* magazine that June Ritchie as Scarlett "looks, sounds, and has many of the mannerisms of a young, fiery Susan Hayward."

Selznick told Hayward to go home and get more experience. "I like oranges; I think I'll stay," she replied.

"Then leave your return tickets at the office," he said.

With hands on hips and jaw firmly set (a stance that, with the withering, over-the-shoulder glare, would become familiar from her screen performances), she answered from the doorway, "I've already cashed them in to live on."

When that money ran out, she and her sister were dispossessed for nonpayment of rent, and Hayward had to

16

borrow to wire an aunt for temporary subsidy. Eventually, agent Benny Medford showed her test to Warner Brothers and they signed her to a six-month starlet's contract; but lean times were not over.

She sent for her mother and brother and worked inauspiciously, sometimes almost invisibly, in several Warner films. For starters, she was in the broadcast finale of Busby Berkeley's *Hollywood Hotel* ('37), with Dick Powell and powerful columnist Louella Parsons, whose weekly radio show had inspired the movie.

Hayward would soon share with Parsons, a great friend throughout her career, a nine-week, coast-to-coast vaudeville "act" that also spotlighted, in four or five forty-minute shows a day, other specially chosen, promising Hollywood newcomers such as Jane Wyman, Ronald Reagan, June Preisser, Arleen Whelan, and Joy Hodges. Traveling part of the time via a TWA plane emblazoned with "Louella Parsons and Her Flying Stars," they enjoyed standing room only audiences. The working Parsons, who sat behind a stage desk, was paid $3,300 a week for herself, while her more ambulatory associates divided $4,200 among them. "The format," related George Eells in *Hedda and Louella,* "cast Louella as a columnist and the actors as would-be stars who hoped to entertain her and earn a plug in her column—which some critics saw as Louella's sly way of sending herself up." Hayward always made her entrance calling out the then infallible, "Anyone here from Brooklyn?" It helped make her a hard act to follow, especially when they played houses like Loew's State Theater on Broadway; but the acrobatic, perky blonde Preisser, rolling herself about the stage like a white-walled tire, managed okay.

During the tour Hayward had a feud with Wyman, teaming up with fellow redhead Whelan against her and Hodges. As part of the act, Hayward had to slap Reagan (whom she had dated briefly, perhaps at the studio's instruction), and Parsons had to speak to her once or twice because she didn't pull her punches. Wyman, then

17

falling in love with the actor who shortly became her husband and much later governor of California, would watch Hayward and Reagan from the wings. Hayward complained to Parsons that Wyman made her nervous.

When her boss mentioned this, Wyman whined, "Too bad about her. If I don't stand and watch she'll knock Ronnie out. She hits him too hard! She just slaps him that hard because she thinks it makes me mad."

Joy Hodges, who today travels between real estate and the New York stage, recounted for this book: "The routines were mainly musical, but Susan had a comedy scene opposite 'Dutch' Reagan that she played with incredible fervor." (Hodges, who had known Reagan in their Iowa radio days and helped him get into pictures, always refers to him as "Dutch.") "I can still see her, the blue velvet dress, with that red hair, the spotlight on just the two of them. In the skit she had stabbed 'Dutch,' and every time he'd try to sit up she'd bop him down again. Susan played it completely straight. The audience howled, but she never faltered, not even when 'Dutch' broke up, as he usually did. We all marveled at how she kept her composure.

"We each had more mileage in show business than Susan, but even then she was special. She'd charge on stage with that bulldog walk, her head bent forward, and plant her feet. The rest of us would sort of float out. And she was *sooo* beautiful.

"Frankly, I was a little afraid of her—that directness, that lack of humor. I never thought of Susan as a girl I'd ever want to know well, one to whom I could say, 'Come on, let's go out and have dinner.' Somehow, she seemed uneasy, withdrawn with other performers then. It wasn't the competitive thing. I just think she felt unsure of herself among people in the profession she had so little experience in. She was always extremely open and friendly with doormen and elevator operators.

"For a while we were concerned about her, though. Night after night she spent practically every cent she had

18

telephoning some fellow in the midwest. I believe she met him on the tour, although she could have known him before. We were afraid she might be wasting all her money on this chap. When Christmas came, he sent her a toy telephone, a gentle hint that she could save her money.

"There was something so alone about Susan. We all had something going for us. I was a brand new bride. Jane and 'Dutch' had each other. Arleen was very gay with plenty of beaux. June already had a career on the stage with her sister Cherry. But Susan—she seemed to have nothing. Except natural talent."

Hodges and Hayward never shared another bill, nor did their paths ever cross again.

Louella Parsons once wrote that the Hayward of this time was actually "ultra moral and conventional—a real Miss Prim, easily shocked by backstage 'stories,' even when they were mild. And her feelings were so easily hurt she dissolved into tears if anyone even looked at her crossly. She seldom went out, even when we hit such big towns as Philadelphia and New York. If she did go, it was usually with a relative or friend from Brooklyn." In 1952 Parsons profiled Hayward as part of a newspaper series she wrote called "Hollywood's Ten Most Exciting Women."

In 1938, though, Hayward played a patient of *The Amazing Dr. Clitterhouse,* with Edward G. Robinson and Humphrey Bogart (who sometimes referred to this one as *The Amazing Dr. Clitoris*); a telephone operator (always a good way to use a contract girl no one knew how else to use) in *The Sisters,* starring Bette Davis and Errol Flynn; and an amateur actress in *Comet Over Broadway,* with Kay Francis. She had a small part, too, as a co-ed in an eighteen-minute "Broadway Brevity" short titled *Campus Cinderella,* which featured Penny Singleton, a versatile entertainer who later that year would get out of the battle and begin her twelve-year run in the undemanding *Blondie* series. To the best of my

19

knowledge, no post-Warners stories on Hayward have ever carried any mention of all these obscure appearances, probably because in most of the pictures she was little more than an extra. A surprising number of reports mentioning this period of her career have claimed—obviously erroneously—that all she did during her brief Warners stay was sit for publicity stills.

Her biggest role up to then was in *Girls on Probation* ('38), a dreary "quickie" with Jane Bryan, a Bette Davis protégée who married and retired a couple of years later, and Ronald Reagan. She was fifth-billed as, of all things, a socialite, albeit a vituperative one—with a thick Flatbush accent. Bryan was a trouble-prone young dumbbell working for a dry-cleaning firm who was loaned a dress to wear to a party by another employee (Sheila Bromley). The frock, it turned out, actually belonged to customer Hayward who, when she discovered it had been "borrowed" and damaged, had Bryan fired and arrested.

Warners named her Susan Hayward, although Edythe Marrener was at least as interesting; and talent executive Maxwell Arnow was to say, "She had a wonderful mind, but no heart. It took a long time to teach her to cry."

In view of the unpublicized care she gave ailing childhood friend Martha Little during the actress' own domestic crises of '54, one can't help doubting the claim that Hayward had no heart. At Hayward's expense the fatally ill Miss Little made several trips West for medical aid, and Hayward sought out doctors for her and paid her costly bills. Maybe it was all an image-building ploy: For the 1944 film *And Now Tomorrow*, Paramount Pictures advertising copy proclaimed that "Vixenish Susan Hayward is cast just as you want her . . . cold, selfish, and a pagan to her fingertips!"

When Warners dropped her there was a stretch when, like any self-respecting folks in a '30s Hollywood hard luck story, the Marrener family survived mostly on beans. Susan thought of working as a waitress or a salesgirl. She continued her dramatic lessons, though, and even when she didn't have the money to pay him, coach Frank Beckwith's belief in her was such that he went on instructing her free. Then Artie Jacobson, who had encouraged the aspirant earlier, was appointed talent head at Paramount and got her a contract at two hundred dollars a week. As he explained it to a magazine writer in 1940: "Susan Hayward walked in here one day, picked up a cold script and read it like a veteran. She was a natural, a neglected Scarlett girl, and we signed her pronto." She became one of that studio's "Golden Circle" of promising young players that also numbered handsome Richard Denning, who a couple of years from then would appear in her first real personal hit, *Adam Had Four Sons*.

Her premiere picture for Paramount was the French Foreign Legion tale, *Beau Geste* ('39), admirably retold almost scene for scene from the 1926 Herbert Brenon-directed version. Gary Cooper starred as the self-sacrificing title hero, played first by Ronald Colman, with Ray Milland and Robert Preston as the other two devoted Geste brothers. Hayward, her accent smoothing out after many viewings of Ronald Colman's *The Prisoner of Zenda,* was English Isobel Rivers ("Poor Awnt Pat!"), the spit-curled, sparingly used heroine and the boys' friend from childhood (when Isobel was represented by a friskier Ann Gillis). She had about three sedate scenes, mostly diddling at the piano in the magnificently appointed Brandon Abbas, and exaggerated only slightly when she later described her part for the press: "I waved goodbye to the boys at the beginning and hello to them at the end." It was Milland she really bid adieu as he left to join his brothers in the Legion. Her final exquisite close-up at this parting, aglow with youthful promise (on more than one level), was a cameo her sweetheart would carry safely in his heart through desert warfare that was to claim his brothers' lives. The acting laurels went to Brian Donlevy, whose close-cropped, shifty-eyed, sadistic Sgt. Markoff ("I make soldiers out of scum like you . . . if I have to kill half of you . . . I promise you!") earned him a Supporting Actor Academy nomination and made him a name. But Hayward received a flurry of publicity, some of it announcing her name would be changed to Mary, much of it promoting her as a discovery of the film's producer-director, William A. Wellman. Her role as ward of the Geste lads' adoptive aunt, Lady Brandon (Heather Thatcher), first announced for Patricia Morison, was played by Mary Brian in the silent version of the Percival Christopher Wren adventure classic. In the poor 1966 remake the character was talked about but never shown.

David Zinman included Hayward's *Beau Geste* among his *50 Classic Motion Pictures* in his recent subjective book, subtitled *The Stuff That Dreams Are Made Of.* Not surprisingly, youthful wonderment had left him particularly impressed with the beginning that showed Fort Zinderneuf, "a soldier in every embrasure, each with his rifle cocked for action. They are dead to the last man. . . . The film grips the audience from the very first frames. The camera work (by Theodor Sparkuhl) is so resourceful that the picture packs more mystery and suspense in the first five minutes than other movies often achieve in an hour. The movie has, in my opinion, the most engrossing opening of any picture made in the 1930s."

4.   QUEEN OF THE "B"S

Beau Geste was followed that same year by *Our Leading Citizen* and *$1,000 a Touchdown,* but not within shouting distance. It may be only coincidental that the *New York Times'* first-string critic Frank Nugent quit his job there and left for Hollywood to become a screenwriter just a few months after he had reviewed (mercilessly) both these pictures. Almost a decade later, he co-scripted Hayward's *Tulsa*.

In *Citizen* Hayward was the ingenue daughter of small-town lawyer Bob Burns, the radio star who was vainly trying to capture a movie following, as well as—it seemed here—the late Will Rogers' niche. Her romantic interest was Joseph Allen, Jr. Nugent's *Times* review was an angry one, taking to task Irvin S. Cobb, author of the original story, and calling the production in its folksy over-simplification of social-political-economic problems of the day "an affront to intelligence and good taste." A recent critique for television viewers indicated that time had worked no miracles, yet Steven H. Scheuer could now see *Citizen* as "a philosophic comedy-drama that never quite comes off as particularly good, but it does interest us today as it concerns strikes, Communists, rabble-rousers, and capitalists *à la* 1939 attitude."

Movies set at institutions of higher learning almost traditionally have enrolled characters of lower mentality, but the ensuing *$1,000 a Touchdown* has few peers even now for sheer idiocy. In this slapstick sortie Joe E. Brown was an actor contemplating suicide because 1) he was terrified of people and 2) those who didn't send him up the wall he couldn't remember meeting five minutes later. Somehow, though, Martha Raye, whose acquaintance he made when he tripped her head over heels, was different: he could talk to her, if not always remember who she was. "All my ancestors were actors. Except my mother. She was an actress," the hapless Brown gulped, once Miss Raye was upright again. A democratic as well as daffy heiress, she took him home to meet her butler (Eric Blore), who almost swooned, "Ah, the son of the great Booth!" Naturally, when Raye converted a defunct university into a dramatic school ("Become an actor in four easy years," said their posters), she made Brown both President and football coach. Starlet Hayward was a faculty member(!) whose most memorable

23

line was "I teach romance"! Known as "that little fire-cracker" to the football team she helped recruit, Hayward enthusiastically instructed well-attended necking orgies during evenings in the school garden. Although teamed with student John Hartley in publicity for the picture, she saw little of him on film—teacher's work obviously came first. A blondined, Brown-smitten Raye recessed midway to warble a song: "Some spell love with an *l*, but I spell love with a *you*." Against this kind of competition, even Brown's complexes took wing. So did he. To quote Frank Nugent: "It ends with Joe E. scoring the last-minute touchdown by being thrown over the goal posts. They threw the wrong man. Delmer Daves, who wrote it, would be our choice—and we'd insist on a field goal."

Touchdown sent Brown back to the stage, and Raye's unspectacular tenure at Paramount was drawing to a close.

More meaningful was *Among the Living* ('41), a top-notch grade "B" thriller that was among the most interesting, unusual films Hayward made at the studio. Rarely were movies of its stratum made with such multi-departmental flair; lucky was the grade "A" film that was as well fashioned.

Living, tersely written by Lester Cole and Garrett Fort with welcome dashes of humor, was directed with nightmarish chiaroscuro by Stuart Heisler. He was coming off one of the National Board of Review's "Ten Best" of 1940, *The Biscuit Eater*, also a lower berth entry but a heart-tugging study of child/pet relationships, and he would later guide Hayward's *Tulsa* and her milestone *Smash-Up, The Story of a Woman*. With his cinematographer Theodor Sparkuhl, Heisler here unostentatiously, deftly utilized some whooshing camera effects and fast-cut collages that would not gain wide usage in pictures for years. His flickering, shadowy images abounded in sinister effect. Heisler also gave Hayward, who played a mercenary flirt, her first decent chance to show audiences the blossoming dramatic actress she had become. Although experience would bring "the Brooklyn Primitive" (one day one of the print medium's many nomenclatures) a more facile shading technique at her calling, Howard Barnes in the New York *Herald-Tribune* joined the numerous yea-sayers: "Susan Hayward is especially good. The film is head and shoulders above most of the filler shows ground out by Hollywood, superior psychological melodrama." Hayward won second billing for the first time, after Albert Dekker, whose dual lead may have been the best role of a long screen career spent mostly in support.

Dekker number one was a rational young businessman, Dekker number two a maniac since childhood when his mother's screams from her husband's beatings traumatized him. The sane brother had married Frances Farmer (who would soon depart pictures and spend many years in a mental institution) and returned to his poor Southern town to reactivate the local mill. At the same time, his not unpitiable twin, locked up in one room of the family mansion for twenty-five years, murdered his keeper (Ernest Whitman) and escaped. He found his way to a seedy rooming house run by a frowzy Mrs. Pickens (Maude Eburne).

In an unforgettable morass of introductory frumpery, Eburne beckoned: "Come in, come in. Oh-oh, don't trip over the vacuum. I was just cleaning the foy-yer—foy-yer's French for front hall. I had one of them Frenchmen living here for three months last year. He had the back room on the second floor, and honest to goodness every time you'd turn 'round that Frenchman was a-grabbing for your hand and kissing until he'd like to pull the skin off. I always admired a gentleman, but if there's one thing I hate it's to have someone slobbering over me. But I must say that he paid his room rent right on the dot, so I just let him keep on kissing. *Millie!* Millie's my daughter. She'll show the rooms. You quite sure you can pay in advance? No cooking allowed and *no* foul language. I didn't always tell my roomers this, but we had a man here last month and honest to goodness the language that man used would have melted your gold tooth!"

"Yes, Ma," said Hayward, poised feet apart at the top of the stairs for her belated entrance. Spotting a man, she quickly removed her cleaning bandana to reveal luxurious shoulder-length hair. A swirl of this dark red silk tumbled obligingly, enticingly over one pre-Veronica Lake eye. Dekker got to see even more of her after he flashed a bankroll. "Say," she exclaimed, "if I had a wad of folding dough like that I'd go right out and buy an outfit that would knock this neighborhood cock-eyed!" As they left one afternoon for a round of what looked like Hayward's second favorite sport, shopping, her mother waved them off from the stoop and muttered approvingly, "Us Pickeneses always had a weakness for refineness." Then she cranked to her feet and turned to go in, pulling a sticking housedress away from her behind.

To complain that this tenementlike, standing Paramount set, a major venue in *Among the Living,* was closer to Delancey than Peachtree Street, and that the players didn't even attempt Southern accents, would be nit-picking.

Dekker encountered his next victim in one of the most intriguing sequences. Wandering about Skid Row, passing poolrooms and a legless man selling puppies (as well as a movie theater showing *Those Were the Days!*), he straggled into an almost surreal, swinging waterfront cafe. He was snatched up by a B-girl who looked and sounded like Ginger Rogers, but who was actually studio contract actress Jean Phillips. "I'm hungry," she pouted as they sat. "You shouldn't oughta eat on an empty stomach. Make it two," she instructed the waiter. The place soon became a whirling inferno of laughing doxies, arguments, and jitterbugging couples, the latter wrigglers used here, uniquely, for ominous ambience. The frenzy climaxed in a dark alley where, triggered by her screams,

26

Dekker strangled Phillips, pressing her hands tightly against her ears in death, as he had his previous victim.

As Dekker became more attracted to Hayward and was buying her an expensive bottle of perfume, the store radio announced that there was now a five thousand dollar reward for him, dead or alive. The unsuspecting girl's already bright eyes beamed. "I could get a fur coat, I could get outa this town!" That night she dug out the family blunderbuss and told him they were going out to his deserted family estate to look for the fiend. "You're not afraid—at all?" gawked the fiend. "For $5,000 I'm not afraid of anything, not even death!" she declared. Which, following an ill-timed scream inside the cobwebby old house, was nearly her fate. Luckily, the rest of the town was equally venal and trooped by virtually en masse in time to save her. "My Millie got him!" Ma Eburne yelped. "It was that dirty Mr. Paul, my new boarder!" A kangaroo court was set up on the spot, where Hayward did her best to arouse the mob to violence. In the melee, Dekker number two was shot and died by his mother's grave.

Hayward, to borrow James Agee's words on another actress, "tackled her role as if it were sirloin and she didn't care who was looking." Her eager, banister-hopping incandescence deserved immediate stardom, but Paramount never really recognized her worth. Perhaps it was reasoned that her excellence in unsympathetic, generally tributary parts would vitiate public empathy in starring roles. Liza Wilson, in an *American Weekly* study titled "The Harder You're Hit," offered another possibility: "Paramount was top-heavy with feminine stars who, after one look at Susan, decided that she was a menace. 'I won't have her in my picture,' more than one movie queen told the front office when casting was discussed. So the parts to which Susan was assigned were few and small, and in 'B' pictures."

Unqueenly Maude Eburne, a rubber-faced harridan,

was priceless in *Among the Living,* perhaps the most consistently mirth-provoking character actress in my ken. She never failed to rise above often meager material. No part was too small for Eburne. Or too far-out: in 1942's *The Boogie Man Will Get You* she was the crazy sister of crazy professor Boris Karloff ("You don't know *how* good he is. Even when he was a baby he never cried—not even when we dropped him") who frequently thought she was a chicken ("Pa-caw! I just laid my 214th egg!"). *Among the Living*—like everything else in which she ever worked—was the richer for Maude Eburne's presence.

Its "B" status, however, limited the movie's prospects. Shortly before he hanged himself in '68, Dekker told me, "*Living* was one of the best goddam things I ever did, but it did nothing at home. It made a helluva lot of money in South America, though."

Also in 1941, Republic Pictures employed Hayward for a wacky, mildly diverting Judy Canova hick opera called *Sis Hopkins* that at least helped Judy's star rising behind the still, and didn't hurt Hayward's either. Studio President Herbert J. Yates had purchased the moldy Rose Melville stage vehicle for $50,000, practically an unprecedented sum for the penurious Republic. Yates had great faith in the rather specialized talents of Canova, a hillbilly from Florida radio with a factory whistle trill. One-time child stage star Joseph Santley directed a large troupe of scene-stealers, including the airwaves' Elvia (of Brenda and Cobina) Allman and Jerry ("Ahhh, yes . . .") Colonna.

Cast as the snobbish daughter of wealthy plumber Charles ("I know my bathrooms") Butterworth, Hayward came on conniving when country cousin Canova, who came on warbling "Wait for the Wagon," moved in with her in college. Many of the resulting jokes, possibly because of the dusty original source, sounded antique even then. For example:

When Sis Canova, who had been burned out of her farm home, uttered her standard "You're tellin' I," college employee Allman (in the kind of giddy, Colonna-chasing old maid part that had to have been meant for Vera Vague) no-noed, "Your syntax is irregular."

"Where?" worried Canova, giving herself a quick double-O.

Hayward, still whipping her hair about, was refining her tactics, though, and now was able to deal with the situation without inciting a mob . . . exactly. Her supreme moment of treachery found her paying to get the guileless Canova a spot in a burlesque show as a sorority initiation ruse.

Hayward: "But you mustn't tell a soul."

Canova: "I'll be a real dummy."

Hayward: "You're tellin' I."

At the old "BQ" Hayward phoned the police to report an "indecent performance," then pulled a thread that caused her cousin's dress to fall off on stage just as the theater was raided.

Jule Styne, who was just starting out, and Frank Loesser wrote the new tunes, one of which, a plaintive pleasantry titled "Look at You, Look at Me," Hayward sang with film boyfriend Bob Crosby, her voice throatily, credibly dubbed. Their setting was a Ziegfeldian *Fall Frolics* school revue, with Hayward and Crosby at opposite ends of a split stage duetting over the telephone. Otherwise, her part, almost as big as that of star Canova (who by year's end was a top ten box office attraction), was among Hayward's most physical. She got drenched with a pan of water; ran in a track meet, with hurdles; and, in what may stand as an unparalleled instance of indignity for any actress, nearly impaled herself walking over a perpendicular plunger.

5. ADAM HAD FOUR SONS BUT ONE DAUGHTER-IN-LAW

That year on loan to Columbia she had her strongest role thus far. It was lubricious Hester Stoddard in the schmaltzy but succinct, enjoyable *Adam Had Four Sons,* scripted by William Hurlbutt and Michael Blankfort from Charles Bonner's novel, *Legacy,* also the title of the film during production. Set early in this century and concerning a devotèd governess (Ingrid Bergman) who held a motherless family together, the narrative watched the lady's four small male charges (Billy Ray, Steven Muller, Wallace Chadwell, Bobby Walberg) grow to manhood (Richard Denning, Johnny Downs, Robert Shaw, Charles Lind), all in eighty minutes. Warner Baxter as the father starred with the ascending Bergman—whom Hayward in a 1958 press conference called her favorite actress. Dispensed with early was sickly mom Fay Wray, her glory days driving *King Kong* right up the side of the Empire State Building now just a warm memory.

It was a third-billed Hayward who stole the show as unsuspecting son Downs' right-off rotten wife in a startlingly uninhibited portrayal of nymphomania for Hollywood in the "forbidden '40s" of twin beds (and, it followed, flat pregnancies). Further unmindful of the booking at the familial Radio City Music Hall, she enacted the first of many drunk scenes in her career.

Hayward reviews around the country were generally fine, with audience response even better, although the New York critics were surprisingly resistant. Cecelia Ager in *PM* suggested that the picture's timing may have had something to do with her chilly press reception there. She began by saying: "A plague of little baby vampires has broken out on the local screens, genuine, old-fashioned baby vampires who snuggle, sidle and stuff.

Not a whole plague, maybe—on actual count there are only two—but Veronica Lake in *I Wanted Wings* on Wednesday, and then Susan Hayward in *Adam Had Four Sons* on Thursday, make it seem like a plague, though it may be nothing more ominous than a trend or a movement or something."

However, the Manhattan dailies couldn't dismiss Hayward, whose ripe peskiness created the only real excitement the faintly musty *Adam* could boast. Lee Mortimer in the *Daily Mirror* also dwelt on her, beginning his review by reporting that returning from seeing *Adam Had Four Sons*, "featuring the redheaded pride of Gowanus," he found a wire on his desk:

> AT FOUR PM IN SUSAN HAYWARDS
> SUITE AT WALDORF ASTORIA
> NOTED ILLUSTRATOR RUSSELL
> PATTERSON WILL COMPARE HER
> LEGS WITH FOUR OF THE BEST
> LIMBED GIRLS IN BROADWAYS PAL
> JOEY TO ASCERTAIN WHETHER
> MISS HAYWARD DESERVES PRESIDENCY
> OF PERFECT LEGS INSTITUTION
> STOP YOU ARE INVITED STOP
> COLUMBIA PICTURES STOP

Mortimer had to decline in favor of writing his notice, so he could not pass on the name of the new president. Although she always called her gams "too thin," it would not be rash to assume that Hayward won.

To titillated contemporary fans, her film name of Hester became synonymous with malevolence. She deserved but did not get an Oscar nomination as Best Supporting Actress for this baleful, musical-bedrooms-playing in-law, whom the family's wise old "cousin" (Helen Westley) recognized as "someone to be reckoned with" as she expired from shock on the spot. She *did* get a first name for one of her twin sons who arrived a few years later: Gregory, after the film's director and early Hayward booster, Gregory Ratoff. The director of Bergman's American introduction, *Intermezzo* ('39), Ratoff was also an actor remembered for his dyspeptic producer in *All About Eve*, Max Fabian.

It has been written that the tyro's unpopularity with some Academy voters—in later years she was venerated —cost her not only nominations but possibly an Oscar or two.

"I was pushed around during those years," Hayward has explained, "so I spoke up. The studio kept referring to me as a promising young actress. What I wanted to know was, just *how* long could a girl be promising? I got the reputation of being, to put it politely, a wave-maker."

One of Adam's four "sons" answered my request for comments on her with the following frank note, his bitterness provocatively undiluted even after thirty years: "Looking back, my respect and admiration for Ingrid Bergman only accentuated the unfavorable contrast with an ambitious, unscrupulous and selfish Susan Hayward. Unfortunately, I can recall nothing complimentary, so I'd prefer to remain anonymous and say no more. As an actress, I cannot criticize her; as a fellow worker, her attitude and selfish ambition left my personal regard for her microscopic."

"From the start, she gave the most skilled directors a bad time," specified another actor who knew her when. "She refused guidance, although there were times when direction would have helped her considerably. She was touchy on the set, and it was a rare day when she mixed with the cast during breaks. Somewhere along the line she learned to act. And she didn't stop at being just good. Every inch of that voluptuous woman is actress. She can portray a lonely, frustrated, desperate woman because she's experienced those emotions. If you look closely, you'll see they've left scars on her heart."

On the eve of her first Academy nomination for *Smash-Up,* she relaxed and opened up to writer Jack Ashland:

"When I arrived at Paramount, I had preconceived notions and stubbornly clung to the belief that they were right. I was a green kid, fresh at times, and it was probably that quality that made them see possibilities in me. Then something happened. They gave a party to introduce all the young hopefuls. Claudette Colbert was there, Paulette Goddard, Dietrich—all the supersophisticated, successful actresses.

"All my life I've been terribly frightened of people. At the studio it was the casting director, the cameraman, reporters, and publicists who asked endless questions. I thought everyone was so brilliant and I felt so inadequate. Then at this party, all those famous stars seemed so poised, so sure of themselves. Or so I thought. That's when I got the idea that I should try and be like them.

"People around the studio had told me that I should change, that my attitude was wrong. So suddenly, overnight, I stopped being myself and tried to copy everyone else. As a result I got so mixed up and was more confused than ever. Some people did try to straighten me out, but their approach was wrong. A word of encouragement produced a glow inside, like good, fine wine. But mostly I was criticized. I guess it never occurred to anyone to find out *why* I behaved the way I did.

"The only way I knew how to protect myself was to try and scare people before they scared me. Other girls were going right to the top, while I got the parts no one else wanted. I was getting a good salary by then. But, being basically an honest person, I felt like a fraud for accepting it. Things went from bad to bedlam—for a while."

6. NOT-SO-DELUXE TOURS

Hayward is said to have warred constantly with her home studio for not using her on screen more often and more advantageously. She had, as another acquaintance put it, "brass knuckles on her tongue then." Her early years at Paramount were spent mainly posing in the still department astride brooms, firecrackers, and—a bathing suit was de rigueur for all seasons—even wearing snowshoes. In other studio promotional activities, she had to go off on frequent tours to plug other people's pictures while her own career went nowhere.

One of her more unconventional jaunts was to a Sioux Indian reservation, incongruously chosen as one of the sites to talk up her employers' *Rulers of the Sea* ('39), which had Douglas Fairbanks, Jr. and British import Margaret Lockwood in the cast but, unsurprisingly, no Hayward. Kissing papooses in the name of Paramount, she almost had to do battle, too, with one Indian mother who so liked the visitor's way with her infant that she kept insisting Hayward keep the child.

Then there were the more conventional promotion tour hazards.

Ann Richards, the beautifully spoken Australian star who graced several Hollywood films of the '40s, recently wrote me that while she did not know Hayward, "I am indebted to her for some advice passed on to me by a mutual friend many years ago. Miss Hayward had been out on a personal appearance tour, and in conversation our mutual friend mentioned that I was leaving soon on a p.a. tour to promote *An American Romance* [Richards' first lead in an American feature]. Miss Hayward said, 'You tell any actress you know going on a p.a. tour to be sure and take along a chaperone of her own choos-

34

ing. Someone to share her room—so that Ann doesn't have to answer the phone or the door; because in many towns the gay blades masquerade as newspapermen and knock on the door at all hours and phone endlessly in an effort to meet the movie actress! They can be quite aggressive, and it's not worth the aggravation to go without a close friend along.'" Richards heeded Hayward's counsel, and was glad she did.*

The breach with her sister seems to date back to such a tour in the early '40s, when Hayward was sent to New York for personal appearances. Florence went along, and has said: "One evening Susan returned to our hotel suite with some of her new, fashionable friends and saw that I was entertaining some of my old friends from Brooklyn. 'How can you *do* this to me?' she cried. 'What are you all doing here? How can I entertain *my* friends if you have the place filled up with *yours?* This is supposed to be a business trip for me!' When Susan returned to Hollywood, I stayed behind. I didn't want to stay in New York. I wanted to be back in California with my family. I have to have family around, otherwise I fall apart. Maybe that's the thing in me that's so weak. I'm not strong and self-sufficient like Susan. I need someone around to want me and love me."

Cameron Shipp wrote, "Susan fought and scrounged for parts, but she never begged. She had a certain angry integrity. She demanded."

And not always to have the main lead. She strove, for instance, to play the good "bad woman" role in Olivia de Havilland's important *Hold Back the Dawn* ('41) at

___

*Although—while visiting one city, at Richards' instruction her companion refused several phone calls from a man in the hotel calling himself Louis B. Mayer, her boss (and for almost a decade the highest salaried man in the United States). "I had just left him in Hollywood," Richards explained. "The next morning on the way to breakfast, there was Mr. Mayer in the lobby!"

Paramount. Paulette Goddard got it. Hayward proved capable when she portrayed this old flame of Charles Boyer's on the *The Lux Radio Theater* soon after.

During a Paramount sales convention around the time of *Adam Had Four Sons,* several exhibitors, beguiled by the effulgent neophyte as she mingled among them, asked Hayward why they weren't seeing her on the screen more. She remembered that when she was chosen to say a few words of welcome. Instead of giving out with the usual gushy salutation, she said, in essence: "Several of you have asked me why I am not in more Paramount pictures, and I have never been asked a more interesting question. Why *haven't* I been in more of the studio's pictures? Well, Mr. Freeman [Y. Frank Freeman, the long-time studio head], do I get a break or don't I?"

At that moment before a stunned but soon cheering assemblage she was living the two-sided Hayward image that can still mesmerize moviegoers: the ambitious, shrewd banner carrier for female viewers, and the audacious, even bellicose, but physically enticing challenge for men. It is her unsurpassed authority which makes her acting so compelling. For if one should begin to toy with the idea, seated in the dark, that there is more Susan Hayward than, say, Mrs. Andrew Jackson in that characterization up there on the screen, Hayward's laser look would soon dispel doubt by zapping out to warn, in effect, "You'd better believe it, brother, *or else!*"

In short, she projects feminine come-hither with a masculine wallop. Other feminist types like Bette Davis, Joan Crawford, Katharine Hepburn, and Barbara Stanwyck also pulled no punches going their determined cinematic ways, but mostly they lacked the natural biological appeal to men of the wholly feminine-looking, petite, and niftily proportioned Hayward. She can appear to be the prettiest, clingingest of vines . . . then, when it's time for action, she can become a land mine that today's Women's Liberation Movement might profitably skip a bra-burning to observe. As John Wayne was saying to me

36

only the other day: "I've had the good fortune to work with Susan in several pictures, in a variety of backgrounds from the sea to war to world conquest.* At no time does her magnetism ever let you forget that she's a woman."

In 1941 Paramount released one of its first Henry Aldrich comedies, *Life with Henry*, with Jackie Cooper. Midway, the ambitious teen-ager's older friend, Rod Cameron, while clipping a newspaper pin-up that in close-up just happened (?) to be a bathing suit shot of Hayward, advised him, "I always say, Henry, the only way to get anything is to go after it."

Reap the Wild Wind, The Fighting Seabees and *The Conqueror*.

II

THE VICTORY

Cherokee Lansing: Killing's too easy. I want to get him where he lives.

—*Tulsa*

7. "A DEMILLESTONE"

Paramount's Cecil B. DeMille, with his renowned eye for the spectacular, could hardly help noticing Susan Hayward's spunk.

He made her the tragic ingenue in his roistering epic of 1840 salvage pirates in Florida waters characteristically shot on studio stages, *Reap the Wild Wind*, released early in 1942. Also aboard were Ray Milland, John Wayne, Robert Preston, and Paulette Goddard who, like Hayward, finally got to use her Scarlett drawl. The film fittingly celebrated the producer-director's thirtieth year in pictures. Adapted from Thelma Strabel's *Saturday Evening Post* serial, the film won the Special Effects Oscar—its Cantor-eyed giant squid was surely the major single contributor to World War II's rubber scarcity—and broke Paramount's boxoffice record previously held by the 1923 DeMille production of *The Ten Commandments*.

"It definitely marks a DeMillestone," reported a perspicacious Bosley Crowther in *The New York Times* when it opened—"Bos" always seemed to favor the big pictures. "It is the master turned loose, with no holds barred . . . A gorgeous panorama—the gentleman spends money on his films . . . *Reap the Wild Wind* represents the quintessence of make-believe. But who, in this time of trouble, is going to take exception to that?"

With one notable dissenter, as we shall see, hardly anyone.

The movie boom was on. Film audiences had never been so large as they were in 1942—an estimated ninety

41

million a week, all prosperous on defense paychecks. Even popular sheet music rolled up its heaviest sales in fifteen years. Civilian and serviceman alike were insatiable in their quest for entertainment. It has been written that only three pictures lost money during those war years: *Wilson,* with Alexander Knox clutching pince-nez as Woodrow Wilson; *Yolanda and the Thief,* a musical starring Fred Astaire posing as Lucille Bremer's guardian angel; and *The Hitler Gang,* with a cast of refugee character actors portraying "the boys in the bund" responsible for their emigration.

Obviously designed to capitalize on the recent success of *Gone with the Wind,* many of the characters reaping wind had counterparts in *GwtW,* as did some of the developments. Watching John Wayne kick down a door, for instance, couldn't help recalling Clark Gable's similar entry to Vivien Leigh's boudoir in the earlier work. And heroine Goddard, called "that little savage from Key West" by one Charleston dame, was paraded in the kind of vermilion dress that had provoked an incident when worn by Leigh's Scarlett. Hoping to give things a briny taste, scenarists Alan LeMay, Charles Bennett, and Jesse Lasky, Jr., made it virtually impossible for sailor Wayne to talk without saying something like "I'm not here to chew blubber" or ". . . as cozy as fiddler crabs on a marsh bank" or "They think they've got me busted flatter than a haddock." The others' language was less picturesque, with lawyer Milland getting temporary custody of the latest variation on scenariodom's hoariest line (to Goddard): "You're very desirable when you're angry"— the line's apogée was uttered in the 1956 Wayne-Hayward vehicle, *The Conqueror* (discussed later).

DeMille wisely, shamelessly chose to stress the derring-do rather than the personal relationships. Action was his main ingredient here, and few directors would have attempted what he managed to pull off: an outdoor adventure picture probably lensed entirely indoors (excluding a few second unit location shots without the leads).

To today's more sophisticated film eyes especially, the actors, whether skimming a lake or wrestling the greenest, roughest of "Florida oceans," were clearly navigating within Paramount's great gates. Rarely have water tanks, miniature models, and rear projection been used so extensively in a major film, or so effectively; and effects creators Gordon Jennings, Farciot Edouart, William L. Pereira, and Louis Mesenkop justifiably were honored by the Academy. Even in 1942 the osmotic unreality for audiences of all its gimmickries could not have seemed inappropriate to the plot's *Whiz-Bang* juvenilia. Indeed, the craftsmanship and *chutzpah*—I mean, almost totally making over nature—now seem infinitely more praiseworthy and remarkable than merely setting up cameras around the real thing.

DeMille lauded technical adviser Fred F. Ellis, a retired captain of the British merchant marine, "whose knowledge of sailing vessels and of all usages, language, and lore of the sea kept us technically correct and gave us so thorough a course that we might all have qualified as old salts after working on one picture with him. Captain Ellis was always punctiliously correct, yet always reasonable, which some technical advisers are not. If any viewer of *Reap the Wild Wind* was shocked to see that the peak and throat halyards were tied close together on the fife rail starboard, I could show him a note of Captain Ellis' in my working script of the picture, conceding that Mr. DeMille wishes to take the dramatic liberty of tying them that way, so that Paulette Goddard could cut both ropes with one stroke of an axe."

Although more suited to Goddard's seagoing Scarlett, here Loxi Claiborne, who ran her late father's salvage business ("Loxi, I worry every time you go wreckin'," said mother Elizabeth Risdon), Hayward continues to be remembered as the Melanie-esque Drusilla Alston ("Mercy *sakes*, Cousin Loxi!"/"Cousin Loxi, you're playin' with gunpowder!"). Bright-eyed with, unsurprisingly, a hint of checked prankishness therein, and more vivacious than another actress might have been in this subordinate, innocuous part, she was the gently raised sweetheart of pariah Robert Preston, the henchman brother of pirate "heavy" Raymond Massey. Her drowning, masterminded by Massey, provided one of the screen's most dramatic death scenes, its impact felt around the world.

Just recently an Australian friend wrote me: "I think my pet movie with Susan would be *Reap the Wild Wind.* What a magnificent production that was. Susan was really lovely, and Paulette was a delight. I'll never forget that beautiful, haunting love theme for Susan and Preston that Victor Young composed. It was used several times during the proceedings, but the scene I will always remember it in was when Susan, to get to Preston, had stowed away on the new steam boat. She was down in the hold trying on the new shawl he had given her and the camera tracked across the hold to give a medium close-up of her, as the ship was being driven steadily onto the rocks. It was a touching scene in a wonderful 'movie' movie."

(The Young-DeMille collaboration began on *North West Mounted Police* in 1940, and the composer did all subsequent scores for DeMille films until Young's death in 1956.)

Hayward was proving her versatility by playing a sweet, lovable type and making it stick without being sticky. With her emphatic coloring, she additionally was proving on this maiden tint voyage to be, as they used to write every time Maureen O'Hara exploded for the lens, one of the reasons Technicolor had been invented. In *The Autobiography of Cecil B. DeMille,* "C. B." noted: "In *The Buccaneer* [which he made in 1938], Evelyn Keyes had gone down in a scuttled ship early in the picture. In *Reap the Wild Wind,* that same fate was the portion of another young actress whose talent would raise her to stardom, Susan Hayward."

DeMille, reputed to be something of a martinet more

concerned with directing crowd scenes than individual performers, didn't treasure her "spunk" in close-up, however. It has long been said that they clashed seriously. Recently she recalled only that "On the first day of filming I said to Mr. DeMille, 'Excuse me, Mr. DeMille, but do you think that . . . ?' He cut me short and said, 'Young lady, I hired you for this film because I want an actress who can think for herself. Do that and you'll take a load of worry off my mind and add years to your own!' "

Ray Milland's memories of the *Wind* days are more vivid. "The role demanded curly hair, so they gave me women's permanents with the electric curlers and all that. After seven weeks of filming, I found my hair coming out by the handfuls. Ever since, I have used a hairpiece." His opinion of the picture for which he made this sacrifice? "Terrible."

8. STAR BILLING AND OTHER PASSING FANCIES

After the DeMille job, Hayward got back on the track that same year via two more typical second lead minxes, jealously suckering a dazed heroine in *The Forest Rangers,* another Strabel story, but getting her own comeuppance on an even wilder scale in *I Married a Witch,* the film of *The Passionate Witch,* Thorne Smith's final novel completed after his death by Norman Matson.

Rangers was an "audience" movie, the kind of bread-and-butter production on which the motion picture industry was founded. If its formula rudiments had been fleshed out a bit, this intended tribute to our Forest Service would have been exactly the kind of tale that DeMille, of the mass-appeal epics, would have loved making. The veteran director George Marshall was probably an even better choice: he kept the pace brisk and—

as was often blessedly his fashion—humor always in the foreground of the melodrama. He also kindled some of the most exciting holocausts the screen would see until Hayward's *Tulsa* six years later, leading his players through flaming mazes and, as it snowed ashes, urgent dialogues. *Rangers* claimed, too, an advance in the Technicolor process plus the hit Frank Loesser-Joseph J. Lilley song, "(I've Got Spurs That) Jingle Jangle Jingle."

Acting honors were glommed by Hayward in her first starring role (third-billed) as the forest fire that Ranger Fred MacMurray couldn't douse by marrying New Yorker Paulette Goddard. It is my favorite of her Paramount performances. The sun igniting her hair, she was young, alluring, vibrant—and a little fearsome. Undiminished by a uniform of baggy overalls and rumpled man's hat, she played Tana (for Montana) Mason, the logging mill owner who had been the leading contender for MacMurray's hand until he was let loose in town overnight and returned with a wife.

"I'll drive that society 'debit number one' right back to the nightclub circuit," pledged an even witty Hayward.

The best part was the scene where she sneaked off and pushed their car into a ditch, stranding the three of them alfresco on a mountaintop on the newlyweds' first honeymoon night. To keep warm they had to "bundle," suggesting, in a scene then considered racy, an early Bob and Carol and Tedless Alice. Hayward's efforts to sleep next to MacMurray under their one blanket (cracking about snakes, goosing Goddard with sticks) and the bride's to keep her from doing so made for some of the blither minutes. Reappearing at the Ranger post the next morning, a suspiciously cheerful Hayward was met by admiring pilot Regis Toomey (who turned out to be causing all the secondary mayhem and forest fires), remarking, "You must have had a swell night in the woods." "Wait'll I go to work in the daylight!" she snickered. Her smiling condescension toward Goddard, who

46

loved her husband and fumfferingly strove to learn forest ways, had positively lethal implications.

Harder to fathom was MacMurray's jocular blind spot towards the captivatingly "regular" Hayward, a far more likely helpmate who knew exactly what to do in case of fire. Hoping to awaken MacMurray, she stashed her trousers for a russet, skirted ensemble but all he came up with was, "You look like a splinter off a redwood." And it only got worse. When Goddard asked him if he would have married Hayward if she hadn't come along, he replied, "Who, Butch? Haha, why she's just one of the boys." Talk about big mooses.

But the viewer was all for this "pixie of the pines" (courtesy of the *Times* review), as were many of MacMurray's cronies. And since she was such a nervy and competent figure, the ending, when Harold Shumate's screenplay made her freeze in the midst of a fire and thus permit the higher-billed Goddard to save her, was out of character for her and unconvincing. Everything considered, the picture adequately conveyed the dedication and bravery of the Forest Ranger but in MacMurray's embodiment left his intelligence seriously in question.

I Married a Witch, co-starring another Brooklyn girl, Veronica Lake, and Fredric March, was an imaginative, thoroughly delectable comedy-fantasy produced and directed by René Clair that featured Hayward in a narrower role as March's witch-plagued fiancée. Although the two stars seemed to work well together, Lake has admitted, "I don't believe there is an actor for whom I harbor such deep dislike as Fredric March. He gave me a terrible time . . . I'm sure that March considered me a brainless little blonde sexpot, void of any acting ability and not likely to acquire any. He treated me like dirt under his talented feet."

Lake was cast as a wraith come back to torment gubernatorial candidate March, whose Puritan ancestor had had her burned as a witch. Naturally, or unnaturally, if you will, she fell in love with the modern-day March, breaking her centuries-old curse that all the men in his family would marry the wrong women.

"A fantastic element," maintained Clair in 1953, "is appropriate in a picture only if its effects are limited. If a witch has so much power that she can destroy her enemies and the world—there is no plot and no show." In *I Married a Witch,* opined Catherine de la Roche in *René Clair/An Index,* a monograph published by the British Film Institute, "Veronica Lake's witchery often seems essentially natural and the machinery of modern society absurdly artificial—hence the logic, credibility, and humor of a screenplay in which fantasy and reality are neatly balanced." The gags and visual tricks such as flying taxis and poltergeists imprisoned in bottles are still a treat.

With script credit going to Robert Pirosh and Marc Connolly, Hayward's human witch had less substance than Lake's ectoplasmic one; she was, moreover, a caricature of the "other woman" and one of the most intensely unrelieved bitches she ever played. Her snottiness was established with atomic dispatch in her opening tiff with March set against thunder rolls and lightning flashes. Her publisher father (Robert Warwick), who was backing March in the election, was entreating her at the engagement party, "Will you try to be a little more pleasant— at least until after the wedding?" Lake then glimpsed her for the first time and gloated, "The curse is working. She has the look of a shrew." Driving home after the affair, March suddenly saw a fire and exclaimed, "That's the Pilgrim Hotel!" To which Hayward grumbled, "It *would* have to be right on our way home." She appeared only slightly overmatched in her livid final wedding scene, smiling over teeth grating so violently they almost gave off sparks as black magic-induced hurricanes and shootings repeatedly interrupted the ceremony.

While the TV producers denied it, the hit series *Bewitched,* starring Elizabeth Montgomery, seemed to have been born of *Witch*. The first show, in fact, with Nancy Kovack getting the witch's zingers instead of Hayward, actually looked like an abridgment of the movie. The major change was a sexual one: Agnes Moorehead, as Montgomery's mother, replaced Cecil Kellaway, who had delightfully played original star Lake's tippling sorcerer father, the inventor of the hangover. The funniest line was got off by stringy Elizabeth Patterson, March's old maid housekeeper, after the mischievous Lake put her to sleep leaning upright against a study door. Brought to by March and Robert Benchley, her wary first words were, "What are you two doing in my bedroom?" *I Married a Witch,* now paired by Lake with *Sullivan's Travels* as the only two really good pictures she ever made, is generally conceded, furthermore, to be the best of the smart set of films French master Clair made in America, including *The Flame of New Orleans, It Happened Tomorrow,* and *And Then There Were None.* Ironically, and inexplicably, *Witch,* like Hayward's upcoming *Young and Willing,* had been shot by Paramount but—apparently thought to be nothing special—was the first of several titles sold outright to United Artists, then suffering a paucity of product.

Next came a fifteen-minute "Victory Short" called *A Letter from Bataan* ('42). Hayward had to cool it this time as a World War II home front girl-next-door prototype, the faithful stateside sweetheart of wounded Pvt. Richard Arlen who in the title missive enlightened his loved ones on ways to support the war effort. Following this reading, a telegram revealed that he had died the day before he had dated his letter, a sophomoric touch of fantasy in a propaganda-sodden featurette containing a war surplus of sentiments like Arlen's sign-off, "And Mom, don't waste any kitchen fat."

As with most contractees of the flush '40s, she got to serve with almost all her studio fellows in a musical mélange, in her case the sparkling *Star Spangled Rhythm* ('42)—"The Greatest Galaxy of Stars Ever Gathered Together in One Picture" said the ads with typical Hollywood wartime economy. Said Bob Hope, who emceed the Navy benefit story peg, phoning: "No, no, I can't tonight. Veronica Lake's going to show me her other eye tonight." A negligée-clad Hayward showed more than that in a short rubber shortage "blackout" opposite Ernest Truex. "I want love, passion, fi-yuh! I want something to bring out the woman in me. You don't even bring out the Gypsy in me!" she raved, strutting her stuff around a stylized alabaster bed. Truex, as an aging sugar daddy, proceeded to satisfy his sweet Genevieve's cupidity not with diamonds or furs—but a girdle.

(Many years later, when things had returned to normal, Truex played a near-repeat of this sketch on television's *Alfred Hitchcock Presents* and had to ply his petulant lass, Sharon Farrell, with pearl earrings.)

Star Spangeld Rhythm's barely existent plot had Paramount switchboard operator Betty Hutton and gateman Victor Moore pulling out all stops—and stars—to convince Eddie Bracken, Moore's sailor-on-leave son, that his father was Executive Vice President in charge of production at the studio, a position actually held by beleaguered B. G. DeSoto (Walter Abel). Veteran songwriter and Capitol Records co-founder B. G (Buddy) DeSylva recently had taken over this post in real life, and there is some irony today in watching his movie counterpart comically worry throughout about a picture he has just made being so bad it will cost him his job, because that was alleged to be what happened to DeSylva a few years later. (The movie: the expensive flop *Frenchman's Creek,* starring Joan Fontaine.)

Among the guest "names" was Cecil B. DeMille, plugging his *Reap the Wild Wind* just as he had in Paramount's *Glamour Boy* ('41), with Jackie Cooper. Who needed television talk shows? Bing Crosby had the big finale, a patriotic tableau called "Old Glory," which asked the musical question, "Do you know any other country where a Brooklyn girl can get to be a movie

50

star?" More inventively staged and edited was the number "I'm Doin' It for Defense," socked across by an inexorably amorous Betty Hutton to a group of sailors in a moving jeep. Bounced out and then dunked in a lake as the bucking vehicle traversed the worst of countryside obstacle courses, the Hollywood newcomer never missed a lyric, even when she had to gurgle them. Such determination had to be rewarded with stardom, and, since the blonde bombshell from Broadway was a special pet of DeSylva's, she soon was. The best remembered divertissement, however, is "A Sweater, A Sarong, and a Peekaboo Bang" by Paulette Goddard, Dorothy Lamour, and Veronica Lake and drolly parodied in drag by Arthur Treacher, Walter Catlett, and Sterling Holloway.

The Academy nominated the film's Harold Arlen-Johnny Mercer song, "That Old Black Magic," sung by Johnnie Johnston and danced in scanties by Vera Zorina who, you can believe it, went tearing about a snowy hillside on her toes. The success of the George Marshall-directed production was responsible for the revival for a decade or more of the all-star revue format which initially had enjoyed popularity with the early talkies.

9.   SONGS, SOCKS, SETTEES!

Three Hayward films opened in '43. *Hit Parade of 1943* was an easy number one in quality and box office for this Republic musical series. It was reissued as *Change of Heart* after its Oscar-nominated Jule Styne-Harold Adamson song. It starred Hayward as a songwriter with a quick, powerful right cross. *Young and Willing* was a simple-minded but likable United Artists farce about a lot of struggling young thespians, among them William Holden, Eddie Bracken, and Hayward as a sharpie with a quick, powerful right cross.

Hit Parade of 1943 was bolstered by Albert S. Rogell's

surprisingly tricky direction. "A 'wolfing' sequence in John Carroll's apartment, with gremlin cut-outs uttering the inner voices of both Miss Hayward and Carroll, makes for some good fun, as Rogell has handled it," exampled *Variety*. The film took some amusing—and, for action studio Republic, rare—satirical swipes at the popular music business in that hustling, bustling "Mairzy Doats" age. There were singing liver pill radio commercials, jokes about the hit novelty song (not in the movie) "Three Little Fishies (Itty Bitty Poo)," and machinations justified by outbursts such as "Just one more plug on this song and it makes the *Hit Parade!*" The film was different becuse its "hero" (Carroll) was a crook, a louse and, as somebody noted, "a couch cricket." Seldom has an audience been asked to warm to a romantic lead with so many negative qualities and who remained devious right through the last chorus. Country girl Hayward met writer-publisher Carroll when she moved in with her New York cousin (Eve Arden) to pursue a career in songwriting. She was soon ghosting tunes for Carroll, who had stolen one of her melodies and was using a huge, round, wall "lyric master" for his June-mooning. "He has something I've always wanted since I started writing. He has an outlet," enthused the forgiving, straight-playing Hayward. "So has a drainpipe," countered Arden, putting a long red fingernail right on it, "but you don't want to hang around one."

The score, frequently performed here by black artists like Dorothy Dandridge in Ringling-scale club revues, was unusually tuneful. Hayward got to "sing" snatches of "A Change of Heart," "Who Took Me Home Last Night?" and "Harlem Sandman," plus, in a duet with Carroll, all of "That's How You Write a Song." Described by Carroll as "smart, ambitious, and quick on the uptake," she was a pert, pretty heroine in this light undertaking, a slight case of the cutes and a tendency to over-cheese for the camera mattering little in the final favorable tally.

Carroll, said to have worked a lot at Republic to pay off loans from President Yates, was a believable scoundrel.

It was Arden, however, who strode off with the most acting plaudits, a habit with her then. Invariably single and cynical, the Eve Arden of this era was enormously popular with a vast audience that recognized the humanity behind the barb, the probability that the right man— but not just yet; maybe in the *next* picture—could turn Our Miss Arden into Little Mary Sunshine. In the meantime, she made a war-concentrated nation laugh with a timing so dryly, casually faultless that it reminded anew that comedy is a born talent and not, like drama, something one can learn. Sitting on her piano keys to read something, Arden heard the plunk-plunk and remarked to no one in particular, "Hmmm, two octaves. I'd better go on a diet." Later, arriving at the office party celebrating a new Hayward-Carroll hit, Arden asked Walter Catlett, Carroll's partner, "Where's Jill (Hayward)?" He pointed to the left. "Where's the bar?" He pointed to the right, the direction in which she unblinkingly breezed.

Young and Willing stemmed from a trivial 1941 play titled *Out of the Frying Pan* by Francis Swann. His inspiration was a *Life* photo story on four young actresses sharing one apartment, among which was Swann's sister who, he hastened to assure, had no facsimile in his theatrical creation. The Broadway production featured a pre-*Oklahoma!* Alfred Drake and introduced a teenage Barbara Bel Geddes.

The picture very contemporarily had all the boys and girls living in one Greenwich Village apartment and was stolen by Florence MacMichael of the New York cast as a snooky-ookum-voiced, nitwit midwestern interloper scandalized to think there might be hanky-panky going on. Used infrequently in movies (although she did show up in 1959's *Woman Obsessed,* starring Hayward), the *Willing* MacMichael might more concisely be described as a white Butterfly McQueen. Also fun was another original cast member, Mabel Paige, the 1940s' bunny faced old darling and great screen character actress who was brought to Hollywood and signed by Paramount on the strength of her zany, confused, rent-chasing landlady. In the role of Kate, originally created by Nancy Douglas, Hurricane Hayward played the sassy operator among the would-be Duses, with the unlikely background of Iowa Queen of Corn—"The Most Beautiful Teeth in America, See?" She was the protective, slightly older sister of Barbara Britton (in Bel Geddes' part), who had married James Brown secretly and become pregnant, disregarding the roommates' oath to stay unwed. The group's main objective was producer Robert Benchley, residing directly below them. Peeping through a hole in the floor at him, one of the unemployed youngsters commented that he was close enough to spit on. "I'd *adore* spitting on a producer," sighed Hayward, just as appealingly wistful, in her own unique way, as Jeanne Crain daydreaming about spring in *State Fair*.

Jack London (United Artists), directed by Alfred Santell, had loftier ambitions than the year's other Hayward presentations but was less successful realizing them. This, even though—or maybe because—both Mrs. London herself and her biography of her husband, *The Book of Jack London*, served as guides. Certainly the subject's tempestuous life contained enough drama and incident for a lively film. "If you wrote it as a novel, no one would believe you," said Irving Stone, who authored a subsequent biography of London, *Sailor on Horseback*.

The castrated story of the great Yukon writer-adventurer, this second Samuel Bronston product (the first: 1942's minor *The Adventures of Martin Eden*, from a London tale) was foredoomed by a miscast Michael O'Shea, who had the literary air of an aging Dead End Kid as London, the San Franciscan, saying things like "I saw it happen in a jernt in Singapore." That same year O'Shea was a far more believable Biff Brannigan, the baggy-pants comic in Barbara Stanwyck's winning,

54

facetiously tawdry (early camp satire?) *Lady of Burlesque*. The more passionate John Garfield, a London aficionado who had just starred in London's *The Sea Wolf*, originally had been sought to play the writer, but his studio, Warners, refused to loan him. The only thing *Jack London* did for Broadway's O'Shea, aside from make him known in Hollywood (where, draft-drained, "victory casting" was the ungallant expression generally used on these occasions), was to introduce him to his future bride, Virginia Mayo. She played a supporting role.

There was also a long, clumsy, propagandistic section in the movie showing the Japanese mistreating Russian captives, and a prediction of the part, as one of "our side" put it, "those little sawed-off runts" would play much later in starting World War II. (Remember, it was made in 1943.) In their book, *Hollywood in the Forties,* Charles Higham and Joel Greenberg viewed *Jack London* as "a cruel disappointment. Ernest Pascal's screenplay sidestepped the more neurotic aspects of the author's personality, concentrating instead on his Asian adventures, realized in impressive sets and attractive sepiatone images. (The film is) little more than an anti-Japanese tract."

A docile, sympathetic Hayward—radiant in bustle and upsweep hairdo and evidencing a settee charm not exactly the *sine quo non* of her appeal—was the only bright spot as the late-appearing, extraordinarily patient Charmian Kittredge, the nomadic London's wife. A manuscript reader, she met him when she recommended his novel, *The Call of the Wild,* to the publisher. "You're not like other men," she was to tell London admiringly. "You've got something in you that won't let you rest." Would that producer Bronston had let him.

10.   WEDDING BILLS

Late in '43 while she was entertaining servicemen at the Bette Davis-founded Hollywood Canteen,* Hayward met South Carolina-born Jess Barker. He was an attractive, promising (there's that word again) newcomer to films who had been in Broadway's *You Can't Take It with You*, among other plays. As master of ceremonies, Barker, whose screen test was directed by Hayward pal Gregory Ratoff, watched her flounce on stage with her highly individual, undulating gait (someone once wrote that "She looks as if she's climbing stairs—to the bedroom") and shout her old Louella Parsons act opener, "Anyone here from Brooklyn?" The ensuing ovation showed she was still a hard act to follow.

Barker, 4-F because of a rapid-beating heart, asked her out but Hayward said no at first: "I didn't want to add my name to the list of starlets I had read he was dating." Eventually, she gave in and they began to see each other. She is said to have socked him when he first tried to kiss her.

After a stormy courtship in which, he later claimed, she soon became the aggressor, they embarked on an even stormier marriage on July 23, 1944, although in later "official" Hayward studio and/or publicists' biographies the wedding date has been listed as April 23, 1944. The only nuptial attendants were her press agents, Jean Pettebone and Henry Rogers. Before the splicing, however, the farsighted, always money-conscious Hayward had lawyers draw up an agreement, which the

---

*Actor Earl Holliman relished those days: "I always wanted to be in the movies, but didn't know how to go about it. So—I lied about my age and joined the Navy. The next thing I knew, there I was, a 15-year-old kid dancing at the Hollywood Canteen with Joan Crawford and Susan Hayward."

couple signed, whereby the actress' income was forever separated from that of a spouse.* This strange move for a pair of young newlyweds—no longer uncommon in Hollywood—was unearthed by their violent divorce action ten years after. One-time Columbia and Universal Pictures contractee Barker, his career potential unrealized and today in *The Filmgoer's Companion* remembered merely as "Lightweight American leading man of minor '40s films" (but more often nominally confused with ex-Tarzan Lex Barker), turned down a pretrial settlement offer of $100,000 to seek community property. But he wound up getting only the family station wagon. Hayward, by now a superstar, was awarded $1,293,319 in assets and custody of their twin sons, blond Timothy and red-headed Gregory, born prematurely on Feb. 19, 1945.

The strain of it all—including her widely reported beating and nighttime nude dunking by Barker in their Sherman Oaks pool, and his charge that she had tried to jab him in the eye with a lighted cigarette—seemed to have taken a terrible toll. Some stories then even accused her of carrying her screen drunk roles over into real life. On April 26, 1955, following the death of her close friend and agent Ned Marin, and shortly after meeting with Barker about their sons' future, she took a near-fatal dose of sleeping pills. When she phoned Mrs. Marrener and drowsily told her not to worry, that she'd be provided for, her mother called the police and Hayward was rushed unconscious to the hospital. Learning this, Barker sobbed in headlines almost as bold as his Hayward's, "I love her! I love her!"

During this period she said, "I married for love and

---

*During the divorce proceedings, Hayward said that the separate income agreement was signed to appease her mother, who disapproved of Barker, who was allegedly hesitant to wed and risk alienating bobby-sox fans; and Barker testified that he had been too busy with wedding preparations to read the document. His attorney called Hayward "an icy woman, corrupted by movie fame and fortune."

security but got neither. I married a man who wasn't in love with me. I bore his children. I did everything I knew to make the marriage work. Then I had to spill my personal life from coast to coast to keep my sons. I'm divorced and I never wanted to be divorced."

Not many months after, Barker was adjudged the father of bit player Yvonne (*The Wild One,* etc.) Doughty's baby daughter. His ex-wife dated Howard Hughes, under whose auspices she did *The Conqueror.* It was because of Hughes, her sister inferred in a magazine piece, that Hayward had taken the pills.

Lillian Roth, the entertainer illumined by Hayward in *I'll Cry Tomorrow* around that time, stated that she had come to know her alter ego well and identified strongly with her emotional nature. Disregarding Hayward's last-minute call to her mother, she didn't believe she intended to commit suicide.

"Susan is too vital and eager, too ambitious a girl to want to end her life. No, I think she was probably highly nervous about the filming of the picture and that night while reading the script she might have had a few cocktails and then, being very tired and knowing she had to work in the morning, took some sleeping pills. The alcohol and the sleeping pills fought each other, slowing her pulse, making her respiration extremely shallow, lowering her skin temperature. When your nerves are a little off the beam, this can happen to you; it happened to me. . . . There were articles that hinted that she did it on purpose to study how I felt, to follow in my footsteps. But who would want to follow in my alcoholic footsteps?" asked Roth.

The husky Richard Egan, who was with her in *Demetrius and the Gladiators* and *Untamed,* was another of her post-Barker escorts. A columnist pondered how a personality of Hayward's brio could have sought happiness with such "an epicene-looking and, to believe the actress' own testimony, lazy man as Barker in the first place," one whom, as the divorce brought out, she had to support while he stayed home and ran the house—badly, she further testified. (Barker's brief appearance as a Gay '90s stage-door Johnny in Rita Hayworth's 1944 *Cover Girl* was especially androgynous.) Acquaintances, though, did credit him with a ready wit plus an impressive erudition concerning his craft. Just before their break-up, Hayward even plugged to Hedda Hopper that she felt he was more talented than she. And the record notwithstanding, the blond actor had a well-bred Southern gentleman veneer not unlike the Ashley Wilkes of Leslie Howard in *Gone with the Wind*.

It was Barker's professional misfortune to come along when war-hero worship was the rage, with the movie business' stalwart leading men soon to return from service and deprived audiences gravitating to newcomers of the muscular Burt Lancaster-Kirk Douglas variety.

Even Leslie Howard, the gentle esthete and polished actor, had he not been lost in the war, would have had a rough time getting on in postwar Hollywood, where Rock Hudson would park his truck forever and Tony Curtis would catch screen notice rhumbaing with a curl dangling from his forehead and a handkerchief dangling from his lapel pocket.

Some ironic lines of dialogue from Hayward pictures are brought to mind—there were many times in her career when, *à la* Mae West, she seemed to be writing her own words.

Robert Preston, frowning on some of her shady business deals in *Tulsa*, evoked this upbraiding from his flammable fiancée: "What are you, a boy scout or a man?"

"I'm not sure anymore," said Preston, usually so assertive on screen himself.

With a toss of her rust-colored mane and a ratatat finality, Hayward shot back, "Well, you better make up your mind. The man I marry's gotta be sure!"

"Where do I find a *man,* someone I can look up to?" communications empire head Hayward implored Major General Kirk Douglas in *Top Secret Affair.*

And, to the towering but cowering Albert Dekker in *Among the Living:* "I guess I made a mistake. I thought you were a man. Sorry!"

"You know, for a little while tonight I thought I'd met a real man. But I was wrong," huffed Hayward, seeking help from *Soldier of Fortune* Clark Gable. "To me, mister, you're just a gangster, a throwback. I hope you enjoy living with yourself!"

After a year of marriage in *I'll Cry Tomorrow* that saw them drunk most of the time, playboy Don Taylor groggily told Hayward, "I'm a man, and I've got to get to work."

"What are you going to be a man at?" sneered his equally groggy wife.

In *Demetrius and the Gladiators,* the slave Demetrius (Victor "Hunk of Man" Mature) wondered, "Why do you choose me?"

Replied Messalina (Hayward), interested in more than a slave-and-owner relationship, "Because you'd never crawl to anyone. You're a man!"

Hayward's choice of a man in real life especially surprised those who recalled she had steady-dated her *Hit Parade of 1943* co-star, the dark, unctuously masculine John Carroll, just before she tied the knot with Barker. Carroll, divorced from actress Steffi Duna, could have been the man in question when *Motion Picture* wrote in 1957: "Even then, highly selective about her personal life, few knew that Susan was engaged to an actor before she met Jess Barker. A GI, he wrote her to have an engagement ring made. And Susan, who has always believed that a diamond is a girl's best friend, let herself go. Her mother had never had an engagement ring and Susan wanted one—though she wasn't certain she was in love. The actor blew up when he found out what it cost, and Susan impulsively broke the engagement then and there, paying for the ring herself. She still wears it as a good luck token."

Many years after this incident, in another magazine feature, she announced her preference for leading men (on screen) with strong sex appeal. She rapped "the pretty boys of the '60s," praised Clark Gable, John Wayne, Dean Martin and Vince Edwards as "great lovers" of the business, men who clearly had "fought for their successes and won."

The same magazine writer described their meeting: "With her bright hair at shoulder length and dressed in a smart suit, Susan Hayward walked into the restaurant. We were going to hold our interview over lunch. She spoke to the head waiter and he brought her over to my table. All the eyes in the place turned to look at this beautiful vision crossing the dining room. One man sitting at a table in the front almost fell out of his chair as she wended her way toward me in the back. I smiled to myself and wondered if some of the new stars of today— the young girls with their pale looks and athletic figures —could match this reception. I sort of doubted it."

11. GONE APE!

Although she was still a ways from being the *grande dame* she is today, Hayward continued her rise in a productive 1944. She received publicity-worthy titles like Miss Pin-Up, but, with the possible exception of Marjorie Main, so did almost every Hollywood female in the limelight then. Completely her own were honorary memberships in the New York Police Department, the Montana State Penitentiary, and the International Boilermakers.

Filmwise, there was another wartime Paramount propaganda short. It was the thirteen-minute *Skirmish on the Home Front,* made for the U.S. Government Office of War Information and written by Stephen Longstreet, under the production aegis of Charles Brackett and Joseph Sistrom, who was then also producing *Double Indemnity* —Hayward wanted the part of the desirable, evil Phyllis which Barbara Stanwyck, more at home when her suits were double-breasted, never seemed physically right for. Hayward shared stellar billing with Betty Hutton and with the male leads in two of her features that year, Alan Ladd and William Bendix. Against the advice of another couple (Ladd, Hutton), marrieds Hayward and Bendix cashed in their war bonds to buy a home, later got caught short in a postwar depression as those patriotic, steadfast "Ladds" moved comfortably into their dream house.

Hayward supported Loretta Young and Alan Ladd in the slick romance *And Now Tomorrow*, which today sounds like tavern humor—did you hear the one about the poor Polish doctor (Ladd) who fixed the deaf heiress' (Young) hearing but couldn't do anything about her smell?

Her last role while under contract to Paramount, *And Now Tomorrow* was one of Hayward's most popular films there, probably because it heralded Ladd's return from nearly a year in the Army Air Force. Co-adapted by Frank Partos and, of all people, "private eye" novelist Raymond Chandler from Rachel Field's last novel, the detergent plot appeared severely edited, almost "condensed" on screen, and missing several of the lesser players who had been cast (Darryl Hickman, Mary Field, Minerva Urecal, etc.). Apparently they were left completely on the cutting room floor. Many times the picture opened on scenes that already seemed to be in progress, while others ended with the actors still talking away.

Hayward's professional proclivities, as usual in those days, were unleashed with little subtlety in this 1930s New England setting. As the heroine's globe-trotting sister, she was brought home and introduced at Young's engagement party where, embracing her sister, she spotted fiance Barry Sullivan over Young's shoulder with forebodingly rapacious glee. During the evening Young collapsed from meningitis, which left her deaf—her vision already had proved faulty. In short order, a scene faded in on Sullivan asking as he drove onto a back road, "Comfortable, honey? Lovely day, isn't it?" "Wonderful, darling," cooed his female companion, whom the camera pulled back to expose as a cuddling Hayward. Assignations over the garage were not beneath the pair, while Young occupied herself learning to read lips. Enter Ladd, whose magnificent obsession became curing her with some new serum.

Hayward was an ornery little wench into the bargain, taking it out on the servants ("Can't you see we aren't finished yet? I'll ring if I need you!") and, as Young clomped through a silent waltz with Sullivan, impatiently exhaling a cloud of cigarette smoke that all but enveloped her struggling deaf sister. She even had a vaguely tipsy minute or two. It was the segment wherein Young announced to everybody that she was finally going to marry Sullivan, whom she'd been putting off nobly because of her debility. Hayward's expression, previously kittenish in her sidelines cups, quickly switched in close-up to bug-eyed, stunned disbelief. She got back at her still unsuspecting sibling after Young had been cured, foxing the lily-livered Sullivan into telling her he loved her where Young could overhear him.

Though perhaps not a pagan *all* the way to her fingertips, as the advertising promised, Hayward still gave a refreshing tartness to the crises under the direction of Irving Pichel—who had undoubtedly picked up some pointers handling predatory women when he played the servant to *Dracula's Daughter* ('36).

Young, overacting, and Ladd, underacting, were the original odd couple. She drew what could be the sourest notice of her life from Bosley Crowther in *The New York Times*: "Miss Young gives a performance which may best be compared to a Fanny Brice imitation of a glamorous movie queen. What ever it was that this actress never had, she still hasn't got." Her simulation of deafness, however, was more restrained than it had been under similar circumstances in 1939's *The Story of Alexander Graham Bell*. Then, every time other players would have a line, an outrageously upstaging Young would bob her head like a yo-yo in front of them to study their lips. As her doctor and eventual sweetheart, Ladd, presumably as balm to reviewers who had taken to calling him expressionless, did force some smiles, but their unnaturalness gave him a weirdly sepulchral look.

On a 1964 set Hayward discussed this period with a reporter who asked why she had survived when so many other actors with whom she had begun had disappeared. "Like the girl said in the story, 'Just lucky, I guess,'" she effused in the blunt, almost flip manner she used with some interviewers. "I think I've taken the business seriously. I was totally reliable and when I was told to be on a set at nine P.M. I'd be there. I was always prompt and ready for work, so as a result I got it. I played Loretta Young's little sister, Paulette Goddard's cousin, and I lost the boy to Veronica Lake. It was all good training. We were all in the same boat, didn't know our hands from our feet. Oh, I knew so little—I knew nothing—when I came to the studios. I remember the day George Cukor had to tell me, 'The camera's over there.'"

Then in '44 there was *The Fighting Seabees* (Republic), an action-packed war drama with Hayward the newshen between Navy men Dennis O'Keefe and John Wayne; and the interesting, more portentous *The Hairy Ape* (United Artists), from Eugene O'Neill's 1922 play about a ship's stoker (William Bendix) who was driven nearly crazy when a rich hedonist (Hayward) called him a "hairy ape."

The Fighting Seabees, however, publicized as this quickie studio's biggest budgeted film up to then, deserves some attention. It helped Hayward by making her "the girl" in another boxoffice entertainment, and found a slender, good-looking John Wayne in extremely comfortable situations. As Wedge Donovan, the construction boss hero, Wayne's hat was not only hard but white.

64

The fictional plot, set early in 1942, concerned the establishment of the real-life Seabees. "Construction battalions?" deliberated a naval officer. "No oomph. We'll call them . . . Seabees!" Wayne's goal, finally achieved, was to win permission for his builders to carry weapons in war zones threatened by "Tojo and his bug-eyed monkeys." His chief adversary was the "gold-braided" Dennis O'Keefe, who just happened to be the boyfriend of ubiquitous wire service reporter Hayward—a dish even with her crowning glory tucked under silly hats and/or those most dreaded of World War II scourges, hair rats. She met Wayne when they accidentally bumped against each other a couple of times on a crowded pier. "Let's not make this a habit," she finally snapped. "The lady's difficult," Wayne grinned in her dust. When he shortly kissed her on a moonlit ship's deck, she gasped, "I'm sorry you did that"—but then she said the same thing to Clark Gable in *Soldier of Fortune*. Eventually, "Connie Correspondent" confessed being in love with both Wayne and O'Keefe. She even stopped a Japanese bullet looking after her interests, but recovered in time for her next assignment.

The action scenes were expansive and generally well handled by director Edward Ludwig and long-time Republic special effects ace Howard Lydecker, although a number of process shots involving the actually draft-exempt Wayne made it sometimes seem as if he had missed this war, too. There was one bit of battling that was *outré,* cinematically, even for the white-hot anti-Japanese period of its filming. During the explosive closing contest, Grant Withers scooped up a screaming Japanese soldier in the jaws of his crane and then, while he was squirming in the air, shot him. When fellow Seabee J. M. Kerrigan* asked why he'd done that, Withers

---

*With character actors like J. M. Kerrigan and William Frawley doddering about the mortar, it looked like the resistance to construction engineers carrying guns was really because they were too old to lift them.

yelled, "I was afraid the fall might kill him." Nearer the end, when Lydecker actually filled acres of California real estate with blazing fuel oil, a superficially wounded O'Keefe told Wayne, "Go on, Seabee. Hold the island." "Can do," sloganized Wayne. He did, and died. This didn't exactly wrap up the war, but it did solve Hayward's problem.

The violence extended to an unusual Wayne foray into jitterbugging with an energetic party blonde called Twinkles Tucker (Adele Mara, whose walk-on here would soon be repaid with featured parts like her co-starring role with Wayne in 1949's *Sands of Iwo Jima*).

Most of the professional assessors felt the romance aspect had been dragged in, especially the New York *Daily Mirror*'s Lee Mortimer, who wasn't complaining. His headline was "Seabees and Susan/Glorified at Globe," and Mortimer's basically affirmative evaluation read in part: "Faced with a problem almost as imposing as any the Seabees ever met, the studio had to figure out how to horn Susan Hayward into a film about mechanics and machines. 'Damn the plausibilities,' cried someone at Republic. 'Full steam a-Hayward!' So, what happened? Susan turns up in the South Seas in the regalia of a war correspondent. With half the Navy going for her, it's a wonder anybody ever did anything about the Japs. . . . I want to see one newspaper gal built like Susan. They'd never send *her* far away."

Re *The Hairy Ape*, which originally had made Louis Wolheim a star and was labeled "indecent" and "socialist propaganda" by some in its day, *Time* wrote: "Deprived of his bitter social implications and his tragic ending, the stoker becomes a not very convincing sailor ashore. William Bendix' natural good temper shines fatally through his industrious soot-and-greasepaint toughness. Susan Hayward (in the part played on stage first by Mary Blair, then Carlotta Monterey, soon to be Mrs. Eugene O'Neill) is much tougher, more convincing; in fact, Hollywood's ablest bitch-player."

66

Robert C. Roman elucidated further in his article, "O'Neill on the Screen," in a 1958 issue of *Films in Review*. "The script by Robert D. Andrews and Decla Dunning was greatly different from O'Neill's play," he said. "Even O'Neill's theme was sacrificed for new, and unimpressive, dramatic elements. O'Neill had subtitled his play 'A Serio-Comedy of Ancient and Modern Life,' and let it be known that *The Hairy Ape* was a representation of man struggling with his fate. The protagonist, wanting 'to belong,' fails to find acceptance in any level of society and, concluding he has a close affinity to the ape in the Central Park Zoo, enters its cage and is crushed in the gorilla's arms. The film has the stoker, given a feeling of inferiority by a self-centered society girl, Mildred Douglas (Hayward), go to her New York apartment, make love to her, and then flip a coin down the open front of her dress."

Other disappointing factors in this Alfred Santell-directed release, continued Roman, were extraneous sub-plots and the updating to the current war. Plus, "the inner feelings of the stoker, called Hank instead of Yank, were not adequately set forth. Nor was the 'ironic life-force,' with its distinct and powerful social meaning."

One of Hayward's biggest personal disappointments around this time was when Buddy DeSylva changed his mind at the last minute and refused to loan her out for the highly dramatic lead in *Dark Waters,* which Merle Oberon then got. "You've been rude, snippy, and unco-operative with stars and directors," he chastened. "Maybe this will teach you." About twenty years later, when some high-priced names were helping with their unprofession-alism to bury the star system in an already ailing busi-ness, Hayward said, "I never held up production in my life. I worked at it. I truthfully don't think I've been a temperamental actress. I've fought for what I thought was right. I don't call that temperament, I call that being honest and fair."

In the mid-'50s she remembered "doing the 'walking

off the set' routine just once, and that was when I was at Paramount in the early stages of my career. The director kept riding me. Nothing I did was right. One day he got particularly nasty and I blew. I then bearded Buddy DeSylva in his den and said, 'I won't go back on that set until that man apologizes.' Mr. DeSylva called the director to his office—and he apologized. I haven't had to do that since."

John Gavin, her co-star in the widely seen *Back Street* in 1961, who a decade later would become President of the Screen Actors Guild, remarked several years after on network TV that while certain people he knew had pitied him when they heard he'd be working with Hayward, "I found her to be not only a great artist but a great lady as well."

World War II was drawing to a close just as Hayward's contract came up for renewal in 1945—events not without their parallels. Her refusal to re-sign, however, did not quite match the image that had evolved by Gavin's time. "They offered me more and more money, but I had had enough of Paramount. I told them in no uncertain terms what they could do with their contract," she confessed.

Only weeks later DeSylva left, too—by request. Hayward shed no tears.

RKO was quick to hire her for the critically applauded *Deadline at Dawn* ('46). This was a diverting if over-written mystery with Hayward as a dance hall girl at a Broadway bunion palace called "The Jungle." She was top-billed (above the title) for the first time, over 1943 Best Actor Oscar winner Paul (*Watch on the Rhine*) Lukas. Again, *Time:* "As hard-boiled Big City cops-and-killer dramas go, *Deadline at Dawn* is one of the better ones. It is lifted out of the run-of-the-corpse routine by earnest playing, good lighting and photography (by Nicholas Musuraca), drum-fire dialogue."

"Go 'way, son," an acrid young Hayward ("Call me June. It rhymes with moon") warned sailor Bill Williams at the start. "I'm in the mood to slug the next ape who paws me in this heat." It was a testament to her skill, another reviewer approved, that the actress, "who looks about sixteen" could call even middle-aged men "son" and get away with it.

Although he thought the denouement illogical, Bosley Crowther liked *Deadline at Dawn:* "In scripting this racy little baffler about a sailor-boy on leave who is compelled to prove, within six hours, that he didn't murder a certain female, scenarist Clifford Odets has assembled a great deal of vivid incident from a novel by William Irish and has blessed it with some bristling dialogue. And Harold Clurman, director, has put it before the camera with a good sense of mood and movement so that the whole thing rolls off fast and well. The feverish intent of the sailor and a few friends he picks up on the way to clear himself, a sordid side of city life in the wee hours and the peril of police intervention—all are pictured absorbingly."

The performances were "thoroughly engaging. Bill Williams is winning as the boy, Susan Hayward is spirited as the night-moth who assists him, and Paul Lukas plays a taxi driver (and the murderer) well. . . . Joseph Calleia, (victim) Lola Lane, and Jerome Cowan are superb as hard-boiled creatures of the night, and Joseph Crehan as a police lieutenant does as sharp a bit of acting as you could ask to see."

Protruding from the melodrama was as self-consciously subversive a portrait of Gotham life as has been made yet. "This is New York, where hello means goodbye," said Hayward. "Where's everybody going?" asked Williams in a crowded subway. "To the dogs," barked a passing traveler. "I'm just a parasite on parasites," avowed a cab driver. There were overworked tenement superintendents, and bums who were refused a night's sleep in jail because they hadn't committed any crimes. Even Hayward and Williams, with the murdered woman only a few feet away, took a sleuthing respite to

69

eat from the corpse's refrigerator. On a grander scale a nationally idolized ball-player named Babe (Joe Sawyer) was characterized as a fat, drunken womanizer

Producer Adrian Scott became one of the "Unfriendly Ten," so named because they refused to testify before the House Un-American Activities Committee during the late 1940s investigations of Communism in the industry. He was blacklisted.

Perhaps the worst criticism for *Deadline at Dawn* appeared twenty years later when Andrew Sarris wrote in *The American Cinema:* "Back when New York's Group Theatre* was camped in Hollywood, Harold Clurman came up with a film which today resembles nothing so much as a parody of poetic social consciousness. Yet, there in the middle of all the fakery was Susan Hayward, pure Brooklyn and pure Hollywood, and infinitely more real and lasting than the WPA."

Thus ended her "ape trilogy"—and an epoch.

12.   ENTER WANGER—UPWARD HAYWARD

Independent producer Walter Wanger, who had made the definitive Garbo film, *Queen Christina* ('33), and was now working at Universal, had been watching Hayward's progress for some time and wondered why she wasn't farther along. He elected to do something about it himself. He signed her to a personal contract, whereupon her career shot upward. Later she would say of the spiffy, cultured Wanger, now deceased, "We both agreed on the sort of roles I should play and went after them. If Walter wants me for anything, no matter what the

---

*The Group Theatre, founded by Harold Clurman, Cheryl Crawford, and Lee Strasberg, existed in New York from 1931–41. It advocated naturalistic acting, while Group writers, including Clifford Odets, explored problems indigenous to the times in their plays.

70

picture is I'll do it. I owe him everything. He was the
first Hollywood producer to treat my desires and wants
seriously, and I'll always be grateful."* She had first answered a call from her old "friend" Selznick, but when
he kept the usually punctual actress waiting an hour
or more, as was his style, she walked out and over to
Wanger's "because I can go in and see him and talk to
him whenever I like."

A couple of the changes wrought by important stardom were wholly sympathetic roles and a certain tem-
pering of the vixens at which she continued to excel.
While in early lower-case jobs she could remain rotten
to the end, patenting "the Susan Hayward-type part" of
sexy meanness, "Hollywood's Hellcat" was now expected
to act a little more housebroken. She would go on to
raise screen hell, but Hayward the popular star, the
"Brooklyn Bernhardt," now found herself frequently re-
deemed at the last minute by her character's hitherto
neatly camouflaged innate decency.

Her new boss used her first in *Canyon Passage* ('46),
an under-appreciated Universal Western by turns lusty
and lyrical. Like Wanger's 1939 classic, *Stagecoach,* it
was based on an Ernest Haycox story. This one was set
in 1856 Oregon and claimed, besides Hayward, Dana Andrews and Brian Donlevy riding shotgun for a heavy-
weight troupe. Featured players included Hoagy Carmichael at his feyest and Andy Devine, who had been on
that stagecoach, and this time he brought along his small
sons Tad and Denny. Directed on location in Oregon by

*She proved a woman of her word years later when she was
big star. She was advised against doing a particular film for
Walter Wanger because he was coming off several flops. But she
didn't forget the major part he had played in her career (all the
while entrusted with the career of his own wife, Joan Bennett),
and she signed for the picture. On the strength of Hayward's
name, he got the necessary financing to make *I Want to Live!*—
which turned out to be a great success for both Hayward and
Wanger.

71

Jacques Tourneur, the film galloped through a Technicolored, flavorful wilderness of slatelike rains, flower-
strewn lakes, buttermilk skies, and hilly town streets trod
by life-size people. It has aged well. Today when seen on
television and compared, especially, to that medium's
studio-bound, claustrophobic, *Gunsmoke*-type Western,
telling their tales mostly via close-ups (Gary Cooper, I
think, once said that these programs dealt so little with
the Old West as such that their stories could just as easily
have been told in a Manhattan skyscraper), the scope
and wide open spaces of this unpolluted *Passage* look
even more inviting than on initial release.

As Lucy Overmire, daughter of frontier lawyer Stanley
Ridges and Fay (Ma Hardy) Holden, Hayward was increasingly drawn to idealistic, ambitious businessman Andrews, although she was engaged to weak, embezzling
banker Donlevy. (An unprincipled banker, played by
Berton Churchill, also figured in *Stagecoach*.) She gave
her rather thankless "man's picture" part a sense of humor
which may not have been in the script, showing a surer
flair for fluff in this essentially straight chore than in most
of her elusive all-out comedies, debunking *Time*'s later
contention that her lightest touch would "stun a horse"
and proving the ability to make merry was there for the
mining. Hayward's puckish, flirty baiting of the honora-
ble Andrews, for example, though it was kept to a
minimum, was a welcome breather from Indian-harassed
pioneering. In a three-way discussion, Donlevy told Andrews he felt the wilderness had a corrosive effect on
man. He asked Hayward what she thought. She grasped
her fiancee's arm and twinkled Andrews' way, "Some men
are more primitive than others, I guess. Some men just
fight it harder." Hayward promenaded through the brush
like that, one arm in Donlevy's, the other antagonistical-
ly akimbo as if to challenge the unseen—a challenge
never really heeded. Nevertheless, her showing was not
without a salty moment or two: "Why didn't you kill
him?" suddenly blazed our crinolined heroine to Andrews
72

after his bloody saloon fight with villainous Ward Bond—which Hayward had watched through a window with a beatific smile. As in other tepid roles, one could almost hear her telling the writer, "Audiences expect me to flare up. Maybe we could put a line in here . . ."

"Amid all this elemental, physical melodrama," reviewed *The New York Times*, "Ernest Pascal, the scenarist, finds time to contemplate normal aspects of frontier life. For instance, the festivities attendant upon the cabin-raising ceremony for a newly married couple are altogether charming . . . A whopping show." If it was hardly the original that *Stagecoach* was, which had repopularized the entire genre with its visual poetry and down-the-line fibrous characterization, the movie did very well. Much thanks were due the exceptional scenic production values and musical director Frank Skinner's lavish orchestral use of atmospheric Carmichael melodies, particularly the jaunty, bewitching, Carmichael-Jack Brooks tune, "Ole Buttermilk Sky." The Academy registered its approval of the song with an Oscar nomination. Unexplainably, the picture is today ignored in the number of tomes and articles written on the history of the Western film.

Considering the demands of her next Wanger entry from Universal, which had Martin Gabel as Associate Producer, maybe it was just as well that Hayward had to conserve her energies in *Canyon Passage*.

13. THE STORY OF AN ACADEMY NOMINATION

It was a decade of dazzling female rule.

Of Mrs. Minivers, Margies, Lady Eves, Mildred Pierces, Incendiary Blondes, Mrs. Skeffingtons, Lauras, (Johnny) Belindas, Bernadettes, Heiresses, Gildas, St. Joans, and Lassies.

But no '40s actress grabbed off a meatier tour de force —or masticated one better—than Hayward in *Smash-Up, The Story of a Woman* ('47), an Academy-nominated original story by Dorothy Parker and Frank Cavett. It is cited by many of her devotees as their favorite Hayward film, although sans her shiny-browed realism the John Howard Lawson screenplay could have slipped irretrievably into suds. Portraying the neglected, alcoholic, ex-singer wife of a popular crooner ("played by Lee Bowman," wrote *Life,* "with all the enthusiasm of a stuffed moose"), she powerfully created a tragic lady with a basic insecurity that first materialized with a drink before going on stage—also Lillian Roth's start with liquor, according to Hayward's case history of her eight years later in *I'll Cry Tomorrow.* Her insight into the drunk's psyche and manner was astonishing, causing many to wonder just how thorough had been her research.

Writer-wit Parker's research has been better documented, and some Hollywood insiders said *Smash-Up* was really the story of a woman named Dorothy Parker. A biographer of hers, John Keats, denied this, allowing only that the chance to work on a film at this particular time may have helped to stay the troubled Dorothy's own smash-up.

If it hadn't followed Paramount's 1945 Best Picture *The Lost Weekend,* which dealt in a similar graphic, sympathetic way with a male dipso (Ray Milland, in his Oscar performance), *Smash-Up* undoubtedly would have been called a film landmark. For Hayward's vulnerable Angie Evans was a different kind of heroine for the rather repressed Hollywood of that day, as well as against-type casting for the rock-ribbed actress—"The trouper's blood in our family ran out when it got to me," she informed her agent when she quit show business to be a homemaker. No perfect wife or floozie with a heart of gold, this advantaged but lonely, even shy woman loved her family but battled an "illness" that caused her

74

at one especially candid point to pass out on the street and wake up in a stranger's bed. Seneca called alcoholism "voluntary madness." Her neurotic need for the then struggling Bowman was established early and subtly when, in their silhouetted coming together in a stage door alley after one of Angie's performances, her desperate ardor showed this was not merely "boy meeting girl."

"Did you ever sit, day after day, night after night, staring at your hands?" a new drowning, poignant Angie later asked someone.

The characterization of her agent also was a departure. Instead of the usual greasy, grubbing flesh-peddler so dear to movie-makers and stand-up comics even now, Angie's agent, as played by inescapable 1930s–40s character actor Charles D. Brown, was a soft-spoken, kindly friend. It is not hard to imagine how other producers then—less daring than the often contrary Wanger—might have reacted to a script whose heroine was a falling-down drunk and which featured a gentlemanly, generous agent.

Even the more familiar material was brightened by the lead's wonderful performance. For instance, the scenes detailing the young wife's pregnancy period were given a conventionally light "Dagwood" treatment—Bowman: "You don't mean—you and me . . . *Steve,* I'm gonna have a baby!" but when her husband suddenly was called to the hospital he found Hayward being wheeled away to the delivery room with a startling look of agony and pleading on her contorted, sweaty face. Another unforgettable bit was Hayward's parched, pinched expression in her march from bed to her bar one dry morning after. This seemed a premature peek at *cinéma vérité,* Hayward striding right past the voyeuristic lens of Stanley Cortez, "that supreme master of light" (Charles Higham in *The Films of Orson Welles*) and cinematographer for *The Magnificent Ambersons, Since You Went Away* and *The Night of the Hunter,* whose work throughout had a sheen that, not inappropriately, made it sometimes also seem as if we were viewing life through a shot glass. Moments like these lent some validity to the confession magazine title addendum, *The Story of a Woman*.

The scene where a drunk Hayward nearly cremated her child when she dropped a cigarette and set the house afire was among the most harrowing the screen had presented. Her screams, furthermore, as she fought with her own body the flames enveloping her little girl were as chilling, resounding and legitimate as any to be found in that movie age of that now archaic staple, the Screaming Mimi. (A grimly ironic footnote to this celluloid conflagration is that early in 1971 a fire broke out in Hayward's Fort Lauderdale, Florida, ninth story apartment that was also started by an unextinguished cigarette. Then living alone, Hayward, who had been sleeping, escaped the blaze by going out on her balcony where she was preparing to lower herself by blankets to the next floor when the firemen arrived and rescued her. A fire lieutenant stated that the actress, who was uninjured, "kept her cool and did everything right. If that balcony hadn't been there, though, she would have been in serious trouble. It was the only thing that saved her.")

Another marvelous Hayward moment came in the flash when, as she was intently drinking and smoking alone at a bar after her daughter had been taken away from her, a rather tight new father (Robert Shayne) nearby counseled, "Don't ever let anybody take your baby away from you!" The seething lady vowed she wouldn't, firing smoke through each nostril like a dragon getting ready for the charge.

On the way to her smash-up, Hayward even got to sing two fetching Jimmy McHugh-Harold Adamson tunes. Her voice was dubbed by Peg LaCentra, whom George T. Simon in his book *The Big Bands* called—accurately, if this soundtrack was evidence—"one of the finest of all girl vocalists." Miss LaCentra has said, "I imitated Susan. By that I mean I got together with her and studied her voice, so that I could sound as she might if she sang. I always did that when I was dubbing, which I did quite a bit in those days," preeminently for Ida Lupino in *The Men I Love* and *Escape Me Never*. Prefaced by a shot through Hayward's sheer entrance curtains of her downing a shimmering bracer, the torchy "I Miss the Feeling" was the more creatively staged song, establishing within one average-length number not only Angie's weakness but her progress along the boite belt from smallish room to medium-size spot to large club. En route, the film audience watched Angie's gowns change to suit each new location; the orchestra augmented until it sounded like the Boston Pops had joined her to finish the song; and the places' names grow more posh until, in a crescendo, the monogram on a crystal goblet revealed—Club Biarritz! Her "Hush-a-Bye Island," a charming lullabye, was sung to Angie's child. The pretty "Life Can Be Beautiful" was given to Bowman, voice dubbed by Hal Derwin.

Smash-Up was the turning point in her career, as well as, a long-time associate pointed out, the first time Hayward really began to feel like an accepted member of the movie colony.

Photoplay's Marian Quinn Kelly called it "an absorbing film," naming Hayward in their "Best Performances of the Month" department. Comparisons with *The Lost Weekend* were inevitable, and the reviewer felt *"Weekend* pictured the subjective battle in Milland's mind: *Smash-Up* tells its horror story by a sometimes melodramatic pointing up of incidents."

That same magazine's Jack Ashland, in a story on Hayward, imparted: "For the first time since serving her Hollywood 'internship' (her name for it), she thoroughly enjoyed the relationship of cast and crew. From the 27th of May until the end of August, 1946, she worked every single day. She was never tired, never unhappy. She had complete trust in her director, felt he completely trusted her, too. Every shot the cameraman took she knew was

77

the best he could do. 'I'm the girl who made all the mistakes in the book,' Susan tells you frankly. 'But if I hadn't, I never would have fully appreciated that great cooperation from the entire company. I've never been as contented in my life, but it took me seven unfortunate years to learn my lessons and profit by them. I guess no one can really tell another person how to change. You just have to learn for yourself, go through it yourself.' "

Incisively directed by Stuart Heisler and supported by stable family friend Eddie Albert and sleek other woman Marsha Hunt (whom a soused Hayward, following a Gale Sayers-worthy piece of broken-field stalking, trapped in a party powder room for a dandy slugfest), Hayward earned her first Best Actress Academy Award nomination. But somehow Loretta (*The Farmer's Daughter*) Young won.

Alfred Hitchcock's erstwhile assistant, Joan Harrison, borrowed the now hot property for one of her own producing ventures in suspense, RKO's *They Won't Believe Me* ('47). Written by Jonathan Latimer and directed by Irving Pichel, it is today considered something of a classic of ironic plotting. Critic James Agee: "A skillful telling of a pretty nasty story about a man (Robert Young) who loves money and women almost equally well, and finds that they get in each other's way. . . . Susan Hayward proficiently sells her special brand of sexiness." Young, if a bit upstanding for his parasitic husband role, and lovely Jane Greer, elevated to stardom as one of his girlfriends, were lauded, too. While Rita Johnson, another eternal other woman, tasted the rewards of virtue in one of her most praised screen appearances, as the wife this time—Young's wealthy, coolly calculating albatross whom Johnson's sensitively shaded performance made oddly sympathetic.

In spite of the reviews, the film was not a big moneymaker. Recently, Young proffered as the reason his unshatterable "good guy" image during palmy 1930s and '40s: "One exception was my 1938 role in *Three Com-*

rades as a Nazi officer, which shocked the fans. They just couldn't get used to my new image. There was a similar problem in the '40s when I made *They Won't Believe Me,* in which I portrayed a heel. The picture was correctly named. The public *didn't* believe me. I went right back to playing good guys after the boxoffice results came in. Fate, I guess."

Cast as a gold-digging brokerage firm secretary reformed by her love for Young, Hayward came on late and left early—dead in a car accident running off with Young. "She looked like a very special kind of dynamite, neatly packaged in silk and lace,"* recalled flashback narrator Young for our first glimpse of Hayward, slinking around the office like some feline predator. Her best scene—or angriest, anyway—occurred at a bar, a setting that always brought out the best in the actress. Thrown over for the moment by Young, she bolted upright and, having the bartender's ear, she decried, "That drink's yours, George. The rat on my left will pay. He's got a rich wife!"

Later in the frequently contrived story, Young was indicted for Hayward's murder. Convinced they didn't believe him, just as the jury was coming in he tried to jump out a courtroom window and was shot dead. The verdict was then read by the clerk (Milton Parsons, appropriately, who was long identified with undertaker parts): "Not guilty."

It is doubtful that the social, American expatriate Henry James, great and prolific man of letters though he was, could ever have imagined that a poor little carrottop from Flatbush would someday play one of his complex heroines, let alone a Venetian one. But that's just what happened in another Hayward late-bloomer, the Walter Wanger-Universal *The Lost Moment* ('47), adapted from James' novella *The Aspern Papers* by Leonardo Bercovici with, in the fashion of Hollywood's Freud-obsessed '40s,

---

*Completing *They Won't Believe Me,* Hayward announced she would pose for no more "cheesecake," or bathing suit, art.

even more "psychological" pivots than the original author had devised. It was probably the star's most stylish vehicle.

Hayward was gripping as Tina Bordereau, the tautly beautiful delusionary (perhaps *too* beautiful for a girl life was passing by) who ran an ancient mansion with a ramrod, reclusive authority but who literally let her hair down at night and imagined herself the adoring sweetheart of a long-disappeared poet, Jeffrey Ashton. In reality it was her 105-year-old "aunt" (Agnes Moorehead) who had been his inamorata and, the crone eventually gasped, his crime-of-passion murderess—that one patch in the garden where nothing would grow. It was she, too, who had helped unintentionally to derange her orphaned niece by reading her over and over from childhood the poet's passionate love letters. Into this precarious household came American boarder Robert Cummings, there ostensibly to write but really a publisher after "the Ashton papers."

"Isn't it a bit lonely here for you?" he quizzed the austere young Hayward upon arrival at the remote, sprawling palazzo—she, wrote James, who "always had a look of musty mourning (as if she were wearing out old robes of sorrow that would not come to an end)."

"It's only being with people that makes one lonely," Hayward stiffened, abiding him at first only because they needed his money.

Cummings—himself "always at home with the past" —soon succumbed to the disturbed "Miss Tina . . . who walked dead among the living, and living among the dead." Their love scenes made tenderest pentimentos— the moonlit waltz in a fading bower, a rapturous Hayward alter ego believing herself in Ashton's arms . . . Cummings' gradual thaw of her rigid, tightly coiffured side with a single rose and a piazza evening by gondola that ended with Hayward, once back behind her door, uncontrollably loosening one strand of hair beneath her lace shawl to signal a spell. Her quivering, glassy-eyed face when she was accosted during the violent lapse in which she discovered "her" letters had been stolen was particularly knowledgeable pretending, haunting my youth; in fact, one of the medium's most effective intimations of madness and "instant trauma." Although a rare involvement in moody, arty filmmaking for the substantial, forthright Hayward, *Lost Moment* contained one of her most luminous, responsive acting jobs and recent viewings show that time has achieved the unique feat of brightening its lustre.

She made it possible to accept a weirdly careening creature who could enter harping, "Amelia, I think you should pull the drapes. The sun is beginning to come into the room." But who, just beyond the next black stairway, was exulting, "No woman since time began has ever received such letters!"

The eerie Hal Mohr photography and Daniele Amfitheatrof music plus almost impressionistic "period" canal-side sets on the backlot and, especially, a fantastically wizened Moorehead—who, while called "the divine Juliana," was really based on Claire Clairmont, Lord Byron's mistress—all contributed to the pervasive lavender romanticism of this wrongly forlorn production. Several years afterwards, producer Wanger told me, "We missed badly on that one." The only place they may really have missed (aside from the till) was with a fiery finale too far removed from James that too patly resolved everyone's problems. Hayward escaped the flaming house that had destroyed her aunt and the letters and, free of all ghosts, embraced redemptor Cummings, a schizoid thus cured on a very hot dime. At the time of release, *Screenland* magazine was one of the few authorities to appreciate *Lost Moment*: "Hayward's highly sensitive performance as the emotionally and mentally unstable heroine . . . forms an absorbing picture. Credit her compelling performance and Martin Gabel's consistent, deliberate direction for maintaining suspense. The story, interesting as it is, is secondary to Susan's engrossing study."

Over a decade later the James story again failed to draw patrons in a Broadway version under its original title. Wendy Hiller assumed Hayward's mantle.

Twenty years after in *Hollywood in the Forties,* perspective was sufficient for the authors to place *Moment* "among the most pleasurably civilized films the sound cinema has yet given us. Lovely visuals (Hal Mohr) accompanied a delicately recorded soundtrack that caught perfectly the tinkle of cut-glass chandeliers, the faintest whisper of the nocturnal household. The early scenes following Cummings' arrival, sombre and melancholy, achieved an intriguing atmosphere, and a nice touch was the use of a Shelley miniature to represent the late poet Jeffrey Ashton."

Even more recently the picture received a certain celebrity in the film *Myra Breckinridge* when movie crazy transsexual Myron/Myra (Rex Reed), playing the "trivia" game with his doctor (Jim Backus), asked him what year *Lost Moment* came out. Understandably, Backus didn't know.

Hayward voiced her agreement with the critical majority to writer Don Lee Keith in 1972. "If there are details of a picture I disagree on, or points I feel are wrong, I have a talk with the director, and we usually work out any difficulties. As might be expected, there hasn't always been a meeting of the minds. I know that years ago, while I was still under contract with Walter, I was filming something called *The Lost Moment.* I played a schizophrenic, and the director went around telling everybody not to talk to me. Yes, even warned the crew not to speak to me because he said I had to maintain a mood for the part. At one point, I lost my temper and crashed a lamp over his head, and to this day I've never felt sorry. Well, it was a disastrous film. As miserable a failure as you've ever seen. Their name for it may have been *The Lost Moment,* but after I saw it I called it *The Lost Hour and a Half.*"

Shortly before, Gabel was asked to discuss *Smash-Up*

and *Lost Moment,* the only film he ever directed—the medium's loss. Working day and night on various theatrical projects in New York and crying harried, the hard-domed Gabel would say only, "It was almost twenty-five years ago, and, frankly, I don't remember much about those days. I do remember that Susan was—is—an enormously gifted girl, with a big, warm, rich, lush talent. I've always thought her remarkable as an artist, and I've always liked her as a person."

Not jogging much better was the memory of *The Lost Moment*'s Joan Lorring, featured as the half-witted maid Amelia—"She's wicked . . . Sometimes she's kind. Sometimes—it's better when she's wicked! Father protect me, I saw her once . . ."

"What I remember best about that production is George Bau, a gentle, talented man who did the most extraordinary make-up job for Agnes Moorehead's grandam only to have the credit go to one of the Westmore brothers. Gordon Bau, George's brother, eventually gained some recognition in pictures, but George, I don't think, ever did," Miss Lorring offered, her own skin having been dipped in Max Factor No. 38 to suggest a swarthy Venetian peasant.

"As for Susan, after all these years the only impression I have of working with her is of a beautiful and very direct lady."

Hayward's zonked traipsings around the old dark house, candle in hand, brought to mind the sleepwalking Lady Macbeth—and, today, the sorry realization that she never played Shakespeare, especially the Lady Macbeth role.

Wanger saw to it that she finally got to play a headstrong Scarlett O'Hara type (named Morna Dabney) in his Universal production, *Tap Roots* ('48), set in a Mississippi valley that tried—bloodily—to remain neutral during the Civil War. There were numerous other similarities to *Gone with the Wind;* even some of Hayward's outfits looked like O'Hara hand-me-downs, including her corset in the obligatory Southern belle waist-cinching scene. When asked recently how she liked working with Hayward, Julie London, who played her younger sister, shrugged, "Fine. She's a real pro." Prodded further to reveal whether or not she saw any truth in Big Sis's then formidable personal image, the languid singer-actress said, "Oh, sure. She was all business. You couldn't get close to her."

Originally planned as a roadshow attraction, uncommon then, *Tap Roots* was from the James Street novel that had as its roots a true historical incident. Van Heflin co-starred as the Rhett Butler figure, Boris Karloff was a dignified, educated Indian, and the George Marshall-directed production, with many scenes shot on location in North Carolina in unusually brilliant color, was handsome, like most Wanger efforts of that time; but the film really didn't jell. Still, *Tap Roots* lives on—in any number of Universal theater and TV productions that continue to borrow its action footage, as well as utilize the Tara-like Dabney plantation set time after time.

The division that sometimes exists between reviewers has rarely been better exemplified than by the *Times* and *Variety* appraisals of Hayward's Morna. Said the former: "Susan Hayward, generously endowed by nature and further enhanced by Technicolor, is, however, defeated at almost every turn by the script." Said the latter: "Miss Hayward benefits from a well-drawn character (in Alan LeMay's script) and plays it to the hilt." Closer to reality was the critic who notarized that Hayward was "on her second-best broomstick" as the temporarily crippled daughter of secessionist leader Ward Bond. Paring the finished product down to standard showing time also saw the cutting of several significant Hayward scenes, which didn't help, either.

Only average, too, was her last credit for Universal then, *The Saxon Charm* ('48), the gabby "inside" story of an unscrupulous Broadway producer (Robert Montgomery). Far from charming, the Matt Saxon egomania reached straitjacket proportions, to my mind, and in Montgomery's broad, smirking, almost campily light interpretation he became intolerable much faster to the audience than to his movie clique. Hayward, her fire banked but exuding intelligence and perceptiveness, was miscast as the *hausfrau* described by Montgomery as "commonplace" and whose own lines had her gagging, "I'm not smart enough in the head to have a career." Married to playwright John Payne (whose dully pained expression throughout suggested retention of the migraines he suffered in 1946's *The Razor's Edge*), she was estranged from him for a while as he fell prey to the corrupting charisma of Montgomery, who was producing his play—about Moliere, no less. "I like the title: *The Comic Spirit, A Tragedy*," chuckled the entrepreneur. Hayward, who cut her signature avalanche of unruly hair short for the first time,* did have one drunk scene, but like her role in general and the rest of the picture, it was strictly from warm beer.

Surprisingly, there were advocates among the more elite fourth estate members who may have been taken in by the literary pretensions of director Claude Binyon's script. The *Times* called it "a scintillating, adult motion picture" and the *Tribune* "an interesting study of a theatrical tyrant."

The Saxon Charm was from a book by Frederic Wakeman, who seemed to be repeating two characters from his *The Hucksters* the previous year: the sedentary wife (Deborah Kerr in *The Hucksters,* Hayward now) and the torch-carrying torch singer (Ava Gardner first, Audrey Totter in *Saxon Charm*). The most memorable thing about the new film—which at least took a more sophisticated approach to soap opera than was usual at the time—was the name given capable Audrey Totter as Saxon's sorely tried girlfriend: Alma Wragge.

---

*Hayward had it written into her contracts of this period that her hair, often called the sexiest in movies, was not to be cut unless she wanted it.

14. FOX TAKES CHARGE—TOO

It would have taken more than a couple of middling movies to thwart Hayward's ascent at this juncture. Many of the screen's long-running first ladies were showing signs of fatigue as the second decade of talkies neared *finis*. Blondie put her last batch of cookies in the oven; Lassie girded her loins for a long romp on television; and poor Mrs. Miniver, rather prophetically, was killed off in a sequel. Film audiences were anxious for pictures starring the impudent, viable redhead. Wanger met with 20th Century-Fox pooh-bah Darryl F. Zanuck over the coveted *The Snake Pit* ('48), perhaps the part Hayward had wanted to do most since losing *Gone with the Wind*. Olivia de Havilland played the insane girl to acclaim, but after the Wanger-Hayward *Tulsa* ('49) Zanuck bought Hayward's contract for a hefty $200,000, with the same sum to go to her annually.

"I let Susan go with a mixture of sadness and relief," Wanger said. "She was always looking for good roles, and if she'd had her way I would have owned more books than the New York Public Library."

Released via Eagle-Lion, *Tulsa* was that short-lived company's most profitable production, a zestful Technicolor gusher with Hayward masterfully feisty as Cherokee Lansing, a yahooing, part-Indian 1920s oil queen not unlike *GwtW*'s Scarlett. The ads even showed a windswept Hayward waving a fist much like that lady in her "pledge to the earth" scene wherein the war-ravaged belle vowed that no matter what she had to do, she would never go hungry again. Which is not to imply that Hayward acting resources were limited. She could emote with even the back of her head, and proved it with a tiny but eloquent bit in *Tulsa*. Following the death of her cattleman father (Harry Shannon) in an opening oil field mishap, Cherokee stuck on her fedora and sought out her piano-plunking, croaking cousin Chill Wills at his speakeasy. As she approached, he segued into an inspirational old Western ballad. From behind we could see her head very abruptly drop—that was it, just a simple, uncluttered, almost reflex gesture that managed in its split second to convey pain, anger, respect, and gratitude. It said more than a dozen glycerine-eyed close-ups could.

Helping things were romantic lead Robert Preston (his fourth picture with Hayward—counting the all-star *Star Spangled Rhythm*), Pedro Armendariz, and Chill Wills (who knew his way around derricks from 1940's *Boom Town* which had, it seemed, more of character actor Wills than female stars Claudette Colbert and Hedy Lamarr). Other assets were Frank Skinner's music, the Mort Green-Allie Wrubel title tune and Stuart Heisler's direction. Likewise, a panoramic night oil strike staged with Selznickian splash and a climactic fire comprising some of the most spectacular, life-like miniature work up to then. Bosley Crowther, in fact, was so goggle-eyed at this "conflagration of vast and horrendous scope" that he referred to the fire in every paragraph of his five-paragraph *Times* review. The film's repeated pleas for conversation, little more than stage waits between the melodrama at the time, today give the project foresight and immediacy when it is shown on TV, which it often is.

Then there was the basic Haywardian dialogue. When geologist Preston was told that the sobriquet the doting Indian Armendariz always called her meant "redhead," the gal (never more femininely attractive-looking, and now come around greedily to oil) whammed, "But to *you* it means boss!" Of the oil king (Lloyd Gough) inadvertently responsible for her father's death, she swore, dagger-eyed, "Killing's too easy. I want to get him where he lives." True to stardom's demands then, her Cherokee was not without virtue, however, and she was indeed someone for all to cheer on while rescuing a pair of old drunks (Ed Begley, Jimmy Conlin) from a sidewalk bully

(Dick Wessel) with a lightning swat of her purse—"Now you git!" The Hayward image of seductive self-sufficiency was near its zenith in this semiunsympathetic character pinpointed in the Frank Nugent-Curtis Kenyon screenplay as "smart, ambitious, and hard as a driller's fist."

In *Tulsa* the parvenu continued her dream of becoming first lady of a state, a goal she first set in *I Married a Witch,* ultimately realized in *Ada* and may have come close to in real life when in '66 columns had her dating Florida's Governor Claude Kirk. In '53, of course, she got to portray the first lady of the land, Mrs. Andrew Jackson, in *The President's Lady.*

Another coincidence (?): an unexpectedly sentimental Cherokee Lansing kept the oil-smeared dresses she wore bringing in wells racked in a glass trophy case; and in the early 1960s Hayward's home was robbed of several thousand dollars in furniture and clothing, including a number of dresses she was saving from her screen performances.

Her tee-off at Fox was the stringent, regenerative *House of Strangers* ('49), directed with a keen eye for the dramatic by Joseph L. Mankiewicz from Jerome Weidman's novel, *I'll Never Go There Anymore.* Sturdily adapted by Philip Yordan (although it has been said Mankiewicz authored most of the dialogue without signing the script), and underscored by a tangy, *Street Scene*-ish theme by Daniele Amfitheatrof, the 1930s Manhattan melodrama dealt with an interfamily vendetta instigated by an Italian immigrant father (Edward G. Robinson). Running his bank and his family like a lower East Side Il Duce, Gino Monett finally was ousted by three of his four sons (Luther Adler, Paul Valentine, and Efrem Zimbalist, Jr.) following a court investigation in which he was called "a lecherous moneylender."

"I have-a no sons," Robinson mourned. "I have-a strangers."

There was one offspring he could count on, though. "The bank is-a my life, my blood. They kill-a me, Max, they take away my blood . . . You got to make them pay!" he cried insidiously to his fourth and favored son (Richard Conte), who was in prison for attempting to bribe a juror on his father's case. His hatred was fired when Robinson next uncovered that it was greedy brother Adler who had turned Conte in to the police.

Impeccably accented and mannered, Robinson was outstanding as the former barber, imbuing him with flashes of humor and (to lesser degree) humanity that another actor would have been hard put to realize.

His introductory scene was creatively handled by Mankiewicz, giving lie to the belief that he was strictly a verbal and not a visual director. (And I can only assume that Mankiewicz was responsible.) The plot's flashback crux was set up when Conte, visiting his family's now vacant townhouse at night, put Lawrence Tibbett's "Largo al Factotum" from *The Barber of Seville,* one of his favorite recordings, on the Victrola and looked up at Papa's portrait glaring nearby. Gradually, Milton Krasner's camera traveled up the dark staircase until at the top curtains rustled in daylight and his father was alive again, scrubbing himself in the bathtub and roaring the aria to a finish.

Robinson won the Cannes Film Festival Best Actor award, but in a major oversight did not even get a nomination from the Hollywood Academy. Shining, too, were Conte, never flintier or better cast as his vengeful son; Adler, the most treacherous of the brothers; Esther Minciotti, their silent, grieving mother; and Hayward in the somewhat peripheral role of Conte's wealthy but inwardly lonely playgirl sweetheart. Rallying, she fought to keep him from being destroyed by his own bitterness and the malignant influence, even from the grave, of his father.

The sex antagonism was rife the minute they met. Entering lawyer Conte's office in his father's bank, Hayward, finding him on the phone, shut the door twice to get his attention. "Who ever it is, say you'll call them back," she ordered. Offered no chair, she straightaway cleared a

place on the edge of his desk for her pelt-wrapped der-
rière. She hired Conte to get a gigolo boyfriend out of
trouble for stealing and passing bad checks—"He was
worth it." Growing interested, Conte mused, "Nothing
touches you. Everything bounces off that chromium finish." Resentful, though, of what he felt was her check-
book philosophy and slumming attitude, he tried to
taunt her by forgetting her name, Irene Bennett: "I'm not
very good at remembering names." "You'll remember my
name," she wheeled, zipping out the door with an awe-
some confidence.

Their relationship had an external I've-got-your-num-
ber/you've-got-mine brittleness that only accentuated the
genuine rapport and depth of emotion and attraction they
shared.

"You're always looking for a way to be hurt by a new
man," the bossy Conte jeered right after they met, instructing her to drop her ermine wrap because they were
staying "home" (hers). "Get smart. There hasn't been
a new man since Adam."

Another time, at the fights, when she began to show
some possessiveness, Conte (engaged to, but uninterested
in, Debra Paget) said, "I thought you were different."

Chaffed Hayward, "You'd love to find one, wouldn't
you? Get smart. There hasn't been a woman in love different since Eve."

In a recent article on Mankiewicz, Andrew Sarris commented that *House of Strangers* seemed to look better
"with each passing year, at least partly because of Susan
Hayward's toughly American brand of emotional intelligence." Her wardrobe has been less durable, today showing up far more New Look than New Deal. But everything else about her work and the picture was smack in
the *bonza*.

Another scene here exhibiting Mankiewicz' more-than-
usual visual clout was the almost silent early one reunit-
ing Conte and Hayward after his seven years in prison.
Arriving at her plush apartment, he went right to the

key still kept under a hallway vase and let himself in. Wandering about the soft, rich furnishings, he took in the skyline from the terrace (*underscore, theme, underscore*) and then entered the bedroom. He picked up a large powder puff, caressed a casually discarded negligée. He began to undress. Then the elevator deposited Hayward who, putting down her packages, heard her shower running. Dropping her purse, she ran to the closed bathroom door, then turned, leaned back against it and hugged herself, breathing, "Max!" Fade-out.

Probably the most evocative scene took place in a dingy New York café with Hayward and Conte, while a black woman (Dolores Parker) sighed "Can't We Talk It Over?" at her piano. There was a late-hours lethargy in the air—even the smoke was thinning out. A waiter (Sid Tomack) passed a slumped-over drunk and put out a candle at an empty table with the bottom of a glass on his way to dumping an ashtray on the floor. As Conte and Hayward engaged in the painful, protracted (and unsuccessful) process of breaking off at one table, they watched a fat, fiftyish man at another crowd a young, midwest-appearing virgin into tears. Finally, Conte tried to patch it up with Hayward, who sat there clinging to her elbows but impassively staring into space with eyes heavy from both the hour and all they had seen in life, breaking the look only for an occasional cynical smirk. Nuzzling her, Conte whispered, "Ice. Even your ears are cold."

The story of *Strangers,* one of the strongest of Hayward's career, was re-used in '54 for a Western, *Broken Lance,* with Jean (ex-Mrs. Howard Hughes) Peters as the girl and Philip Yordan picking up the Best Motion Picture Story Oscar for what was essentially a re-write of his earlier screenplay; and again in '61 for a circus saga, *The Big Show,* with Esther Williams in Hayward's part. Unaccountably, it has never been done as a musical—yet.

The *House of Strangers* boxoffice was very good in

Europe, perplexingly less so in the States for a plot that would be so lasting. It has been called, however, the only portrait of Italians ever brought off successfully by American cinema craftsmen—even though most of its creators, including several of the tale's focal Italians, were American Jews.

15. ELOISE WAS A NICE PART

> The night is like a lovely tune,
> Beware my foolish heart.
> How white the ever-constant moon,
> Take care my foolish heart.*

Supersophisticate Amanda in Noel Coward's *Private Lives*, besieged by her ex-husband and memories and the song "Someday I'll Find You," scoffed unconvincingly, "Strange how potent cheap music is." Certainly a popular theme never had a more profound effect on a film than in Hayward's next appearance, *My Foolish Heart*. Many still recall with affection the Samuel Goldwyn-RKO production in which Hayward's suds-busting edge, particularly, earned her a second ('49) Academy nomination—she lost to Olivia (*The Heiress*) de Havilland.

"Can a Woman Ever Escape the Memory of Love?" dribbled characteristically pandering advertising.

Not Eloise Winters.

My Foolish Heart originated in the wry badinage of the J. D. Salinger *New Yorker* short story called *Uncle Wiggily in Connecticut*, read to this day in the perennially selling Salinger collection entitled *Nine Stories*. Its greatly expanded screenplay was by Epstein twins Julius

---

*Lyrics excerpted from the song "My Foolish Heart"—written by Ned Washington and Victor Young—with the permission of the publisher, Anne-Rachel Music (ASCAP).

J. and Philip G.—who with Howard Koch had scripted another momentous bittersweet love story, *Casablanca*—and offered Hayward the moving, gamut-running role of the sweet Boise college girl whose World War II PFC lover (Dana Andrews) died in an airfield explosion, leaving her pregnant. Disillusioned, she tricked an officer friend (Kent Smith) into marriage and found herself drinking, raising a neurotic child (Gigi Perreau) and turning virago. When her post-war commuter husband phoned her during a deluge to pick him up at the train station, the slightly blotto wife refused, lying about the reason and haranguing, "Why don't you boys form a platoon and march home. Then you can say that hup! hup! hup! hup! business and be the bigtime major again."

MFH also gave Hayward one of her more striking entrances. As her plain school days roommate (Lois Wheeler), whose beau Hayward had married, drove up the winding driveway of the affluent young matron's mini-Tara in the rain for their reunion, the windshield suddenly revealed a cloaked Hayward standing there in front of the car, glass in hand. Her first line: "Shall we go in or shall we stay out and wait for the rainbow?"

In short order, but after a few tall ones, Hayward was quavering, "I was a nice girl, wasn't I? . . . He was the only boy I ever knew who could make me laugh . . . I was a nice girl, wasn't I?" Her romance with Andrews was covered in flashback after she unearthed from a closet the dress worn the night they met. The "Uncle Wiggily" of the Salinger title had several mentions, too. It was the expression Andrews borrowed from the children's Wiggily tales ("The little rabbit, always in trouble, always getting hurt") to use when Hayward accidentally cut her finger, sprained an ankle, or otherwise was discomforted —"Poor Uncle Wiggily."

There was a terrific, ingratiating performance of award quality by pouch-eyed Robert Keith as the protagonist's remarkably understanding hardware salesman father; while Jessie Royce Landis regally got around the sillier

93

aspects of Hayward's hysterical mother who when crises arose locked herself in the bathrooms of hotels and speeding trains. "Hear that, Martha?" called her husband. "Run the cold water for yes, and the hot water for no." Keith, who had come to Hollywood from Broadway's *Mister Roberts,* had one especially well written and touchingly played speech to the adoring Hayward at a café table en route to his check-up that would disclose heart disease. With his inexperienced daughter enmeshed in what she felt was her great love affair, the now even more drawn but chipper-acting father suddenly decided it was time to admit what had prompted him to propose to her mother: ". . . it was the last dance, Japanese lanterns, a song by Irving Berlin. . . . We were both trapped by the war, our youth—and by Irving Berlin."

The Academy-nominated, Victor Young-Ned Washington theme song, sung in long-shot by Martha Mears in a war-frantic nightclub setting, is generally acknowledged to be the first title tune that helped to sell a movie. Emanating not only from hot spots but dances, car radios casually switched on at Inspiration Point, and the mellifluously active soundtrack, it was a major mood-setter in this intelligently treated, even sardonic "woman's picture."

But, directed by Mark Robson, fair-haired after his ballsy, dissimilar *Champion* and *Home of the Brave,* and photographed by Lee Garmes, it was still Hayward's day. The part must have looked so good to her that she didn't veto billing behind the definitely secondary Andrews. Twenty years later "Mother" Landis recalled her daughter, the star, as "a very charming person and a lovely actress." At the time, *Look* said: *"My Foolish Heart* tells a simple wartime love story that ended in heartbreak. These are ingredients for a typical soap opera. But *My Foolish Heart* rises above its material every step of the way . . . proves that freshness can be given a much-worn story if it is approached with a light touch, an adult point of view and a warm understanding for the weaknesses of recognizable human beings. It emerges a rich, delicious movie that every grown-up moviegoer should cherish . . . In her best screen job to date, Miss Hayward makes the tragedy of a girl in love in wartime very real indeed." *Variety* chorused: "Her performance is a gem, displaying a positive talent for capturing reality." This was especially true in the jaded, juiced, Salingerish early scenes, before her Eloise was seen as a starry-eyed, peter pan-collared student who looked more like Kitty Foyle. (Hayward was, after all, now 31.)

When chum Lois Wheeler told her that their old dean, who had expelled Hayward when she caught her after hours with Andrews in a school elevator, had died horribly of cancer—"she only weighed sixty-two pounds, isn't that terrible?"—heroine Hayward deadpanned over her drink, "Not particularly."

Another swig. "Who was it said 'To forgive is divine'?" Still another. "Probably nobody I'd care to meet anyhow."

There was something slapped together and soppy about the ending, though. The husband finally "hupped" home and announced that he and old girlfriend Wheeler had been conspiring for some time to skip but, being kindly if fed-up souls, they would leave the child with its mother. The camera faded out as the abandoned drunk was attempting to calm the whimpering little girl whom her behavior had helped give nightmares.

"Poor Uncle Wiggily," sobbed Hayward, also forced by the censors to make a verbal statement of repentance.

Early in 1972, the New York *Daily News'* Ann Guarino authored a piece called "Flicks—Then and Wow!" "How times have changed in filmmaking!" she wrote. "I was reminded of this when I caught a good old-fashioned love story called *My Foolish Heart* recently on television. . . . When the movie opened at Radio City Music Hall, Kate Cameron warned 'Bring out the handkerchiefs' . . . The film holds up well due to Miss Hayward's performance. But today it would be a different story. Were the film made now, it would wallow in nude bedroom scenes.

The sex theme would be accented, the war would be updated to Vietnam and the plane accident would be shown in all its gory detail. The heroine would have a drug problem, instead of an alcoholic hang-up, to forget her lost love. This would cue lurid fantasy sequences. And the somewhat innocent love story of yesterday would be a vivid vehicle for 'now,' 'with-it' trash.

"The film would exploit sex, violence, and realism, for those are today's hang-ups. Handkerchiefs may still be necessary, not for tears, but to conceal what's happening on the screen."

Years later, Dana Andrews talked freely about his own drinking problem, one that was more severe than that of the picture's Eloise. As hero Walt Dreiser, he had the ladies sighing as well as crying in one of his best-remembered—if not lengthiest—star roles, even though he was a bit doom-spouting and, by then, craggy for the Greenwich Village fun fellow Hayward described. Andrews did a little remembering himself recently: "Susan? She was a most attractive, hard-working girl who was always very pleasant to me. We almost never saw each other socially, but we worked extremely well together. She reminded me a lot of another redhead with whom I worked: Maureen O'Hara. All you had to do was study their signatures, which were so brash and bold. I could say Susan was self-centered, but almost everyone in our profession is. She was a very strong young woman with a steel will. I felt that if she ever married an equally strong man, it might prove interesting to watch."

Gratifying, time would show, was more like it.

III

THE SPOILS

Harriet Boyd: I've been pinched, patted and
kissed. I've learned the business.
—*I Can Get It for You Wholesale*

16.   A FIRST LADY "FIRST"

Susan Hayward, a redhead, became the first lady of 20th Century-Fox, a lot that always seemed to specialize in blondes, all sizes and shapes, from little Shirley Temple to leggy Betty Grable to lanky Charlotte Greenwood.

The '50s: Hollywood's "decade of disruption." It was a rough time to be a movie star. Television was showing itself to be perhaps the industry's greatest-ever nemesis. The McCarthy witch-hunts frightened the town away from controversial themes. The major studios and their mogul fathers—who, whatever their gaucheries, loved the motion picture industry they begat—were losing their total control. In 1972 pioneer Jack L. Warner said that "the decline of the movies was really precipitated by the early-'50s government edict forcing the studios to sell the many movie theaters they owned around the country. We were told we were either in the film business or the theater business." Meanwhile, the independent producer and foreign filmmaker were gaining power. And the advent of wide screen, to be crowded with as much landscape as possible, paradoxically narrowed the medium's chances to examine the human condition. Someone said that Fox' CinemaScope, especially, was like watching a picture through a mailslot.

"The competition for top roles was murderous, and Susan rarely relaxed," a 1950s article went on. "Always there were story conferences, wardrobe fittings, subtle and not-so-subtle maneuverings for the important pictures. While Susan had a first-rank agent and business manager, it was she who made the decisions for both her career and her business investments."

The following quote was ascribed to Hayward then: "My life is fair game for anybody. I spent an unhappy, penniless childhood in Brooklyn. I had to slug my way up in a place called Hollywood where people love to trample you to death. I don't relax because I don't know how. Life is too short to relax."

"She has an implacable core," said her friend and *With a Song in My Heart* co-player Thelma Ritter, another Brooklyn girl.

Eventually, Hayward routed such 1940s fixtures at the studio as Grable (that decade's top boxoffice draw), Jeanne Crain, Anne Baxter, Gene Tierney, Linda Darnell, Celeste Holm, and June Haver. By 1952 she was the company's vanguard ticket-seller, bringing approximately $12,000,000 through tills that year—no mean feat as TV grabbed more and more of the motion picture audience. In 1953 the theater owners of America as canvassed by *Boxoffice* voted Hayward the nation's most popular female star. Most popularity polls, in fact, were showing her in their annual top ten lists, usually along with only one other female: Fox' inevitable new blonde superstar, Marilyn Monroe. And both popularity *and* acting awards were coming in from all over the world—like Britain's *Picturegoer* magazine 1953 Best Actress honor.

During a busy 1951 she stepped in for the ever-pregnant Jeanne Crain in *I'd Climb the Highest Mountain,* neglected, humane color Americana from a Corra Harris novel set around the turn of the century. It was fortunate casting, with Hayward an undomesticated, pampered city girl who married a country "circuit rider" minister (William Lundigan) and moved to the Georgia hills, where her nearest neighbor was five miles away. In no time she was crying over peeled onions, battling a typhus epidemic, and suffering a miscarriage, among other hardships. But she made her marriage work, as well as dialogue like the following passage from her gently intoned voiceover narration: "I had begun to commit the gravest sin a woman can commit against her husband. I had ceased to care how I looked." In their front porch confrontation, Hayward was able to snap, crackle, and almost pop Lynn Bari one, the latter making a stylish last stand in the sticks for "the other woman," a theatrical drawing room staple then becoming, with the profession's move toward the kitchen sink, almost as extinct as the butler. As the wealthy but unhappy-at-home Mrs. Billywith, Bari had been over-enjoying private sessions with Hayward's husband who was helping her interpret parts of the Bible. "Especially the Second Book of Samuel," smiled Bari, alone with the preacher's wife, "one of my *favorite* Books of the Bible." Fumed Hayward, "What you need is to stay home more and try to interpret your own Samuel." The increasing velocity with which she now chattered and fanned herself convinced Bari to bolt—for good. Hayward, usually in sunbonnet and gingham dress, was a picture, her hair matching the red clay of Georgia where the whole film was shot. Lundigan had possibly his most personable showing as the sometimes unappreciated, frequently uprooted but always dedicated, resourceful and liberal-minded young backwoods cleric.

The location filming, with mossy white woodland churches and winding crimson roads, the use of American Gothic natives as extras and supporting players added inestimably to this Henry King-directed/Lamar Trotti-written-and-produced charmer. It was a simple matter to forgive the ill-meshed genuine cornpone accents and the round actory tones. *Modern Screen*'s Christopher Kane chose *Mountain* "Picture of the Month": "There's something very nice and warm about this picture. The hill people, the kind of parties they hold, the way they talk and look, the scene where the mourners at a small funeral walk along slowly singing an old hymn—these seemed wonderfully authentic and flavorful to me." The big picnic, too, was nostalgically picturesque, replete with furtive young lovers (Rory Calhoun, Barbara Bates); long rows of children eating watermelon; sack races; horseshoe games; a hillside of local folk singing "In the Shade of the Old Apple Tree"—and tragedy when atheist Alexander Knox' small son drowned. Despite what may sound like a plethora of plot, *Mountain* was surprisingly short—under an hour and a half. At least one promising filmed scene is known to have been cut from the release print: the meeting of the country churchwomen when Hayward, spurred by the Lynn Bari episode, advised the ladies to use missionary funds to improve their appearances.

In a 1971 *Films and Filming* retrospective on director King, Roy Pickard wrote: "Like King's earlier essays in Americana, the episodic structure works in the picture's favor and helps develop the different characters living in the minister's small parish. *I'd Climb the Highest Mountain* is a rambling, sentimental account of rural joys and sorrows and belongs with King's half-a-dozen best films (of a total 105). Today, sadly, it is all but forgotten."

Not by Richard Cuskelly, who during a 1972 Los Angeles *Herald-Examiner* chat told the leading lady it was one of his favorite Hayward movies. "You gotta be kidding," she laughed—about to minimize unjustly the reverend's lady. "I never saw myself as much of a preacher's wife. I didn't like wearing all those pretty dresses or having to be so genteel. I liked myself better in movies like *The President's Lady,* where I got to play a gutsy Rachel Jackson. I've never been the prim and proper type."

Ruth Donnelly, long-time mistress of the snappy comeback, found herself among *Mountain* people, too, as Hayward's "near-neighbor" and, in turn, found Hayward "charming, intelligent, and a hard-working trouper. I seldom get to know the stars I work with. I try to respect their wishes to keep aloof while at work. They all have a lot at stake when they star in a film and most of them like their privacy. So, I didn't see much of Susan except

102

Hayward rehearses for an elementary school play in Brooklyn.

Among the Living, a praised "B" film of its day, featured
Maude Eburne, Albert Dekker, Hayward.

Hayward first earned wide attention tormenting Ingrid Bergman,
among others, in *Adam Had Four Sons*.

A Cecil B. DeMille spectacular: *Reap the Wild Wind*, boasting
Ray Milland, Paulette Goddard, a rising Hayward, John Wayne.

Hayward received star billing for the first time in
The Forest Rangers, with, from left, Paulette Goddard,
Clem Bevans, Fred MacMurray, Rod Cameron, Kenneth Griffith.

Hit Parade of 1943, the most successful entry in this musical
series, found Hayward via-à-vis John Carroll, with Gail Patrick.

The first of many Hayward portrayals of real-life people:
Mrs. Jack London in—*Jack London*.

Hayward and husband-to-be Jess Barker during their courtship.

And Now Tomorrow, here also showing Cecil Kellaway,
Loretta Young, Beulah Bondi, displayed quintessential
second-lead Hayward bitchery.

Canyon Passage, co-starring Dana Andrews, was Hayward's
first picture for producer Walter Wanger, her mentor.

Neglected wife Hayward turns to drink in *Smash-up, The Story of a Woman*—Academy Award nomination No. 1.

The Lost Moment, the only movie directed by Martin Gabel, starred Hayward, Robert Cummings, with Agnes Moorehead (mostly hidden by chair).

Scarlett O'Hara seemed the inspiration for Hayward's character in *Tap Roots*, opposite Van Heflin.

Tulsa, with Robert Preston holding off feisty oil queen Hayward, was the top money-earner for short-lived Eagle-Lion studios.

Hayward invades Edward G. Robinson's *House of Strangers*.

Gigi Perreau is comforted by errant mother Hayward in
My Foolish Heart, observed by Lois Wheeler, Kent Smith
—Academy Award nomination No. 2.

Georgia, later to become Hayward's home state, was the
location site for *I'd Climb the Highest Mountain,*
co-starring William Lundigan.

An early "adult" Western, *Rawhide* teamed Tyrone Power,
Hayward, with Judy Ann Dunn.

Archetypal Hayward: *I Can Get It for You Wholesale*, with, from left, Hayward, Dan Dailey, Marion Marshall, Sam Jaffe.

Hayward as crippled songstress Jane Froman in *With a Song in My Heart*—Academy Award nomination No. 3.

Mrs. Ernest Hemingway No. 2 was the model for Hayward's wife in *The Snows of Kilimanjaro*, topcasting Gregory Peck.

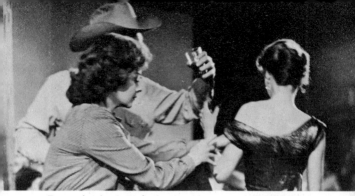

Protecting her marriage to Arthur Kennedy in *The Lusty Men*, Hayward dispatches vamp Eleanor Todd.

Hayward, twin sons Gregory and Timothy in 1952.

Hayward, *The President's Lady*, expires as husband
Andrew Jackson (Charlton Heston) looks on.

All hail Hayward in *Demetrius and the Gladiators*,
including Charles Evans, William Marshall, Victor Mature,
Ernest Borgnine.

As alcoholic entertainer Lillian Roth, Hayward carouses
(with bit player Henry Kulky) in *I'll Cry Tomorrow*
—Academy Award nomination No. 4.

Hayward (with Kirk Douglas hoisting) in a rare film
comedy, *Top Secret Affair*.

One of Hayward's most awarded roles: executed murderess
Barbara Graham in *I Want to Live!*—Academy Award
nomination No. 5, and the winner at last.

Hayward with her newly won Academy Award
as 1958's Best Actress for *I Want to Live!*
At left, Burl Ives; Best Supporting Actor
winner, and at right, David Niven, Best Actor.

Hayward and husband Floyd Eaton Chalkley
shortly after their marriage in the late 1950s.

Governor *Ada* (Hayward) lays down the law.

Hayward has one of her most glamorous parts in the latest *Back Street* remake.

Two screen *grande dames* square off: Bette Davis, Hayward in *Where Love Has Gone.*

New star Patty Duke snatches old star Hayward's wig in *Valley of the Dolls* rumble.

Hayward with son Greg Barker at his June, 1969,
graduation from Auburn (Ala.) University.

when playing my role with her. It was hot in 'them thar hills' and hard work so we had little time to indulge in any frivolities. I enjoyed working with Susan very much, though. She has a delightful sense of humor, and is a devoted mother to the twins, besides being a most beautiful woman."

Rawhide was a workmanlike, lean "adult" Western with, under Henry Hathaway's to-the-point direction, a seemly sandy, sun-dried look. "Not the biggest Western you've ever seen, nor the most original, but it's very, very good," said Louella Parsons of this first Stateside film in about three years for the roving Tyrone Power, long king of the Fox lot. In *A Concise History of the Cinema, Volume 2*, Peter Cowie did find its detailing of the operation of a stage line off the beaten path, and commended the "well-developed suspense situation."

Its greatest novelty, however, was seeing the usually swashbuckling Power as an early antihero, a young Eastern-bred fumbler "learning the business" at a remote 1880s relay station who had his mettle tested when a gang of outlaws took over the place. Fouling up his bugle call, then dropping luggage, soon knocking over lamps and taking blows, as well as doing all the cooking, he left his partner (Edgar Buchanan) to snort, "It's no wonder those mules don't take kindly to you." Hayward, a detained traveler with a chip on her shoulder the size of Squaw's Head Rock, also gave Power plenty of guff. Because he had to change the animals on the "jackass mail," she started off by calling him "mule boy." Just before the desperadoes descended, Power saw her locking the bedroom she had confiscated from him and inquired, "What are you afraid of, coyotes?" Yeah," she scowled, "the kind with boots on."

Hayward was cast in a more familiar mold as Vinnie Holt, her abundant curly hair seeming charged with electricity in time of stress. She was a former Mississippi riverboat entertainer heading East with her niece—or—

phaned by a California gun battle—to make a new life.
When she mentioned to the grizzled Buchanan that the
child had been born in a mining camp, he sympathized,
"Poor thing. That's tough." "It's tough to be born anywhere," she answered. Hayward's short fuse and plucky
presence vivified the Dudley Nichols-scripted proceedings
mainly concerned with attempts by her and Power to out-
wit their captors. Aside from the mutuality of their di-
lemma, there were no Hollywood romantics slipped in.
"I'm just like you, sister. *I want to live!*" Power argued
in the room they were forced to share by the criminals
who thought they were man and wife. At the end, she
was able to shoot degenerate heavy Jack Elam as he drew
a bead on the anomolous Power.

Her stiffest acting competition also came from the lecherous, incomparably repulsive Elam, leering menacingly
with what looked like a single working right eye as the
villain among the villains. Or as Louella Parsons noted
in her *Cosmopolitan* "Newcomer of the Month" citation:
"Jack Elam is cast as a mere follow-up villain to Hugh
Marlowe, but he looks like the type who haunts the man
who hires out to haunt a house. He is terrifying in a role
for which he will long be remembered." Elam was signed
when the originally set Norman Lloyd was thought "too
Jewish-looking" by Darryl Zanuck and was let go to avoid
any "misunderstandings."

Although it was never called a remake, *Rawhide* still
closely resembled another Fox film, 1935's *Show Them
No Mercy,* directed by George Marshall. In this, Rochelle
Hudson, Edward Norris, and their baby were held at bay
by a gang of kidnapers led by Cesar Romero and Bruce
Cabot. *Rawhide* was retitled *Desperate Siege* when it was
sold to television to keep it from being confused with the
Clint Eastwood TV series. Regardless, it's 86-minute ex-
pedition and succession of silvery, TV-like, Milton Kras-
ner-photographed close-ups make it look very much at
home on the small screen.

Coming soon was *David and Bathsheba,* about which Hayward, when she first received the script and was asked how she liked it, chortled prophetically, "I'd like it better if it were called *Bathsheba and David.*"

DaB was a sluggish, unspectacular spectacle in Technicolor solemnly written and directed, respectively, by Philip Dunne and Henry King. There was plenty of Gregory Peck as the covetous King David, stolidly if sonorously speechifying at the drop of a rod or a staff, but low-key, insufficient Hayward doing little more than starlet duty as the adulterous Hebrew woman named Bathsheba.

Her most fruitful dialogue was probably: "David, did you really kill Goliath? Was he as big as they say?"

"I will admit he grows a little bigger every year," Peck tushed, leading his lover away from the knoll where they had proved both the depth and emergency of their passion by trysting among the sheep.

Posthaste, he sent her husband (Kieron Moore) off to perish in battle and got her with child, which died soon after birth. Mostly, though, Haryward had to stand by while Peck orated, once in a while being directed to sit or kneel as he flapped on. "Bathsheba has sinned, and she must render payment according to the law of Moses," denounced perambulating prophet Raymond Massey, strong for a stoning. "She has brought adultery and murder. She has brought the draught and the famine. She has brought the wrath of God upon Israel." All from listening to Gregory Peck.

Following a flashback to the shepherd David's "chosen" childhood and his sling-slaying of threatening giant Goliath, both Biblical errants were forgiven by God in the end. But critics, only human, were less charitable, and one of them had something when he regretted, "David and Bathsheba spend nearly as much time suffering and repenting their sins as committing them." None of the major reviewers, however, noticed that its Oscar-nominated original screenplay was written "mainly in blank verse, possibly a stylistic innovation in screen writing," according to scenarist Dunne in a recent story.

The movie, one of Hayward's least colorful outings personally, drew large crowds who probably thought they were going to get some of the razzle-dazzle of DeMille's 1949 temple buster, *Samson and Delilah.* Produced by Zanuck, *David and Bathsheba* was by some tabulations the year's biggest money-making film.

17.   WHOLESALE TEMPERAMENT

A '51 highspot was *I Can Get It for You Wholesale* (called *Only the Best* for TV), more ideally presenting the Hayward you love to semihate. Indeed her environment was almost uncomfortably fertile. Her character (Harriet Boyd) had been a man (Harry Bogen) in Jerome Weidman's 1937 book and was male again (Elliott Gould) in the 1962 Broadway musical version that had Lillian Roth at the top of the cast but is known as the show that made Barbra Streisand a name. *Time* decreed: "The picture shrewdly cashes in on the superficials of the New York garment center scene, slightly altered for Hollywood slickness and stitched out with some sharp dialogues. This background, plus Michael Gordon's spirited direction, Dan Dailey's breeziness, and Hayward's fire brighten the old scenario [written by Abraham Polonsky, adaptation by Vera Caspary] about the ruthless career woman."

Years later, the frenetic, expense account hustle of the Manhattan business world in general looks very smartly drawn.

Watching Hayward—that incredible torrent of hair backlit in wee-hours disarray—set a diabolically timed and staged scene to bamboozle her sister (Randy Stuart) out of her wedding savings, or—practically having to stand on her toes—brush off her own querulous salesman boyfriend (Dailey) by jamming taxi money in his breast pocket and calling him "the all-American slob," was to see the "divine bitch" at her most disarmingly devastating. With the de-Semitizing of Weidman's original concept that now saw the (chicken) fat very much out of the fire, Hayward was inspired casting as the model—her darting, crafty, ravenous eyes X-raying every angle—who formed her own dress firm. "I know plenty, and I've learned it the hard way . . . I've been pinched, patted, and kissed. I've learned the business," she boasted to Dailey whom, with tailor Sam Jaffe, she would cajole into being her partner in Sherboyco Dresses, Inc. (for Sherman, Boyd, and Cooper). Riding next to her in a cab during an early round, Dailey, pitching, said, "I've been studying you all evening, Harriet, and I have a question. When do you come out of the deep-freeze?" She parried, "I've been studying you all evening, too, Teddy. How much've you got in the bank?"

Her character's blistering intensity was further conveyed by such miniscule but pertinent "business" as Hayward's habit when completing a fashion sketch of absently flinging the crayon across the room. The designing woman—herself a doll-like knockout in business beanie or white-tiered lace gown—fast provoked the observation from a long-suffering Dailey that she had "the simple and astonishing beauty of an old-fashioned straight razor," a line that had to have been borrowed from the ever-epigrammish, supercilious George Sanders in his department store magnate role; while her careworn mother (Mary Phillips), also sounding like she'd been shopping at Sanders', reproved her as "a throwback to an Irish bandit in the hills of Killarney."

Less emotionally involved and perhaps therefore less critical were Sanders, noting as she reached to light his cigarette first, "You really pride yourself on your independence"; and Jaffe, arguing in the wake of a rage feigned to break her contract so she could become Sanders' protégée, "After all, in a genius we got to expect temperament, not good manners." Able Marvin Kaplan's comedy relief was, if not show-stopping, certainly plot-halting in its incessancy. He was the omnipresent four eyes, the Brooklyn-nebbish office boy who left the dress firm that had employed Hayward, Dailey, and Jaffe to administer a broom at their new company. Departing, he pompously notified boss Charles Lane, "I've been offered a situation . . ." Smote Lane (who seemed to have spent his long film career in chronic distemper), "Well, what do you expect, a counter offer?"

Wholesale holds the record for footage of Hayward shot on her home island of Manhattan—where she has returned at infrequent intervals over the years. For our first glimpse, she was seen dreaming her dream during a cigarette break from a Seventh Avenue window, sleeves rolled up; then operating in Central Park, on Fifth Avenue and Sutton Place, where the double-crossing Harriet was soon able to reside. "You know how I feel about you," ladies' man Dailey 'fessed up during a romantic row over her using his tactics "wining, dining" a buyer (Harry Von Zell). "Sure," she salvoed, "I'm one of Teddy Sherman's circus. I've worked and schemed to get a business started so I'd be free of men like you!" She nearly achieved this when her selfish stunts almost bankrupt her two partners. Her change of heart occurred barely in time for a fade-out clinch with Dailey.

Some still think there was more of the off-screen Hayward showing in *I Can Get It for You Wholesale* than in any of her other pictures. For one, film scorer Sol Kaplan, whose indigenously lively background music contributed much to *Wholesale* and several of her early Fox films (especially another of her many personalized titles, *I'd Climb the Highest Mountain*). Shuddering, Kaplan told me, "Her smile was like the kiss of death. I remember we had a party on the set at the finish of one of our films, and Susan was across the room chatting with a young reporter. Suddenly, we all heard her castigate

108

the poor guy as only she could and then turn and walk off the set. I don't know what he could have said to merit what he got, but there was a pall over the party after that."

Ruth Waterbury, on the other hand, who has pro-filed her for fan magazines many times, wrote on the oc-casion of *Wholesale:* "I will tell you right now she's not like its ambitious, hard-boiled heroine. She is a working wife and happy-minded mother of two boys. Susan doesn't take her characters home with her." She conceded, though, that "Every twice in a while Mrs. Barker's temper blows and when that happens all the dishes rattle out of the cupboards and all the bystanders run for the hills. But really, it is over much more quickly than you would imagine. Her one big problem is trying to discipline her emotions and her temper."

A publicity man who knew her when she first came to Hollywood remembers that "Susan was painfully shy, a trait which took the form of brutal frankness. She was almost sullen with people she didn't know well; certain-ly she made no effort to please them. Even with her close friends—and they were few—she was undemonstrative. But when Susan *was* affectionate, you knew she meant it."

During the first flush of super-stardom, she was re-puted to tell approaching studio executives, "What ever it is, the answer is no!" Or, in reply to a casual "nice day isn't it": *"Is* it?" causing the perpetrator to wonder if indeed it *was.* Hayward chroniclers during this era seemed to feel that the star suspected everyone of wanting some-thing from her. With the repetition of these stories as time passed and such as the "witty" quote credited to prob-ably a dozen people in various articles that had her "as cold as a polar bear's foot," it is not beyond reason to suspect that Hayward's tantalizingly irascible image could have been helped along purposely by the zealous lady herself. Surely she was aware that it was most often a dis-tinct and peculiar personality that made the great star during the movies' "Golden Age"—an epoch that Hayward, with her vehicle-type roles, did her best to extend well past its natural late-'40s finale. Off-camera, she's worn glasses for many years, and her near-sightedness is known to be an explanation for at least some of her seeming aloofness.

Then, too, her difficulties with husband number one were spread over several years. They were coming to a head while she was filming *Demetrius and the Gladiators* in 1953. After completing this, she announced she was filing for divorce. It was recalled that she was "even more moody and insular than usual" during the shooting. "Susan acts like someone a hundred years old," Victor Mature, her co-star, had remarked. "I don't know what the trouble is—we're practically on a Mister and Miss basis—but something is worrying her. We all wish we could help her, but we just don't know how to go about it."

18. THE WINNING STREAK CONTINUES

A third Best Actress Academy Award nomination was Hayward's via *With a Song in My Heart* ('52), written and produced by Lamar Trotti for one of the top-earning pictures in history. (In 1966 *Variety* listed her at number thirteen among movieland's all-time top female boxoffice stars.)

The Technicolor telling of U.S.O. heroine Jane Froman's courageous comeback after the 1943 plane crash in which her right leg was nearly severed, necessitating years of hospitalizations and endless operations, it merged Hayward's dramatic know-how and animated song-selling with Froman's own rich contralto to stunning effect. Jeanne Crain had pleaded with Zanuck for the lead, as had, I daresay, any number of other actresses who remembered the huzzahs that greeted the similarly handled

The Jolson Story in '46. *Look*'s enthusiasm wrought a Hayward cover and a big hand for the little lady inside: "In *With a Song in My Heart,* Susan Hayward steps into the character of Jane Froman—and makes her so alive that from now on the two women may be one in the public's mind* . . . Hayward, with the warmth and range of the artist she has become, makes the Froman story a convincing experience."

When the year was up, in the annual poll conducted by *Film Daily* of more than 450 American critics, *Heart* placed among 1952's ten best films.

The star, who also got to dance in some of her numerous routines, prepared by taking vocal and showmanship lessons with an entertainer heroine from the earlier world war, Elsie Janis; by playing Froman records continually at home and at work; and by rehearsing eight hours a day at the studio. The end result brought Froman's encomium, too: "I wanted Susan Hayward in the first place not only because we looked somewhat alike, but because her speaking voice had a throaty quality similar to mine, which would make believable my singing coming out of her mouth. I found her a remarkable person. I worked two months in advance to record twenty-six songs for *With a Song in My Heart.* Every day as I walked into the recording studio, there would be Susan sitting quietly in a corner watching me. It was uncanny! When I saw the first rushes I was astounded by her pantomime. Did I move my arms that certain way? Afterward, I rushed to a mirror to discover with what accuracy Susan worked! Susan *looks* like a singer. Every singer knows that when you breathe—it shows. She understands how to stand, to

---

*This had happened to Larry Parks, who played "the world's greatest entertainer" so brilliantly in two film biographies that moviegoers—and Hollywood—were never again able to think of him as anyone but Jolson. This did not happen to Hayward. (Of course, Parks was blacklisted in the film capital after the early-'50s Communist investigations.)

111

move, and that gestures mean something. She didn't copy me slavishly, either. She had tricks of her own up her sleeve."

Rebutted Hayward: "Let's face it. What would the great Froman story be with the *Hayward* singing voice?"

She even cut her hair again for the part—this time it was worth it. Froman, who had sung in just about every medium, profited as well, gaining a whole new career and audience from this exposure. *Heart* got Froman her own network television show and remains one of the best-loved movies Hayward has made.

Hayward also likes it. *Heart* was the first time she allowed sons Greg and Tim to see their mother on screen. Ft. Lauderdale *News* Amusement Editor Bob Freund recently asked which of her "quieter women" she enjoyed portraying most, and she said, "Jane Froman in *With a Song in My Heart*. I think it was a lovely picture. I'm really a nice, quiet girl, except at times. I usually get along with directors, except sometimes. Most of them I've admired, but when I made *I Thank a Fool* in 1962, that man [newcomer from TV Robert Stevens] and I didn't get along at all."

She got along—greatly?—with Walter Lang, the director of *With a Song in My Heart,* who wrote me just before he died in 1972: "Many years ago I met Susan Hayward at the home of Louella Parsons. At that time she was touring with Louella's act which introduced future potential stars. I was most impressed with her great beauty and determination to succeed. Less than ten years later, I worked with Susan and found her to be a most dedicated actress, one with great talent and wonderful to work with. I made two pictures with her and still feel that she is one of the screen's greatest stars."

Especially easy to recall from this expensively mounted *Heart* are Hayward's sprightly, red-spangled prancing to "Get Happy"—proving Judy Garland had no copyright on this number; her expressive, humorous pantomime on crutches to "They're Either Too Young or Too Old"—

112

proving Bette Davis had no copyright on this number; and the elegant, velvety vocal on "Blue Moon"—proving that henceforth Froman *had* a copyright on this number. The pièce de résistance was the rousing "American Medley" closer, with Hayward/Froman interpreting state-titled songs in a European hall bursting with our servicemen and patriotism. Although the Froman injury precluded leg movement, Hayward's palpable vim made the longish potpourri rocket by. Backed by a large chorus and Froman on pipes, of course, she brought tears to a wounded soldier (George Offerman) evoking the moonlight on the Wabash in his Indiana home and an insistent group to its feet as she finally clap-clap-clap-clapped for the stars at night, big and bright, deep in the heart of their Texas.

Most of these renditions, along with other specially recorded Froman selections from the film, were reprised by Capitol Records who released them on a 10-inch, best-selling LP named after the movie.

All the tunes, a couple of dozen "standards," were a pleasure, and the voice synchronization was nearly perfect. More significantly, the story—its factualness extending to an unusually honest depiction of the singer's first marriage as one of convenience, and some twists surpassing fiction—was much sturdier than that of the general run of movie musical and an advance in light years for the Fox studio, which in its peroxide-drenched prime seemed to remake again and again the same one or two musical plots. (I'd like to have a nickel for every feather plucked off the gaudy get-ups of Alice Faye or Betty Grable by Tyrone Power or George Montgomery to give the girls class.) David Wayne, as Froman's manager, and Rory Calhoun, as the pilot of the crashed plane, were just right as, in that order, subsequent Froman husbands. ("It isn't easy for any man being married to a woman in the spotlight," she tried to comfort an emasculated number one.) Richard Allan, Hayward's singing-dancing partner in the title production piece, an explosion of sequins

113

and chiffon, looked for a year or two then like he might become a major screen heartthrob. But it took a thief named Robert Wagner, a newcomer, to steal male honors in his bit as a shy, piano-grinned young paratrooper Froman serenaded in a night club and next met overseas as a shell-shocked battle veteran. As always, Thelma Ritter was a blessing as a caustic, wise, fictional Brooklyn nurse who became Froman's companion and whom scenarist Trotti had Froman meet in Lisbon right after the accident. What, you might well ask, was Thelma Ritter doing in Portugal? Escaping her relatives in Flatbush, she said. The trip paid off: her own Academy monimation, supporting class, awaited.

Alfred Newman won the Best Scoring Academy Award over, among others, *Singin' in the Rain* (sometimes called the film musical apex), and *Photoplay* readers voted *Heart* their favorite picture of the year. Hayward received the magazine's venerable Gold Medal as "The nation's most enjoyed actress during 1952." Shirley (*Come Back, Little Sheba*) Booth got the Oscar, but Hayward was named the World's Favorite Acrress by the Foreign Press Association of Hollywood and took home their Henrietta.

She was also a favorite of co-star Rory Calhoun, who had survived a similar underprivileged Irish background and as a youth had been imprisoned for stealing. On a 1972 Merv Griffin talk TV show he was asked if there were any players he remembered with special fondness and immediately responded, "Yes, Susan Hayward."

She wound up in 1952 with *The Snows of Kilimanjaro* and *The Lusty Men*. Both in different ways continued her winning streak.

Snows received a tremendous promotional campaign from Fox. Commemorating Darryl Zanuck's twenty-fifth year as a producer, it also marked the fortieth anniversary in films of Henry King, who directed Hayward four times and whom Frank Capra, in his autobiography *The Name Above the Title,* called "the most under-publicized filmmaker in Hollywood, belongs on anybody's 'First Five' list [of directors]."

The result: a glossily ambitious, only intermittently effective yet big boxoffice elongation of Ernest Hemingway's short story into another Gregory Peck vehicle. Its growing pains, said *Time,* had brought on "an atmosphere of whining self-pity and the resolute backing-away from any issues except sugar-coated love."

The opening, set at the foot of Mt. Kilimanjaro, was encouraging. There was a close-up of a prostrate Peck woozily watching vultures stationed in a nearby tree while the shadow of a leafy branch passed back and forth across his perspiring face. His gangrenous leg had turned numb. "A filthy bird, but they know their business," he grunted pessimistically to his attentively fanning, hopeful, but increasingly less indulgent wife (Hayward). Only the sharp edge of their sarcastic volleys cleaved the stagnant, hot African air as they awaited a plane bringing aid.

The film quickly began copping out. From his cot Peck recalled that his illness stemmed from a scratch incurred in a thicket—cut to the couple hunting. His wife challenged this version, said the leg was the result of his trying to photograph too closely a herd of rambunctious hippos which caused one of their native hands to fall into the water—cut to the couple boating. Peck jumped in to save him. According to his spouse, he had insisted on driving back to camp with the injured lad across his lap, and "it was from all his blood and dirt that you got the infection."

"How does a man miss the boat?" Peck, becoming nearly delirious, moaned, cueing the numerous flashbacks that examined the life of his hedonistic writer. Along with a today dissipated reverence for the hunt, there was an even more outmoded, stereotypical Hemingway dissertation (by safari guide Torin Thatcher) on What Makes a Man.

Ava Gardner, featured earlier in another celluloid stretching of Hemingway, *The Killers,* as a girl who didn't even exist in the original story, was again a totally fabricated Hemingway heroine and, although billed below

Hayward, bagged the fancier, and boozier, female role as "Harry's lady" in Casey Robinson's script. Her characterization was almost complete in the single line, "I'm only trying to be happy." She obviously had seen Gene Tierney in a previous Fox production, *Leave Her to Heaven:* to settle a pregnancy she felt would shoo lover Peck, she threw herself down a flight of stairs. Hemingway himself suggested that Gardner replace the first-cast Anne Francis (deemed unsuitable because she did not closely enough resemble Hayward, whom Peck had to mistake for the Gardner character in one scene), and she garnered rare kudos, despite such improbable '20s "lost generation" readings as "Now we can get that lovely apartment on the 'Sane.' "

In the author's original *Snows,* Hayward's character was modeled after the second of Hemingway's four wives, Pauline, and was described as "a rich bitch." She was required to be somewhat less than that in the picture, often playing, furthermore (and surprisingly, in view of the healthy budget), against all too recognizable bogus backdrops and rear-projected process footage. This gave her an ill-suiting stepchild aura. Hayward did reign in the emotional closing scenes. It was then she explained to Peck for the first time the depth of her love and—to provide an upbeat ending also at odds with Hemingway—was forced to lance her husband's leg in their tent, thus saving his life.

Particularly inventive, the kind of minute detail for which movie actors were not famed, was the moment when Hayward, having crouched in vigil all night alongside her husband's sickbed, had to jump up suddenly and run out of the tent to hail their plane. Realistically giving in to her leg as she scrambled about, she indicated that it was stiff from being curled up beneath her during the long night.

But her part as the brave, wealthy wife who also had rescued him from dissolution was cut harmfully after filming to favor Gardner's more romantic, audience-pleas-ing assignment as the husband's idealized lost love, Cynthia. ("Cyn," smacked Peck. "That's nice.") Absurdly absent on release was the character-establishing duologue in which Hayward, getting to know Peck, told him of her own restless existence and difficulty finding another man to compare with her late husband. Some of the missing footage was deemed fit enough to be used in the trailer for this color enterprise that ended the friendship between the producer and a growingly cinema-cynical Hemingway. Although Zanuck claimed "Papa" never saw the picture, Hemingway—his breast not soothed by the exhibition of Ava Gardner's—called it *The Snows of Zanuck*.

Director King, who shot the whole thing (battlefield scenes and all) in forty-eight days, is more kindly disposed. *The Snows of Kilimanjaro* is one of his favorites.

A 90-minute dramatization several years later on TV's *Buick Electra Playhouse,* with Robert Ryan, Ann Todd, and Jean Hagen, was even less valid.

Lusty Men (RKO)—titled *This Man Is Mine* during production—was superior, coming "so close to art," felt *Modern Screen,* "that all its makers must be credited with the kind of creative imagination that all too seldom comes from Hollywood." A moody, engrossing, unvarnished, probably definitive screen study of modern rodeo life, it boasted persuasive work by Robert Mitchum and its lusty woman, Hayward, as the disapproving wife of circuit novice Arthur Kennedy. *The New York Times* found things "vivid and pungent. With a literal and candid use of camera [manned by Lee Garmes] . . . director Nicholas Ray has captured the muscle and thump of rodeos." Hayward's own muscle and thump came to the fore in the amusing scene where she booted a party tramp (Eleanor Todd) who "branded" Kennedy by lingeringly biting his arm—"Men, I'd like to fry 'em all in deep fat!" snarled Hayward.

The film's reputation has expanded with the years, due largely to Nicholas Ray's popularity with proponents of the "auteur" theory of filmmaking devised around the late 1950s by French movie intellectuals to extol those directors felt to be total creators, or authors. If hardly the top commercial success of her career, *Lusty Men* has become one of Hayward's more prestigious credits. English critic-author-magazine editor Allen Eyles lately has alluded to it as "Ray's greatest picture"—from a list that also comprises such other brooding worthies as *They Live by Night, Knock on Any Door, In a Lonely Place, Johnny Guitar,* and *Rebel Without a Cause.*

Mitchum was at his laconic, world-weary best as the worn "rodeoer" who took on the training of money-anxious cowhand Kennedy. He has never lumbered through a more poignant sequence than the early silent one in which, limping away from a darkened, dusty, paper-strewn arena after his goring, Mitchum wandered back to the ramshackle farm where he was born and recovered from a childhood hiding place small mementos of his, and every boy's, youth. And Hayward was never more scalding as the "hash-house" graduate wife who immediately—with some of her most intimidating size-ups and glares—recognized Mitchum as a threat to the "decent, steady life" on some ranch she craved with Kennedy.

She didn't spare the invective, either:

"Look, Buster!" . . . "beat it!" . . . "It stinks!" . . . "Get lost!"

"My folks were fruitpickers. My Pa was a drifter. I grew up in tents and camps. I never knew what a pair of silk stockings was like until I was nineteen. We never had a house. Got so I was always jealous of people who stayed in one place and had someone to love . . ." she bristled in the aria to Mitchum that explained why she valued her marriage above everything. While Kennedy had a swell-headed, frivolous lapse as his fame in the arena grew, Hayward never wavered in her loyalty to him— "You ain't the biggest, you ain't the richest, you ain't the strongest and you ain't the prettiest; but you're the only one that wanted what I wanted . . ." Mitchum, however, seemed to be falling in love with her. "You're real small

118

with your shoes off," the older cowboy began in one close-quartered scene. "You're real small with your shoes *on*," she finished. Ultimately, Hayward at least came to admire and respect the ill-fated Mitchum. The horse sense of the Horace McCoy-David Dortort screenplay, especially in the idiomatic dialogue, helped to make *Lusty Men* a fine entry from the briefly existing (1951–52) stable of [Jerry] Wald-[Norman] Krasna Productions, Inc.

The following year was off to a good start, too, with a more subdued Hayward as befit her new status as *The President's Lady*.

Based on Irving Stone's popular biographical novel about "the most maligned woman in American history," the Fox film gave Hayward the title role of Rachel Donelson Robards, the simple Tennessee farm girl who married Andrew Jackson (Charlton Heston) before her divorce from Lewis Robards (Whitfield Connor) was final, and was charged by Robards with adultery. The Jacksons wed again, but Rachel, the John Patrick scenario avowed, was cruelly ostracized for the rest of her days. At best, a touching, modestly presented romance, it was, as Paul V. Beckley estimated in the *Herald-Tribune*, "a story not so much of a general or a president as of a life-long devotion, and the story is told well. Susan Hayward portrays Rachel with insight and restraint, and Mr. Heston is a convincing Jackson whether in rage or in the moments of quiet dignity." At worst, *Lady* was sometimes patronizing ("Then Andrew and I aren't married!") and primerhistorical (it proved too easy too often to sit the stars down on camera and let them sum up verbally what was happening, instead of revealing events in a more natural flow of action).

No fault, however, could be attached to Hayward, as she deftly eroded to silver-crowned infirmity. At the end, death relieved her misery, and not a minute too soon: the bonnets, white hair, the slight Hayward's scrappily curled lower lip, and Rachel's pipe-smoking shortly might

119

have invoked a comparison between the first lady and Dogpatch's Mammy Yokum.

This Henry Levin-directed *President's Lady* was her one film excursion into extreme old age. Despite the wide range of talent she has displayed, throughout her career Hayward—not necessarily by her design—has appeared in parts that have required a minimum of character costuming and makeup. This certainly has not been true of co-star Heston, who, with barely enough time to doff his *The Ten Commandments* Moses shrubbery, repeated his white-maned Andrew Jackson in 1958's *The Buccaneer*.

Nineteen fifty-three then brought Fox' faint answer to MGM's *King Solomon's Mines* (1950), titled *White Witch Doctor*. Or, a kind of *Perils of Susan,* with its lady light terrorized by African natives, witch doctor curses, and assorted lions, snakes, and spiders.

The arachnid caused Hayward personal discomfort. In one scene an envious witch doctor was to deposit a tarantula on her cot while she slept. Unexpectedly, the spider eluded the special attendant and actually crawled up the actress' arm. In the confusion she tumbled to the floor, suffering torn ligaments of the shoulder.

The new release was entertaining but conventional jungle pulp with Robert Mitchum as the cynical trapper-guide and Hayward as the widowed missionary nurse guiltily embarking on the humanitarian work she selfishly had kept her successful city doctor husband from pursuing. Laid in 1907, it opened as she landed at the jungle's last port of call, from there to journey up river to assist Dr. Mary, an aged, beloved missionary. After no little travail, she arrived to find "Big Mama" dead and, upon delivering a healthy baby to a black woman whose previous children all were born dead, was ordained "Little Mama" by the loinclothed locals.

"Plot is a mixture of tried-and-true situations, neatly fashioned by scripters Ivan Goff and Ben Roberts to suit the tastes of average filmgoers," attested *Variety.* "Distaff appeal is okay also, for it's a sort of jungle soap opera with action, to which Henry Hathaway has given expert direction, spelling everything out in fundamental dramatics to make it easily followed . . . Miss Hayward and Mitchum make a good romantic team, and Walter Slezak is an oily heavy."

It might have stacked up more sanguinely if the leads, unlike those in *King Solomon's Mines* who filmed for months in Africa, had not been confined mainly to the Hollywood backlot. Six months before the *White Witch Doctor* stars got going, producer Otto Lang and his cameras penetrated the Belgian Congo interior. There, among other sites, they shot the rarely photographed Bakuba villages, where the houses were built in movable sections so that each time a new king ascended the throne everybody could literally pick up and switch to the new capital. But what showed up in the picture of this second unit location work consisted mostly of the principals' stand-ins seen boating and trudging, natives gamboling and fishing, etc. Adroitly intercut with the studio footage, this lent some Technicolored atmosphere, but not quite enough.

19. THE FOX FALTERS

Hayward returned to truculent dames in two more for Fox ('54), *Demetrius and the Gladiators* and *Garden of Evil*. They turned out to be generally undeserving of the moxie she gave them.

First, and much lustier boxoffice, there was the color sequel *Demetrius,* clanking along right on the hem of *The Robe*. *Demetrius* at least avoided much of *The Robe's* first century pseudopiety and got right down to the sex and gore, early '50s off-camera style. Left over from the 1953 picturization of Lloyd C. Douglas' novel, the first CinemaScope feature, were its ribbon-like screen, plywood sets, and slave Victor Mature, with Hayward introduced as a lushly decadent, power-driven, but rather twentieth century Messalina who was forced to do one of her most dizzying about-faces for a finale. As the wife of the weak Claudius (Barry Jones), her busy agenda included operating as a pagan priestess; pitting friend against friend in an arena death struggle; procuring girls like Anne Bancroft (too new on the Fox lot to know better), and then, veiled, watching their revels with the gladiators from a loge seat; throwing Christians to the tigers; turning Demetrius' virginal sweetheart (Debra Paget) over to horny gladiators who shocked the girl into catatonia; tossing a drink into the face of the Apostle Peter (Michael Rennie); and sentencing her own uncle and cousin to death when they bungled her planned assassination of the mad Emperor Caligula (Jay Robinson, recreating his shrill faggoty ruler from *The Robe*).

"If I were a man I'd have killed Caligula and won the empire for my own," she throbbed, sweeping about quaking thronerooms draped in beaded '50s "formals" and the cunning authority of an over-compensating woman executive.

Next to the empire, what she wanted most was the burly, Christ-liberated Mature, who was appointed guard outside her rooms. To get him into her boudoir, she sat at the foot of her bed, leaned back, and casually kicked over a large vase, which brought him running. "Where shall I put these?" he asked, having gathered up the pieces. "Back on the floor," she answered, her eyes fixed on his. "Be careful, Demetrius. My claws can be sharper than the tigers'." Backsliding for a time because God had stood still for his girlfriend's ordeal, he joined Hayward for a lengthy dalliance at the seashore. Suddenly, when her husband became emperor she renounced her past and with a straight face declaimed to a roomful of Romans, "I am Caesar's wife, and I will act the part."

Herb Kelly in the Miami *News* objected to this screeching switch, too, but evidently on grounds more historical than dramatic: "Susan enacts the role of the sadistic, sinful Messalina to perfection. The only weak spot was toward the end when she first begged Mature not to endanger his life in the arena, even offering to turn Christian for him; and again after the murder of Emperor Caligula, when she promises everyone to be a true and noble wife to Caligula's uncle and successor, Claudius. History shows this false. She was a wicked trollop all her life and died that way." Philip Dunne did the script for *Demetrius and the Gladiators* (and why not *Demetrius and Messalina?*), with Delmer Daves directing.

Then *Garden of Evil*, a tritely plotted color western with, allowed *Sight and Sound*, "a ferociously determined attempt by Susan Hayward at a femme fatale" who hired Gary Cooper and Richard Widmark to rescue her husband (Hugh Marlowe), hurt mining in dangerous Indian country. While locationing in Mexico to essay this venal catalyst, she got in some real-life rescuing when she risked serious injury jumping to grab an Indian child who was about to fall into an extinct volcano. Hayward sprained an ankle.

Zanuck, who more or less had hand-picked her properties at Fox, resigned as production head around this time and Buddy Adler, who did not seem as interested in Hayward's career, took over. CinemaScope, after all, had become *the* star at the studio, with everyone looking for big stories to show off the "innovative" anamorphic wide screen process actually invented in the 1920s by a French professor named Henri Chretien. In '55 Hayward had her last two pictures at Fox until '59, *Untamed* ("It's Africolossal!") and the Adler-produced *Soldier of Fortune* ("Hank Lee, adventurer for hire . . . and Jane Hoyt, woman in no position to bargain!").

The former title was a color action spectacular that had an undeniable sweep under Henry King's direction, but was jerkily edited and gummed by teeth-cracking lines. The first half, especially, looked like a demonstration film for CinemaScope, the makers compounding their preoc-

123

cupation by seeming to confuse the new toy with the short-lived 3-D: they hurled everything from covered wagons to Hayward's mammaries at the audience. Its vivid, hellbent, and—such was her special magic—appealing feminine cynosure made it worth seeing, though.

Once more "a bush-league Scarlett O'Hara" (*Photoplay*), she was Katie O'Neill, whose good life in Ireland was blighted by famine in the field and in the sack by escape artist Tyrone Power, a visiting commando chief interested only in helping build the Dutch Free State in South Africa. "Find a new land, a more merciful land," advised her dying father (Henry O'Neill). She married John Justin, had a baby, got a nursemaid (Agnes Moorehead), and set sail for Power's wilds, where she fast was spearing hostile natives. By the time she caught up with Power, whom she'd loved all the time, she was conveniently widowed. He could only marvel, "I can hardly believe it. *You,* Katje, here in Africa fighting Zulus!" When she stepped out of mourning right into a bright green dress to join him at a dance, Moorehead glowered that it was "too soon." "It's never too soon to live," Hayward prognosticated over a bare shoulder.

Her New Yorkese reasserted itself in this of all roles, an Irish accent manifest briefly, suddenly, in the last half-hour. Mostly, Hayward's deliberate vocal cadences recalled Bronx emigré Tony Curtis, of "Yon-dah lies the castle of my fod-dah" fame. The dashing Power largely acted as a foil for his untamable co-star. He had always been able to lord it over Henie, Faye, Young, Darnell, Fontaine, Baxter, Tierney, Blondell, and even O'Hara; but he backed off whenever working with the BMT Valkyrie. It was definitely the irresistible object meeting the movable force.

Movie Spotlight reported that Jane Wyman, Eleanor Parker, Joan Crawford, and Lana Turner all had wanted to star in the movie of Helga Moray's novel. And no wonder. *Time* said that *Untamed* was "a Zulu lulu—the

124

sort of costume adventure that may, in a generation or two, produce a race of movie-goers with their eyes popped out on stalks. The picture offers: 1) a full-dress Irish hunt in full cry after a fox; 2) a formal ball in an Irish country house; 3) the great Irish potato famine of the 1840s; 4) the Great Trek of the Boers from Cape Town to the fertile valleys of the interior; 5) the war dance of three thousand Zulus and their attack on a wagon ring; 6) a savage fight between two men armed with bullwhips; 7) a cloudburst, during which a huge tree is felled by lightning; 8) the gruesome amputation of a leg; 9) another formal ball, this time in a South African mansion; 10) a battle royal in a mining town." Running time: 111 minutes.

Soldier of Fortune was an almost unqualified misfortune that wasted the aging but still virile Clark Gable, whose Parkinson's disease head tremor of later years looked worse here—maybe there was a connection. There were DeLuxe Colored Hong Kong locales, and Hayward was husband-retrieving again—this one (Gene Barry) was a photographer arrested in Red China. She had replaced Her Serene Highness Grace Kelly Rainier, a hint as to how much chance she had to detonate as the distraught American wife who charmed Chicago renegade Gable into going after her wandering spouse. Before the climactic rescue, there was some of the most banal dialogue (by scenariest Ernest K. Gann, transferring his own novel) since —*Untamed*.

Such as:

"I wish (your husband) were sitting here right now so I'd stand a chance with you," advanced Gable at dinner. "I can't fight a ghost."

"I wish you hadn't done that," a somber Hayward murmured right after Gable had stolen a kiss he plainly didn't have to—causing audience titters.

There were a couple of slight variations from the mundane.

Instead of loosening his lady with Jackie Gleason playing music for adulterers only, "Cap'n Hank" Gable slid on recordings of Chicago street sounds—toots, whistles, and plunks.

It has become a wheeze for screen couples to come together passionately during rainstorms. *Soldier of Fortune* went this chestnut one better by having the leads kiss for the first time while "Hurricane Rita" rampaged through Hong Kong. For stars of Gable's and Hayward's panache, anything less would have been unthinkable.

The film at least permitted her to play queen to the king of the movies, whom she got at the end. For some reason, the same basic plot was used again in a TV segment of *I Spy* a decade later, with Sue England spelling Hayward.

"People think I'm the most traveled actress in pictures," she said then. "But the truth is, while *The Snows of Kilimanjaro, White Witch Doctor, Demetrius and the Gladiators, Untamed,* and *Soldier of Fortune** had foreign backgrounds, which Fox crews usually went on location to film, all of my scenes in them were shot on the studio backlot here in Hollywood."

20.   NO TEARS AT METRO

Finishing up '55, she got to travel over to MGM for a one-shot that in achievement compared more to a moonshot: *I'll Cry Tomorrow,* from Lillian Roth's million-plus selling autobiography written with Gerold Frank and Mike Connolly. Mentioned early for, among others, little June Allyson, then a Metro contract player, and big Jane Russell, who recently had done her best work in *Gentlemen*

---

*Hayward had planned to go to Hong Kong for *Soldier of Fortune,* bringing her vacationing sons along for the trip; but when her ex-husband legally prevented her from taking the twins out of the States, she refused to leave them behind and did her scenes in Hollywood.

Prefer Blondes, the campaigning Hayward wrote a letter to the studio boss asking for the part in this picture whose title paraphrased Scarlett O'Hara's motto, "I'll think about that tomorrow."

"I'll Cry Tomorrow combines the best elements of my two favorite films, *Smash-Up* and *With a Song in My Heart,"* she reasoned—convincingly—to Dore Schary, who had dethroned L. B. Mayer a few years before.

Her strongest ally was Roth herself, an entertainer since childhood in vaudeville, theater, films and, later, night clubs. "After the book came out," she explained in her less worthy sequel, *Beyond My Worth,* "almost every studio in town wanted the story. But, at an earlier date, I had given MGM a verbal option and I held to my word. Also, they had promised that Susan Hayward would be given the title role, as I had requested. I had followed her career and thought she was an extremely skilled and sensitive actress.

"I met Susan Hayward first in Las Vegas, where I was working, and she came to see my performances several times. About a month later, she visited me again at the Beverly Hills Hotel in Hollywood. It was in the early afternoon and she arrived in her black Chinese pajamas with a coat thrown over them. We talked for several hours. By the time she left, I didn't know whether she was imitating me or I was emulating her. We were both so emotional about things that when we faced each other it was almost like looking into a mirror; I was looking at Lillian and she was looking at Susan."

This reporter's review of the film in the Newark [New Jersey] *Evening News* opened: *"I'll Cry Tomorrow,* the Lillian Roth story, differs in many ways from the usual biography of a musical personality. There is no glossing of a sordid although eventually inspiring life, nor is there song after song popularized by Miss Roth. CinemaScope and color are absent, too, so is dubbing of Roth's singing to star Hayward's gesticulations [her favorite in most numbers: a karate-like arm chop]. Hayward sings professionally for the first time in this frank, engrossing picture. Her sure contralto is quite appealing. Hayward's acting of the unwilling musical comedy star who lapsed into a sixteen-year slough of alcoholism is superb. Drunk roles are fair game for actors, but I've never seen one portrayed with this detail. Hayward sweats, shakes, twitches, and rants in unforgettably revolting fashion."

Roth was not sorry she had asked for her. "Susan's performance was magnificent. My throat tightened as I suffered with her (at a special press preview in Chicago). I began to fill up with tears. I wiped them away quickly, hoping none of the newspapermen in attendance would notice," she recalled.

Hayward's Skid Row carousing and collapsing, in particular, had a documentarylike, almost embarrassing explicitness heightened by 1) the realization that the degraded woman on the screen really lived and 2) Hayward's bravura brilliance, reaching, in one emotional climax after another, a peak of acting versatility yet to be scaled by someone else. One is hard put, in fact, to think of more than a half-dozen roles that have demanded as much of an actress as the raw-nerved Roth—and a couple of them would probably also be Hayward's.

"Filmed on location . . . inside a woman's soul," said the ads. Its leading lady made this claim seem almost reticent.

Images that still flicker include a wanly smiling, sly, kerchiefed Hayward's self-conscious strut past backstage help—one hand on her hip, the other hugging a purse containing a bottle—to some "secret drinking" in her dressing room . . . then, as "Miss Lillian Roth!" was announced on stage, her raspy peal of "Here we goooo!" . . . the drunken waterfront conga with an equally smashed playboy husband number one (Don Taylor), her growlly whiskey falsetto raised to shatter the night's stillness . . . the bar bit with Hayward blathering to strangers, "I'm watcha call a real A-number-one drunk. He's a real doll, though, and I've got the scars to prove it,"

128

whereupon sadistic husband number two (Richard Conte) tripped her flat on her face . . . her sotted dive scene where, singing incoherently and flailing her arms at a table, she was recognized by several other derelicts who joined her for a laughing jag, Hayward going through the wildly euphoric motions but no sound seeming to escape from her own sauce-clogged throat.

It was "a great performance" (*Variety*), and one that relied notably less on her natural fire than on her natural talents. Indeed, for once in her career Hayward was cast as the victim of *someone else's* ambition and domineering ways: the high-strung Roth's "stage mother." Jo Van Fleet, who was slightly younger than Hayward, played this juicy lady in a breast-clutching, Method travesty of overbearing Jewish momism. Roth was somewhat kinder to her: "I thought Jo Van Fleet did a fine job though she was directed to act the part in a way that was not quite true to fact. In the picture, my mother spoke with a foreign accent, whereas she was actually born in Boston and justifiably proud of her speech. There is nothing wrong with a foreign accent, our ancestors were all immigrants, but it just wasn't the way my mother spoke. Nor did she go around in furs and jewels. She was always neatly and modestly dressed, not at all an extrovert." Eddie Albert, of Hayward's first big booze bout, *Smash-Up,* again was comfortingly, creditably on tap (pun intended) as a crippled member of Alcoholics Anonymous (where Roth finally was cured) and, presumably, husband number three. Representing Hayward as a Tenth Avenue preteen, sensitive little Carole Ann Campbell was the rare child player who actually resembled the actress she was supposed to be during early years. Coincidentally, the star made this film, which had Roth attempt jumping out a window in one scene of the Helen Deutsch-Jay Richard Kennedy screenplay, right after what was generally reported to be Hayward's own real-life try at ending it all. *I'll Cry Tomorrow* was said then to be MGM's third biggest money-maker, after *Gone with*

129

the Wind and *Quo Vadis,* and Hayward later lamented that she had done it only on a straight salary deal.

She even had some MGM label recordings released as a result of the film which she felt, probably rightly, contained her finest work. Hayward's records included an Extended Play soundtrack disc carrying the "standards" in the film, "Happiness is a Thing Called Joe," "Sing You Sinners," "When the Red, Red Robin Comes Bob, Bob, Bobbin' Along," "The Vagabond King Waltz" and (not used in the release print) "I'm Sittin' on Top of the World." There was a single record released, too, coupling two songs not in the picture, the oldie "Just One of Those Things" and the new Alex North-Johnny Mercer title tune, "I'll Cry Tomorrow" (the latter melody was used only as instrumental background music in the movie.). Miles Kreuger, film music critic, record producer and author of *The American Musical Film,* recently asked me: "Why didn't she sing more on screen? Susan Hayward had a fine, gutty instrument, not a plastic movie star-turns-singer voice but one you really wanted to hear more of. Her voice had character. I went back to see *I'll Cry Tomorrow* a second time at Radio City Music Hall just for her 'Sing You Sinners'—terrific!"

Charles Henderson was Hayward's arranger-conductor on the film; but it was studio music supervisor Johnny Green who got her to do her own singing as Lillian Roth. "We had planned to dub her," Green informed me, "but just for the hell of it, I asked the front office how much it would add to the grosses if we could say she did her own singing. They told me a couple of million. No matter what she might sound like, it was our policy to get a recording track of the actress whose voice was to be dubbed so we could get a dubber to match it. Suse arrived at my office to make the tape scared to death of singing, this great big star—with that self-confident image. I got her to the piano, but she froze, just stood there. Finally, I said, 'Make a sound, any sound! Fart!' Well, she started to sing and we got the recording. She sounded great! I played the tape for the big brass, and at my suggestion they decided to let her do her own songs. We worked hard and everything came out fine. Suse can do anything she sets her mind to—once she sets her mind to it."

The studio was so pleased with her vocalizing in the finished film that they played up this fact in the trailer and in the picture itself devoted a whole credit panel to this point—"Miss Hayward Sings!"—followed by a list of the songs. She was sufficiently het-up to let it be known she would not be adverse to singing and acting Nellie Forbush in the film of *South Pacific*. Several major night-clubs wanted to book her, but she never got an act together.

Meanwhile, Roth denied column buzzing that, because she was angry at not being allowed to sing her own songs on the soundtrack, she had taken to doing an impression in her act ridiculing Hayward's impersonation of her.

Hayward gave much credit for *Tomorrow*'s bullseye to Daniel Mann, also her favorite director. "Danny Mann checked every detail. He wouldn't let me cheat with lipstick or even a curl. If he thought my hair wasn't mussed enough, he put water on his hands and mashed it down," she revealed. "I read the book several times, and before we started filming Danny, the producer, Lawrence Weingarten, and I went to jails and hospitals and even AA meetings, because I had to know that woman's life and what it had been."

Nevertheless, she lost the Oscar for the fourth time—to Anna (*The Rose Tattoo*) Magnani, also directed by Mann who additionally had guided Shirley Booth in her *Come Back, Little Sheba* Academy-winning performance the same year that Hayward was up for *With a Song in My Heart*.

"The groans in the audience when Anna Magnani snatched the award from under her nose were heard throughout the world," wrote Beverly Linet in *Screen Stories*. Hayward, escorted to the presentations by her sons, told another magazine, *After Dark*, that she "managed not

131

to shed any tears until everything was over and my company had gone home. Then I sat down and had a good cry and decided that losing was just part of the game. Three years later, I knew what an awfully nice feeling it is to win. I've done both, lost and won. And believe me, winning is the best. By far."

She was consoled by best actress awards at the Cork and Cannes film festivals, where she received a ten-minute standing ovation and was the only Hollywood winner, and from *Redbook, Motion Picture Exhibitor, Picturegoer,* and *Look,* whose best actor that year was James Cagney, who could be called Hayward's male counterpart and with whom, more's the pity, she never teamed in a movie—although *Look* did have them pose together for the cover of its awards issue.

Hayward made news in connection with *I'll Cry Tomorrow* on at least two other counts. The first was when starlet Jil (*Swamp Women,* etc.) Jarmyn, who coincidentally shared Jess Barker's lawyer, dropped in on friend Donald "Red" Barry (a bit player in *Tomorrow* as an AA member but remembered as lead in the serial *Adventures of Red Ryder* and dozens of Republic "B" Westerns of the '40s) one morning "for coffee" and found the two redheads together. She riled the pajama-clad Hayward, apparently, because Jarmyn filed—but later dropped —an assault and battery complaint against the star, who claimed to have stopped by for coffee, too. "That Barry must serve good coffee," commented Marlene Dietrich, among those not present.

Hayward made news again when she arrived at Cannes and immediately asked reporters, "Where are the men? Not actors; I said men!"

"Poor Susan Hayward," a columnist around then tsk-tsked. "Some Hollywood stars spend a lifetime transgressing and often stay undetected. Whereas Susan has always taken pains to maintain a sequestered personal life. So wouldn't you know that the rare instances when she

132

slipped would be discovered and detailed on front pages around the world."

Today, Don Barry, who dated Joan Crawford, Ann Sheridan, and Linda Darnell and married two lesser known actresses Helen Talbot and Peggy Stewart, says: "If a man is lucky enough to know a woman like Susan Hayward, he is lucky indeed. She's one of the finest ladies I've ever known."

21. CONQUERED—TEMPORARILY

In '56 Howard Hughes "presented" *The Conqueror*, made over a two-year period just prior to *I'll Cry To-morrow* at a cost of $6,000,000. Color-filmed on location in exotic Utah, it asked viewers to swallow John Wayne as a Fu Manchu-mustached Genghis Khan—only months after they had spit him up as an anti-Nazi German ship captain in *The Sea Chase*—and was produced and directed by Dick Powell—who was a long way from both Busby Berkeley and Raymond Chandler himself. Furthermore, Hayward, brandishing swords in "a dance of death" which guileless publicity from RKO (understandably going out of business) boasted took her six weeks to learn, was Bortai, the Asiatic heroine captured by Wayne en route to her wedding—freckled, with newly slanting eyebrows and long drop earrings. "Duke" had an easier time conquering the world than Hayward. When he turned his back, for instance, she tried to lop off his head with one of her dance props. In the line most quoted by film reviewers that year, the twelfth century invader gushed "Yer beoodiful in yer wrath." Hayward, unruffled, continued to call him a Mongol dog, spawn of the jackal, cur, etc.—until, sitting alone in her tent, she exercised a lady's prerogative and changed her mind: "To reach his arms I'd betray my people into Mongol bondage."

133

If there's one thing critics have always loved, it's the chance to pass on a good chunk of bad dialogue. *The Conqueror* afforded those so inclined a feast. William K. Zinsser, one of the wittiest reviewers ever on a Manhattan daily, as well as one of the shortest employed, recapped 1956 at the movies in a funny *Herald-Tribune* "think-piece," writing: "Spare a final grunt for the year in which John Wayne played Genghis Khan. He and Susan Hayward proved that the sands of the Gobi Desert were good for more than war. Who can forget how the Khan's brother (Pedro Armendariz) warned him to steer clear of the girl because she was Tartar, he Mongol? Who can forget his swift reply, so touching in its restraint: 'There are moments for wisdom and moments when I listen to my blood; my blood says 'Take this Tartar woman.' Yes, it was a grand year for history."

Apparently the vile, Oscar Millard-written proceedings traumatized a large number of patrons, because, unfortunately, *The Conqueror*—close to its leading lady's professional nadir—is remembered today by a depressingly large number of moviegoers as a Hayward credit.

Far from depressed herself, she recently said, "I had hysteria all through that one. Every time we did a scene, I dissolved in laughter. Me, a red-haired Tartar princess! It looked like some wild Irishman had stopped off on the road to Old Cathay."

When he sold RKO, presenter Hughes repurchased *The Conqueror* and another John Wayne vehicle, *Jet Pilot,* for a reported $12,000,000. One trade paper called this "the most incredible deal in Hollywood history. *Pilot* was every bit as good as *Conqueror.*"

In '57, a change of pace—sort of—and her first profit-sharing film venture: *Top Secret Affair* (Warners), directed by H. C. Potter, who had helmed Loretta Young's Oscar-winning *Farmer's Daughter* ten years before on the occasion of Hayward's first Academy nomination. The new picture was something of a throwback to the hey-day of Hollywood male-vs.-female comedy, although its two stars, Hayward and Kirk Douglas, were a considerably more martial pair of steel-jawed jokers than, say, Irene Dunne and Cary Grant.* One reviewer said, "Miss Hayward doesn't enter a room; she *takes* it." Seasoned supporting player Roland Winters told me that in person Hayward was "charming and highly professional."

Affair, from the novel *Melville Goodwin, U.S.A.,* by John P. Marquand, was a spoof of the magazine field and Army brass. Hayward was Dottie Peale, the dictatorial *News World* publisher out to discredit "Ironpants" Major General Douglas who had gotten a diplomatic appointment she wanted for someone else. Her first seismic appearance was well managed. With the Douglas news just revealed to her pacing executive staff, voices on the intercom periodically announced, "Miss Peale just drove up . . . She's in the elevator . . . She's *here!*" "Miss Peale, you can't attack the Army!" soon gaped employee Charles Lane. "Why not," she retorted, "are they such big advertisers with us?" In this unusual (for her) framework of farce, familiar Hayward attitudes appeared almost self-parody, especially in the gangbuster abrasiveness of the opening scenes, with Hayward commanding her office troops and cursing Douglas, and her late low comedy drunk rondo when Douglas, seeming to step out of the script, chided, "You seem to be used to this." There were certain dialogues, though, at which Hayward was without peer. Growing suspicious of her romantic attentions, Douglas said to aide Jim Backus, "There are only two kinds of women in the world, mothers and—the other kind." Fast cut to Hayward telling companion Paul Stewart, "There are only two kinds of men in the world—and I can handle both of 'em!"

Hayward, rather puffy-looking after many months fallow waiting for "the right role" to follow Lillian Roth, was shown no mercy by scenarists Roland Kibbee and

---

*Humphrey Bogart and his wife, Lauren Bacall, originally had signed to star shortly before Bogie died.

Allan Scott. In pursuit of her laughs for this Clare Boothe Luceish part, she had to engage in a knockabout samba, fall into a swimming pool wearing an evening gown and allow Douglas to best her in a judo match.

Some critics were reluctant to accept her in this rare light hope, but there was evidence in her performance of a latent, roguish talent for sophisticated as well as slapstick comedy that remained regrettably uncultivated through the years. Editor Stewart, exposed to Hayward's boss lady in a coy mood, could have been voicing popular opinion on *Top Secret Affair* when he demurred, "I like you better with your fangs out." The actress herself called this return to the studio that first employed her twenty years earlier "a bomb."

IV

THE PEACE

Cop: What do you do? Barbara Graham: The best I can.

—*I Want to Live!*

22. EATON AND OSCAR

"Women are soft," Susan Hayward once reflected. "They're only hard until they meet the right man and fall in love. Then it all changes. Any woman would put true love before a career."

This woman did. After she'd received her long-sought Oscar, along with New York Film Critics, Golden Globe, David di Donatello (Sicily), Silver Bear (Berlin), Golden Gaucho (Argentina), and Mar del Plata Festival (South America) 1958 best actress awards for the Barbara Graham story, *I Want to Live!* said one Hollywood wag, "She's got the Academy Award at last. Now we can all relax." Said Hayward, "I won it for my three men," meaning the twins and Floyd Eaton Chalkley, whom she married on February 9, 1957.

In '55 an interviewer had asked her what qualities she desired in a husband, and Hayward replied, "Reliability, tenderness, strength, and an equal income." She found these virtues to a considerable extent in Chalkley, whom she met at a Christmas week, '56, party at the Hollywood home of her friends the Vincent X. Flahertys. Like her first husband, he was a Southerner. They were introduced by her escort, a stagestruck Georgia restaurateur named "Uncle" Harvey Hester whom Hayward had "adopted" when he did a bit in *I'd Climb the Highest Mountain.* A strapping one-time football player and FBI agent, Chalkley personified her physical ideal of a man, and also was now an attorney as well as owner of several automobile agencies and an insurance and loan business.

"Eaton," as Hayward called him, divorced his first

wife in '50 and had a son and two daughters who lived with his ex-wife. In '58 he formed a corporation with his sister and with Hayward as president for film making, building, and operating motels and restaurants. It was based in Carrollton, Georgia, his home. The newlyweds constructed a modern, ranch-style house there on 450 acres that also contained a guest house and their own private lake. A few years later they took over and rebuilt another ranch, this one on 600 acres in Alabama, retaining the Carrollton residence as their permanent address. The bride did her own gardening, cooking, "put up" food ("which nobody ate"), raised frying chickens ("which *I* couldn't eat. I had *raised* them. For years after that, I couldn't even *look* at, much less *eat,* fried chicken!"). Together, the Chalkleys rode and swam and fished, even motorcycled and went to Ireland for the hunt.

"I don't know why a farm or ranch should attract a Brooklynite," she said, "but I've always had dreams of living on the land."* She certainly had owned her share of it, to believe Dorothy Kilgallen, who around this time printed that Hayward had just sold her West Coast real estate properties for $2,000,000.

Her sons, "as different as night and day" according to their mother, attended Georgia Military Academy. Gregory went on to be graduated from Alabama's Auburn University in 1969 with a degree in veterinary medicine and in 1972 opened his own building in Neptune Beach, Florida. The more restless Timothy went to the University of Southern California for a while and then joined the Army. Coming out he professed interest in photography and writing, becoming a long-haired press agent in Hollywood. "For a while he wanted to be an actor," his parent noted recently, "but, thank God, he got over *that!*"

---

*Gerald O'Hara had told his young daughter, Scarlett: "Land is the only thing in the world that amounts to anything . . . the only thing that lasts . . . the only thing worth working for, worth fighting for—worth dying for . . . 'Twill come to you, this love of land. There's no getting away from it, if you're Irish."

She called herself "just a country lawyer's wife," and Earl Wilson—whom she once walked out on during an interview when his questions became too personal—tagged her "Scarlett O'Hayward." Although very active in local charities and the Heart Fund, she worked less and less in pictures, her corporation apparently functioning mainly as partial backer of a couple of Hayward films. She was content with her quiet, outdoorsy new life and, for excitement, mostly fishing trips from their Fort Lauderdale, Florida, condominium into the briny between the Bahamas and Cape Cod. "She has certainly reformed," observed one veteran scribe of the actress whose once feverish career ambition now looked increasingly directed toward a new kind of angling—the watery sort. Next to her sons and spouse, it was fishing on her succession of yachts, Little Susannah, Big Susannah, and Oh, Susannah, that became her primary passion and, almost obsessively, all she wanted to talk about when she granted a rare interview.

Her husband's people were her people, and she was willing to fight for her neighbors' respect. Early in 1959, while she was in a heated Oscar race for *I Want to Live!* and completing *Woman Obsessed* at Fox, columnist Harold Heffernan wrote that during a temperament fit Hayward caused the firing of her cameraman, William C. Mellor. In a long-distance call to Paul Jones, Amusement Editor of the Atlanta *Constitution,* she vehemently refuted this: "I am an actress, and I do not have the authority to discharge anyone on a set. Mr. Mellor left the set after complaining of headaches. He later entered Cedars of Lebanon Hospital near Hollywood, where it was discovered he was suffering from a brain tumor and underwent surgery for its removal. Fortunately, it was not malignant. From now on I am going to fight every lie that is spoken about me. I don't want the people in my part of the country to believe these vicious stories." Leon Shamroy took over on *Obsessed,* but Mellor got full screen credit as cinematographer. Hayward further intimated that Heffernan's allegation might have been devised purposely to weaken her chances with Academy voters.

Such minor brouhahas apart, for almost a decade the Chalkleys shared an idyllic existence, marred only by the deaths of Hayward's mother in 1958 and Chalkley's son Joseph in a plane crash in 1964.

Then late in 1965, while she was shooting the comedy called *The Honey Pot* in Italy, Chalkley contracted hepatitis, the result, she says, of a contaminated blood transfusion he had received during an operation some time before. He was flown back to a Fort Lauderdale hospital. Hayward went, too, flying back and forth from her European film location whenever possible to be with him. It was written that she might have to be replaced in the picture because of this, but director Joseph L. Mankiewicz shot around her and she got through it. "My husband wouldn't have been very proud of me if I hadn't finished what I'd already started," she explained afterward. On January 9, 1966, Chalkley, age 56, died from hepatitis complicated by pneumonia six days after release from the hospital. His wife was at his bedside.

Six months later, Hayward, who had married her first husband in an Episcopalian ceremony but who had never paid much attention to formalized religion, traveled incognito to East Liberty, Pennsylvania, a suburb of Pittsburgh, where she converted to Catholicism, Chalkley's faith. Officiating was her husband's friend, Rev. Daniel J. McGuire. Soon after, reported columnist Mike Connolly, she sold the ranches and "departed the Taralike Georgia estate to reside beachside in Fort Lauderdale."

"A woman can't manage a cattle ranch alone," she articulated, "at least not this woman. The cows scare me. You need a man like Eaton to run things on a ranch and know what should be done. Selling was a difficult decision. I'd loved our life there, so had the boys, we enjoyed every minute of it. But in Fort Lauderdale I can get to things I never had enough time for before, like music and reading. I keep very busy. People from all over the world come and visit me. And I never want to be too far away from my fishing."

In a 1968 magazine piece, Jane Kessner wrote: "Susan has changed, of course. Isn't that what life is all about —changing, becoming? The volatile girl has become a strong, thoughtful woman who is one of Hollywood's all-time greats and boxoffice champions. Nothing has ever been really smooth sailing for her. 'Nothing,' she says, 'but the wonderful ten years of total happiness with Eaton. When you say ten *years* it sounds like a long time. When you live it and are truly happy, it is only a moment!' "

23.   LIVING IT UP

As for *I Want to Live!*, the following excerpt is from Bosley Crowther's *New York Times* panegyric:

"Susan Hayward has done some vivid acting in a number of sordid roles that have called for professional simulation of personal ordeals of the most upsetting sort. But she's never done anything so vivid or so shattering to an audience's nerves as she does in Walter Wanger's sensational new drama, *I Want to Live!* In this arresting prison picture which is based on the actual experience of a West Coast woman named Barbara Graham, Hayward plays a candid B-girl who gets hooked on a murder rap, is railroaded to a conviction, and condemned to die in the gas chamber. Hayward plays it superbly. From a loose and wise-cracking B-girl she moves onto levels of cold disdain and then plunges down to depths of terror and bleak surrender as she reaches the end. Except that the role does not present us a precisely pretty character, its performance merits for Miss Hayward our most respectful applause."

The director, Robert Wise, added this endorsement: "In motion pictures, Susan Hayward is as important a figure as Sarah Bernhardt was to the stage. Somewhere within her is a chemical combination that can excite and hold audiences as surely as Garbo [who had portrayed Bernhardt in a 1928 film titled *The Divine Woman*] and very few other greats of the screen. Susan is one of two or three actresses who can hold up a picture all by herself." He further called her the most professional actress he ever directed, revealed Samuel Stark in a 1963 *Films in Review* article on Wise, "always on time, up on her lines, interested in the picture and generous with constructive suggestions, some of which he found useful. When he rejected others she merely said, 'Okay, boss.' " During the weeks of shooting, Stark continued, Wise nevertheless came close to learning what made her tick only once. They were filming at night in a Los Angeles slum district and a group of urchins came near to watch. Hayward remarked to Wise, "Those are Park Avenue kids compared to the gang I grew up with."

Realistically, finally horrifyingly staged by Wise for the Joseph L. Mankiewicz-founded Figaro, Inc., and released through United Artists, *I Want to Live!*, ventured *Variety*, was "probably the most damning indictment of capital punishment ever documented in any medium." Many believe that the death penalty's loss of ground in recent years is directly traceable to the impact of this picture written by Nelson Gidding and Joseph L.'s nephew, Don Mankiewicz—whose father, Herman J. Mankiewicz, co-wrote with Orson Welles another socially conscious film milestone, *Citizen Kane*. The screenplay was culled mainly from Barbara Graham's own letters and various articles by a newspaperman named Ed Montgomery (acted by Simon Oakland) who at first believed her guilty but later recanted, leading the fight to save her. Apparently, the theme had intrigued producer Wanger as far back as his 1935 *Mary Burns—Fugitive,* when Sylvia Sidney, as the unjustly imprisoned Mary, said the line, "I'll never get used to seeing women caged up like animals."

The newer film's gestation, however, could have begun in 1952 when Wanger himself spent three months in prison for the jealous shooting in the groin of his wife's (Joan Bennett) agent, Jennings Lang. When he was released, Wanger launched into an attack on the United States penal system. "It's the nation's number one scandal! I want to do a film about it," he stated.

A decade after he had made his movie, Wanger recalled: "When I made *I Want to Live!*, which I thought was a very important picture, I had the Police Department of Los Angeles trying to stop me; I had the motion picture industry trying to stop me; I had the people who had the money trying to stop me. But I was working under Joe Mankiewicz' contract at United Artists, which gave me complete autonomy. That picture could never have been made had it not been for Joe's contract. There was no story purchase at all. It was just an actuality that I built up. I took a lot of legal risks because I was liable for the rights-of-privacy invasion, which is the reason the District Attorney's office fought me all through that picture."

The multifarious Barbara Graham was another of the once-in-a-lifetime roles that have come to Hayward several times. She was on nearly every frame of the two-hour film, and not just present but, excluding a redundantly hysterical outburst or two, doing colorful things in a characterization which had "the strength and sharpness of a master drawing" (Paul V. Beckley in the New York *Herald-Tribune*). From her opening ecstatic squeal in the dark at the foot of her latest "trick's" bed, to the closing execution, her strapped-down body jerking briefly, helplessly, the star was at her galvanizing best. Because of Graham's many sides, it was an enormously difficult part. There was some decidedly un-Hayward *shtick,* as when she mimicked with the abandon of a Danny Kaye the geet-gat-gittle of some shop machinery she happened to be passing. The lady definitely wanted to live, all right—at the ring of a phone on Death Row, her riveted, searingly anguished face was held in close-up by film editor-turned-director Robert Wise until the celluloid almost scorched. Yet, sometimes her carelessness for so practiced a law-

145

breaker indicated an even greater rage to self-destruct—it was easy tailing her to a hideout where she was called out, standing legs defiantly spread, to face policemen, reporters, and food-munching crowds.

Graham, in this delineation, was like some ancient maenad who, after compulsive Bacchanalia and still enraptured, suddenly leaped to her death at age thirty-two.

"The hardest cookie I ever ran up against," groaned one interrogating officer. It was in the grisly verbal sieges that the actress seemed to make the deepest personal impression on viewers as well. When one policeman asked during a grilling if she was on drugs and she said no, he wondered, "Then why are you squirming?" "I've got a worse habit," she blasted back, contorting her delicate mouth. "I have to go to the powder room every six or eight hours!" When she quelled a slavering hood (James Philbrook) who later fingered her for the 1953 pistol-whipping murder (never shown in the picture, which was momentarily confusing) of a Burbank, California, widow during a robbery, it was with the kind of lip haymaker that had become highest art in her hands. One believed, too, when she called a prison matron "fat stuff," even though the woman cast, oddly, was no such thing. Another arresting cop inquired: "What do you do?" Her rejoinder: "The best I can."

The execution near, she showed a sympathetic nurse (Alice Backes) a pair of lounging pajamas and said she could just see the newspapers: " 'Barbara Graham spent her last night decked out in her favorite color—flaming scarlet.' That's what they always call red when I wear it." Backes was a welcome gust of warmth down clammy corridors, although improbably sensitive and tremulous for a young woman who, after all, had chosen to set up shop outside a gas chamber.

Hayward's tortured wait for death, the reprieves and, penultimately, execution by cyanide—the guard (Dabbs Greer) whispering that it would be easier if she counted to ten and took a deep breath and Hayward recoiling from

146

the chair, "How do *you* know?"—yielded memorable drama. Its effectiveness was augmented by the sudden substitution of John Mandel's jangly jazz score with the stark, reverberating clang of cell living, and dying. So distressing, in fact, was this documentarylike section—director Wise's research had included viewing a genuine San Quentin execution—that British censors refused for many years to allow the film to open in England, and then cut most of the gas chamber footage. The last scene still plays well, too. After the execution and his reading of Hayward's—Graham's—letter of thanks for his help, newsman Simon Oakland winced as the witnessing reporters burst through San Quentin gates to proclaim Graham's death to a noisy gathering in the streets. He turned off his hearing aid and everything went silent as he drove away.

Some complained that *I Want to Live!* twisted facts to martyr a murderess. But many of those involved in the production, like Theodore Bikel who played the criminal psychologist dying of heart disease, as well as critics and mere moviegoers, maintained that Barbara Graham's guilt or innocence was no longer the real issue, that it was actually man's inhumanity to man that was under scrutiny.

At the time of the film's release, Hayward expounded on how she came to portray Graham: "Two years ago Walter Wanger called me, full of excitement, to tell me about reading a 200-page outline on her life by Ed Montgomery, Pulitzer Prize-winning reporter for the San Francisco *Examiner*. I read the outline and was fascinated by the contradictory traits of personality in the strangely controversial woman who had an extraordinary effect on everyone she met. She was first a juvenile, then an adult delinquent, arrested on bad check charges, perjury, soliciting, and a flood of misdemeanors. But somewhere along the line she was a good wife and mother. I read her letters, often literate, sometimes profound. She loved poetry and music, both jazz and classical. None of this seemed to square with the picture drawn of her at the time of the trial. I studied the final transcript. I began to wonder myself whether she was really guilty or innocent. I became so fascinated by the woman that I simply had to play her."

Along with a number of others, Hayward eventually deduced that "Bloody Babs" as the papers called her, was innocent of the actual murder of Mrs. Mabel Monahan; but she did feel that although Graham claimed to be home the night of the killing she had been present when the murder was committed. A few years later when asked if she believed in capital punishment, Hayward said, "My only feelings about capital punishment are simply that if somebody murdered the man I loved and didn't get the death penalty, I'd murder him or her myself!"

Undoubtedly because she knew what the success of this film could mean not only to herself as owner of a third of it but to the skidding Wanger, she went out and promoted it more vigorously than any other picture of hers, even going to several overseas openings.

New Jersey reporter Bea Smith, long an admirer of Hayward's work, remembers going to Manhattan to interview her then with some apprehension about meeting the in-person Hayward. But the star, drinking coffee throughout the cocktail time confab, "couldn't have been more charming," Miss Smith recollected. "Oh, there may have been a little reserve at first; but when she saw that it was more than 'just another job' to me, this changed. We spent a couple of hours talking about *all* her films. I remembered particularly my college days when I saw *My Foolish Heart* and so empathized with that poor girl that for several days after school I went back again and again to see the picture. I told Miss Hayward I would send her a tearsheet of the story when it appeared and she said, 'Just address it to Susan Chalkley, Carrollton, Georgia. They all know me there.' I did, although frankly for personal reasons it had not turned out to be one of my better stories; and a while after she had picked up all those awards for *I Want to Live!* I received a lovely thank-you note from her, with an apology for being so tardy acknowledging my article. 'I have been rather busy lately,' she wrote with that twinkle I had come to recognize so well by then."

On this fifth and at last successful nomination for the Oscar, her competition had been Deborah Kerr in *Separate Tables;* Shirley MacLaine in *Some Came Running;* Rosalind Russell in *Auntie Mame;* and Elizabeth Taylor in *Cat on a Hot Tin Roof.*

Right after the ceremonies, and the actress' acceptance speech thanks to Wanger, Hayward, who always had prided herself on being strictly a product of motion pictures, said, "I guess this proves you don't have to be a Method actor." Many years ago, when trying out for a role she needed bad, her up-and-at-'em method was rejected by the director, George Cukor. "Listen," the fledgling demanded, "who's reading this part, you or me?" Sometime later, another director who persistently corrected the Brooklyn traces in her speech was warned if he did it again she'd punch him in the nose.

Her smoky, expressive tones, likened by one writer to "black coffee without sugar," as well as called by others "a voice of intense voluptuousness" and "pseudo-Bryn Mawr interspersed with authentic Flatbush," actually were an asset during the halcyon days of radio on such programs as *The Lux Radio Theater*, where she reprised many of her picture parts; *Hollywood Premieres;* and *The Screen Guild Players*. Plus, on a Bill Stern interview show on the first of many visits the sexy newcomer told her startled host and friend, "Bill, I'm going to win the Academy Award before I'm through."

24.   IT WAS A VERY BAD YEAR

Britain's Thomas Wiseman dined with Hayward in '56 for his book *The Seven Deadly Sins of Hollywood* and concluded: "She had the look of a highly polished diamond with many facets, but one that is still sharp enough to cut. There are girls in Hollywood whose outer hardness conceals only an inner hardness. Susan, I would say, is not in this class. She has miscalculated too often to be accused of being calculating. She struck me as being intelligent, gifted, and blunt—down to earth without being earthy. An acknowledged glamour girl who does not talk with her hips, but in a normal way, and has things to say which are worth hearing. I liked her."

So does Theodore Bikel, who was featured in one of her biggest hits, *I Want to Live!*, and one of her biggest stiffs, *Woman Obsessed*. "And," he assured me, "I'd say so if I felt otherwise. I've worked with some real bastards. Susan was most agreeable, never temperamental. Despite all the fussing about her on the set that a star of her stature must endure, she never put on airs or behaved like the superstar she was. She is, though, a fantastically intense performer who concentrates totally on what she does. Sometimes she tenses up because of this. I remember such an occasion on *I Want to Live!* when Bob Wise asked her to loosen up. It was very tough. I said, "Hold it for five minutes," and went over and told her a joke. She laughed. Then I told another. She laughed even louder this time. I said, *"Now*, Bob." Early in 1968 when I was doing *Fiddler on the Roof* in Las Vegas, she came backstage afterward to see me, which I thought was very nice."

Surprisingly, *Woman Obsessed* and *Thunder in the Sun*, immediately following the smash *I Want to Live!*, were complete flops, and 1959 was probably her worst professional year as a star.

Obsessed was from a very readable, touching novel called *The Snow Birch*, by John Mantley; but stripped down to incident by scenarist-producer Sydney Boehm it all looked almost ludicrous. Hayward, an ex-schoolteacher, was a struggling Canadian farm widow with a droopy little son (Dennis Holmes) who took on a dour widower

Massive volume finally does justice to the greatest film studio –in its golden era

(Stephen Boyd) as handyman and then husband. She overcame both of them, ditto a forest fire, blizzard, flood, and a miscarriage—everything, in fact, except the movie itself. Although this was their fourth project together, she was scarcely directed by Henry Hathaway, who was always more comfortable when male stars were the center of attention, as when he goaded John Wayne to an Academy Award in *True Grit*. Hathaway, writer Wendel Mayes' idea of "the toughest son-of-a-bitch in Hollywood," let Hayward give one of the screen's more snortingly unbridled, literal demonstrations of bosom-heaving histrionics. The whole DeLuxe tinted debacle, with its grainy, poor-man's *Yearling* nature inserts and close-ups of the mother sweating while lost in a snow storm, had the chintzy, Cinecolored look of a 1940s Producers Releasing Corporation number, not a major 20th Century-Fox production.

To give the picture its due, there was a certain fascination watching the mostly sound stage-confined Hayward poised on the cabin set steps for a trip to the barn, followed by a long-shot of the actress' double sprinting across the Colorado location site toward her destination and then back to Hayward for the breathless arrival on the studio barn set.

Thunder in the Sun (Paramount), its title aside, was an even darker hour (and 21 minutes). Her own Carrollton, Inc., co-produced in Technicolor, and co-starring was old Flatbush school chum and frequent mid-1950s escort Ira Grossel (now Jeff Chandler). While *Woman Obsessed* conceivably might have been turned into a decent vehicle, it is impossible to imagine what attracted Hayward to this asinine, unsuitable story of emigrating Basques toting their grapevines to California. She played a beret-wearing, Flamenco-dancing firebrand, and though her French accent was a shock at first, it was better than anyone had a right to expect. Hayward was the wife of wagon train leader Carl Esmond and Chandler was the guide whom she kneed in the testicles when he first tried to kiss her. After Esmond's accidental death she took charge of the train and, following one of the noisiest Indian battles on record, wound up with Chandler who, from the odd way he ambled into her arms, had suffered more from her kick than from the redskins' raid.

The veteran Blanche Yurka, an interesting presence in support, has said, "On paper I had a perfectly lovely part, but after the editor got through there was nothing left of the film but the Indian attacks."

The Marriage-Go-Round ('60), a color comedy and the last assignment on her Fox contract, was better although Leslie Stevens' changes adapting his own play gave Amazon Julie Newmar from the original cast more footage, even, than nature had. Hayward had been slightly overweight for a few films now, a fact that did not go unnoticed in the scenario—"Every time you eat banana cream pie, it shows up on my hips," she told co-star James Mason. She was back in shape for her next movie appearance. Former husband Jess Barker once described the actress as having "the soul of a ballet dancer and the appetite of a truck driver."

In *Marriage-Go-Round* she was the wry but cordially accommodating Dean of Women whose happy marriage was threatened by the arrival of "well-stacked Swedish sexpot" Newmar who wanted professor Mason, Hayward's husband, to father "a perfect child" with her. More dialogue alterations to suit the Hayward cachet included Mason's teasing "I remember you now. You're from Brooklyn."

Bosley Crowther, the foremost film critic through the '40s, '50s, and late '60s, who was perversely cool to some of Hayward's finest performances, crowed about her in this trifle. He called it "giddily clever and witty . . . Susan Hayward is excellent as the intelligent wife who finds herself being casually unseated by a disarming guest in her own house. Being a dandy with poison-tipped sarcasm and plenty of a looker herself, she easily holds her own against the menace and makes the standard moral ending bearable." By then, finally steamed at discovering her husband and Newmar necking, she held the dirty end of such "clever" repartee as "I came, I saw, and I frowed up!"

On the set, Hayward—whose Content [sic] alluded to Newman's Katrin as "Tiny Tim" and "Baby Snooks"—was presented the Spanish equivalent of the Oscar as that country's favorite actress. In general, however, critics and public alike, conditioned by her imposing dramatic efforts, still refused to flock to anything wherein "Hayward laughs." Overall, *The Marriage-Go-Round* lacked the proper light touch, due in part to the all-seeing monster CinemaScope screen, which the studio had developed to revitalize interest in theater movies during the TV panic of the early '50s but which was now proving destructive to creative filmmaking, especially where intimate stories like this were concerned. (The studio would abandon the process quietly by decade's end.) Directed by Walter (*With a Song in My Heart*) Lang, the picture also missed many of the naughty punchlines that helped make the Claudette Colbert-Charles Boyer play a couple of seasons earlier so successful on Broadway.

25.   SHADY LADIES, SORT OF

Hayward's credits for '61 included *Ada* (MGM), co-starring Dean Martin, the saga of a self-educated ex-whore (Hayward) appointed governor of a Southern state (unnamed), in color (Metro).

Daniel (*I'll Cry Tomorrow*) Mann directed, again displaying a keen appreciation of the leading lady. As did *Motion Picture Herald* Managing Editor Richard Gertner when he wrote: "Ada is the kind of determined dame that no actress can play with the gusto and assurance of Susan Hayward, and that lady gives a no-holds-barred performance. From the moment that Miss Hayward makes her delayed entrance, no male in the story—or actor in the cast—stands a chance. Armed with irresistible feminine appeal and the amazing technical virtuosity she has steadily developed over the years, Hayward makes much of this far-fetched melodrama fun—even for a lowly male. Typical is a scene in which she parries at a tea with a group of society women who snobbishly try to put her in her place. Conciliatory at first, the new governor's wife suddenly turns fiercely on her tormentors, her eyes snapping fire, red hair aglow, and admits the truth: 'I'm a sharecropper's kid from off the Delta Road!' She proceeds to tell everybody off. A preview audience applauded her at the end of this scene, as they did in several of her big set-tos. The audience recognized the truth: *Ada* is a vehicle for its female star."

Writer Bob Freund summed her up in this one more succinctly as "guts in a girdle . . . a redheaded switchblade."

The picture was from Wirt Williams' novel *Ada Dallas,* but both the Hayward and Martin roles—he the singin', pickin' governor, she his lieutenant governor wife who inherited his duties when he was injured by "boss" Wilfrid Hyde-White's men—were whispered to have been inspired by living people. Although the Arthur Sheekman-William Driskill scenario slackened the elegiac momentum of the original to a fairly routine political potboiler recalling, especially, Joan Crawford's 1949 *Flamingo Road,* and despite the characterless Klieg light glare to most scenes, Hayward was operating at full throttle. She was able to bark at virtually everyone in sight, co-stars, featured actors, and bit players; she showed no favoritism.

Arranging a blasé Hayward's first meeting with the campaigning Martin, madam Connie Sawyer said, "Now don't tell *me* you wouldn't be impressed if you were going to entertain the next governor."

"Do they make governors different from other men?" drawled Hayward, wedging a cigarette between her pretty teeth.

"You want a drink?" Martin asked when they'd retired to her rooms.

"Not while I'm working."

Much swearing-in later, Hayward leveled one-by-one a
tableful of corrupt politicians as a cabinet meeting was
closing. The last man to retreat stammered, "Oh, ah,
give our best to the governor when you see him."

He was sharply notified, "You're talking to the governor!"

Her asperity made Ada (oops, the governor!) a gal
worth watching—and watching out for.

Universal's *Back Street* was a blatant weeper, the
continuing story—as they have said for generations on
"the soaps"—of the long affair between a fashion designer (Hayward) and a married department store heir
(John Gavin). No screen couple, however, has had lusher,
plusher surroundings in which to rendezvous. Our hero
held our heroine by the lakeside, the oceanside, the
countryside—every place except, it is too tempting to
resist saying, by the backside. It was a relationship on the
highest fantasy level, so it was only fitting that this particular errant but noble lady's symbolic back street turn
out to be nothing less than her very own small chateau
outside of Paris.

Hayward was the Nebraska shopkeeper's daughter
caught in a whirlwind wartime romance with serviceman
Gavin. "When you love somebody, that's it," she told him
one afternoon in the daisies. "Just that simple?" he wondered—warning signal, girls. "It is for me," she smiled.
When he flew off without marrying her, she went to New
York and dedicated herself to designing. "You're a
shrewd, conniving, opportunistic female," admonished
her boss, Reginald Gardiner, just before making her his
partner. She became "rae"—"all small letters, very chic"
—of Dalian *et* rae, soon an internationally famous combination. Gavin, far from idle himself, had married a
suicidal drunk (Vera Miles) and sired two unnervingly
creepy children (Tammy Marihugh, resembling a dis-

placed Munchkin, and Robert Eyer, an orthodontist's nightmare). Some of the more remarkable coincidences in all fictiondom began to bring him and Hayward together again. Once they bumped into each other on a crowded Fifth Avenue in New York. Next, scripters Eleanore Griffin and William Ludwig brought on a collision in a Roman restaurant, when Gavin's wife stumbled and fell right at Hayward's feet. That country place near Paris was waiting for them just around the next coincidence.

Hayward was never more flatteringly (Eastman) color photographed (by Stanley Cortez, her cameraman in *Smash-Up, Top Secret Affair,* and *Thunder in the Sun*) or more extravagantly outfitted (by Oscar-nominated Jean Louis), although the several mink-trimmed ensembles sometimes resembled altered overflow from Kate Smith's costume trunk. Running the show was David Miller, who has had one of Hollywood's more erratic but diversified directing careers and who next year made the arty contemporary Western *Lonely Are the Brave,* Kirk Douglas' favorite of his own films. Produced by glamour merchant Ross Hunter (who had to talk Hayward into doing an out-and-out love story—she said she felt more at home fighting for something) and her own Carrollton, Inc., *Back Street,* predictably, received poor reviews but was listed among *Film Daily*'s top-grossing pictures of 1961. Shortly afterward, Hayward defended the movie, under Miller's astutely star-aware direction perhaps the most affecting of Hunter's suds series.

"These days unless you have incest and a couple of rapings, the critics are not impressed," she contended. "But there are many people who want to see a decent picture. *Back Street* is a love story. It's simple love, old-fashioned love. And I think audiences have liked it. You don't feel dirty when you come out of the theater. *Back Street* is about rich people and women love this. Women don't like to see rags on the screen."

As the character created by novelist Fannie Hurst and essayed in earlier pictures by Irene Dunne ('32) and

Margaret Sullavan ('41), Hayward's careerist was much more successful than her predecessors, a miss who looked like the last thing she needed was "keeping." Her most dramatic scene probably was her almost lineless closing one. Sitting alone in unrouged mourning after the car accident deaths of her lover and his wife, she was suddenly visited by the two Gavin sprites who asked if, since they were now orphans, they might come and see Daddy's friend from time to time. Welling up (like the ladies in the audience and Frank Skinner's contributory, concerto-like background ripplings), she embraced them, the gesture reflected in the glass covering the nearby wall sketch she had done of Gavin that girlish day in the daisies. The end.

Being glad to see those two kids, though—that was *acting*.

Ironically, Hayward's personal happiness and fulfillment were showing in her work for perhaps the first time, and her eyes in this effort and succeeding ones appeared, when occasion demanded, notably more tender and compassionate. This was not lost on Louella Parsons. She knew Hayward better than most people and was one of the few "critics" the studio was able to quote in the ads: "Susan Hayward is so warm, so beautiful that she tears at your heart."

The Harvard Lampoon was among the unmoved. They voted her the year's worst actress for *Back Street* and *Ada*. In a way, it was something of a compliment that after twenty-five years in films Hayward still had the attention of young people. Always a favorite with audiences and, therefore, theater owners and managers, she continued through most of the '60s to be listed by exhibitors among the industry's moneymaking stars while eschewing that decade's blockbuster/hand-camera moviemaking extremes.

In a 1971 *Show* interview with the banner title "I Want to be Susan Hayward!" TV comedienne Carol Burnett said she would love to get into pictures, possibly doing a satire of *Back Street*-type stories—"I want to be Susan Hayward, Olivia de Havilland, Joan Crawford, all those suffering ladies in one movie and do a total camp take-off on all those pictures."

Joseph L. Mankiewicz' most celebrated film, 1950's *All About Eve,* contained a reference to the play *The Hairy Ape* which Hayward did on screen plus—as did the following year's *The Frogmen,* also from Fox—an allusion to Hayward herself as an example of a Brooklyn success story. He has worked with her on several occasions and was asked to comment for this book. "I must congratulate you on your choice of subject," he wrote back. "I should think that, of all the actresses I have directed, Susan's talent has been the most underestimated. Almost more than any other other young actress of her generation, her capabilities were smothered by overexposure and exploitation of her physical attributes—something called 'glamour.' 'Glamour' was benediction which Hollywood executives used to bestow impartially upon all boxoffice attractions from Rin Tin Tin to Greta Garbo."

Adding, "Of my own work with Susan, I consider her performance in *House of Strangers* to be as sensitive and satisfying and fully realized as any in my experience."

She liked Mankiewicz, too. Perhaps remembering his understanding during her grief-stricken *Honey Pot* shooting, she said not long ago, "He has heart."

26.   THE SCENE CHANGES

Although her blissful role as Mrs. Chalkley had pushed films into the background of her life, Hayward was not oblivious to her husband's pride in his movie star wife. She kept a hand in.

A change of scene seemed in order after *Back Street* and *Ada.* Besides, the couple was in a traveling frame of mind. Hence, *I Thank a Fool* ('62), a mysteriously titled mystery attractively color-filmed in England and Ireland and Hayward's first Anglo-American picture. *Variety* regretted that the "co-starring of Susan Hayward and Peter Finch has not produced the chemistry that might have been anticipated. It is not the fault of the principals, but simply that the somewhat turgid screenplay and the implausibilities of this meller are too much for the case."

Hayward was a Canadian doctor, the daughter of a janitor—"My father died when I was twelve. I worked my way through McGill University." She fell in love with a married professor and followed him to England, where she became his mistress. When he became incurably ill, she also became his doctor and as his pain deepened administered a lethal injection.

"He'll sleep now," she whispered, looking guilty as hell, although among many points never satisfactorily clarified was whether she *had* purposely killed him.

Still, she was called a "mercy killer" and convicted of manslaughter, spending eighteen months in prison. Peter Finch, the lawyer who had helped send her there, was waiting when she got out to whisk her off to his north country estate as keeper to his schizoid wife (Diane Cilento, who in the early '70s joined a commune in that area to write—and commune). As the latter grew more unmanageable, and player Cilento's directionless, Eloise-cum-Mr. Hyde ravings and escapades more irksome to viewers than seemed absolutely necessary, the wife suddenly was found dead of an overdose of sleeping pills. Suspicion, naturally, fell on Hayward. One critic funnied that the shock for once of having to dog another actress in the throes of a smash-up could have unhinged Hayward.

"It's all too much like . . . what happened before," she ruminated, beginning to suspect the charming but enigmatic Finch (who grew poison flowers as an avocation). And with plenty of justification.

"A very ingenious man," one character squinted. "He never does things without a reason."

159

The film, in fact, which the *Herald-Tribune* called "a washed-out descendant of *Jane Eyre*," had been building steadily and inexorably toward a conclusion that would reveal Finch as a wily murderer. To provide the weariest of romantic endings, however, the dead girl's libidinous Irish father (Cyril Cusack) was rushed on to blame in a thoroughly unpalatable climax. As best as I could tell from some very untidy tidying up, Dad knew she had just taken the pills but because of her admittedly accelerating nuisance value opted not to do anything about it.

Not bloody likely. Withal, the denouement of *I Thank a Fool* was as unconvincing as any in the annals of the mystery movie genre. In keeping was the final scene, which showed Hayward happily driving into the Irish horizon with Finch—"Christine, you going to give me a lift?" Only a short time before at the inquest, staged in a country schoolroom swathed with colorful children's paintings, he had told the residents of her manslaughter conviction, and she had accused him of murder.

"Please enjoy the shock, but don't reveal the surprise ending to your friends!" was the advertising come-on. Producer Anatole de Grunwald and company had nothing to worry about: hardly anyone saw their film. Well into shooting, Hayward—who throughout played it very "foreign intrigue" in her indivisible gray raincoat—disclosed that there was trouble when she confessed she didn't know how it ended "because that part hasn't been written yet." New director Robert Stevens worked hard, though, among some adequately Gothic settings, and so did Hayward in the physically arduous but emotionally one-key role of the abject, probable euthanasiast.

She might have used this medico's services in United Artists' *Stolen Hours* ('63), also in color, British-made, and demanding of her stamina. It was a remarkably reactionary endeavor for the young producing team of Stuart Millar and Lawrence Turman, in view of the fact that four years later Turman would make the revolutionary *The Graduate*—for which, incidentally, Hayward early had been mentioned for the Anne Bancroft lead. Directed by Daniel Petrie, *Hours* (first called *Summer Flight*) was a Jessamyn West-written remake of Bette Davis' 1939 hit, *Dark Victory*, done on the stage by Tallulah Bankhead. The story of a frivolous, dying young jet-setter "who came to terms with life and herself at the eleventh hour" (as the ads had it), the new film, if scarcely a sensation, was decidedly refreshing in its tastefully wrought, time-tested man-woman romanticism and self-sacrifice.

"The heroine, given a superb reading by Miss Hayward, is never allowed to go off the deep end," related Robert Salmaggi in his very quotable New York *Herald-Tribune* review. "Her first fears of the unknown malady that afflicts her with blinding headaches and blurred vision are honest and real, as is her refusal to face up to the seriousness of her condition and her terror-stricken resistance to medical help. Equally impressive is her reaction and those of the people around her when she discovers that she has only a few months to live. There is no hand-wringing, martyred posturings, or playing to the grandstand.

"When Miss Hayward, completely blind at the film's conclusion, gropes her way to her bedroom, lies down, and closes her eyes, waiting for the inevitable, Petrie slowly darkens the screen. Tears will cause a lot of mascara to streak, and the men may fight a tight throat as well."

Commendably, her approach to the once "poor and barefoot" oil heiress was more restrained than La Davis' overdone playgirl. Hayward's best bit, moreover, probably was her silent, unfocusing look of almost numbed betrayal when, in the midst of her first deeply felt love affair with Harley Street doctor Michael Craig, she accidentally found her file in his office and learned that her illness was terminal. But she was not inert, as Ronald Gold pointed out in *Motion Picture Herald:* "A past-mistress of anguish, Miss Hayward gets ample opportunity to display this facet of her talent. Briefly, also, when she learns her fate and decides to 'grab as much of the world as I can lay my hands on,' she shows a hoydenish streak reminiscent of previous 'devil-may-care' roles. Oddly, however, Miss Hayward and the film as a whole are most effective in the idyllic sequences of the film's final third (after her marriage to Craig). Here, no little assistance is provided by Robert Bacon as a cherubic English ten-year-old, and by the stunning background of the Cornish coast."

The early section's plusses numbered the scene where Dr. Craig and Hayward, who thought he was simply a good-looking guest, retired to a private room during one of her palatial blasts. Surreptitiously, he began his diagnostic questioning, obtusely at first, ingratiating himself to the secretively sick young woman, then waxing more bold in his interrogation. Finally he owned up to being an MD. Accurately spieling out her string of symptoms, he added, "And your sense of direction . . ." Furious at his deception, she threw her drink in his face—"What do you think of my sense of direction now, doctor?" After a walk in the garden and maybe the first real stock she had taken of a starry night since her Texas girlhood, a contrite Hayward meandered back to the room and found the doctor waiting for her.

The opening credits were as efficacious as any adorning a Hayward picture. Names bloomed against a skylike background that suggested seasons by changing colors, while the petals of dead flowers blew dustily away in the breeze to Mort Lindsey's autumnal musical motif.

There were a couple of unfortunate lapses by the makers of *Stolen Hours,* though. One was the awkward cutting out of Hayward's whole party twist dance, which Chubby Checker had spent a week teaching her and which she said was the hardest part of her entire performance. In the long run, it was thought that this terpsichorean turn would date the picture too quickly; but its omission left a jumpy continuity and a star who was breathless right after with no real explanation. Another miss: the thick-legged woman who doubled for the slender, Fabiani-frocked Hayward in some location long-shots.

Hayward's physical exertion also included winning a school sports day egg-and-spoon race, replacing the alcoholic mother of young, attentive Master-Bacon—whose university education she made her husband promise he would see to. The festivities took place along the remote Cornwall promontory where Dr. Craig had been born and where, in her final ecstatic, sea-blown months, she now had convinced him to switch his practice.

Hayward herself had become so docile at work that one columnist yawned: "Just for some excitement, the crew at Shepperton Studios in London where Susan Hayward is finishing *Stolen Hours* wishes Judy Garland, who recently completed *I Could Go on Singing* there for the same producers, were back. Susan spends most of her time between scenes knitting."

27.   WHERE LOVE WENT AND STAYED

Then in '64 came what first looked like Hayward's most attention-getting, controversial assignment since *I Want to Live!*, Joseph E. Levine's Embassy-Paramount production of *Where Love Has Gone*. Co-starred was Bette Davis, and there were a number of reasons why a Hayward-Davis set might have been expected to rival in fireworks Zanuck's *Tora! Tora! Tora!* To enumerate some:

1) A bit player in Davis' *The Sisters* vehicle over a quarter of a century before, Hayward was top-billed in *Where Love Has Gone*.

2) *Time* once labeled Hayward "a bargain-basement Bette Davis."

3) When Hayward returned home from the hospital after her sleeping pill episode in 1955, she unknowingly

commandeered a miffed Davis' studio-assigned limousine. (Hayward was set then for *I'll Cry Tomorrow* at MGM, where Davis was well into *The Catered Affair*.)

4) Hayward had just remade Davis' favorite Davis picture.

5) Davis was just coming off an extensively talked-about feud with another august actress and co-star, Joan Crawford.

6) Davis and Hayward were both fighters for what they believed in.

On *Where Love Has Gone,* the publicity department admirably refrained from flacking "The Screen's Two Great Ladies of T-N-T (Talent and Temperament)." The ladies limned high-handed society mother (Davis) and glamorous 'sculptress, pagan, alley cat" daughter (Hayward) in Harold Robbins' story of a murder that couldn't help suggesting the Lana Turner-Cheryl Crane-Johnny Stompanato tragedy of 1958. Joey Heatherton was Hayward's fifteen-year-old daughter who stabbed her nympho mother's boyfriend to death. "How about it, kid. Was he your lover, your mother's, or both?" probed a newshawk. In some handy psychology, it eventually was uncovered that daughter, resenting mother for having already deprived her of one man, her father (by divorce), and now feeling the not-so-old girl was at it again with the stud they shared, actually wanted to kill her parent when the victim got in the way. Heatherton's perpetual squint made this particular slip at least semibelievable. Traffic allowing, opposite Hayward as Joey's ex-drunk dad was Michael Connors (born Krekor Ohanian), who earlier had been Touch Connors and later would be Mike Connors (TV's Mannix), sleazy-looking under any name. Jane Greer, returning to films after seven years and a recent heart operation, played the youngster's probation officer; and the overall results were eagerly awaited not only because of the touchy, potentially explosive subject matter, but because of the inherent electricity in a Hayward-Davis bout. Between them Hayward and Davis—coin-

164

cidentally, both Scarlett O'Hara rejects—had earned fifteen Academy Award nominations.

But . . . while there were a few minor rumbles rumored, word had the set surprisingly cool. Joey Heatherton told interviewers the two female stars had been "lovely" to her. *Where Love Has Gone,* although grubbing some bucks, seemingly kicked up no fuss anywhere at the time and was a thoroughly negligible, trashy, garishly colored film that somehow missed casting Lana Turner. It was distinguished mainly by one of Bette Davis' worst performances. Delivering each line as if it were a declaration while crowned with a white marcelled fright wig that literally began turning green toward the finish (from envy at Hayward getting the lioness' share of the nasty dialogue?), Davis gave her co-star little visible hassle snaring acting laurels. And Hayward achieved the not inconsiderable feat of making sympathetic an impossible woman (scripted by John Michael Hayes). "The only truth she's capable of is in her work. Nothing else matters" groused DeForest Kelley, yet another of her lovers. She was especially forceful in the juvenile home hallway square-off with Davis, the mother she despised and whom she blamed for everyone's troubles. Wielding a finger like the sculpting tool that had skewered her lover, she railed to Davis that no matter what happened she would never let her get custody of Joey—"NEVER!" Hayward's "never" meant positively.

Off-camera, she was somewhat less successful finding appreciation, responded Bette Davis recently, practically by return mail, to my inquiry: "It is with sadness I tell you Miss Hayward was utterly unkind to me on *Where Love Has Gone.* The title was prophetic. There was no one whose performances I admired more *up to* working with Miss Hayward, and if I said otherwise when Miss Hayward reads your book she would know I was dishonest." Davis' honesty did not extend to any details then, but she did explain to *Sight and Sound* that there had been a dispute about her interpretation: "So I said to

165

them, if the mother has to be shown as a monster, at least give me one scene being really monstrous to the daughter so that people will really believe it. Unfortunately, Miss What's-her-name didn't see it that way, and she did get top billing, so . . ."

I must admit being rather heartened to hear that the domesticated real-life Hayward might not have lost her bite completely.

Her only related comments were to a reporter who mentioned that she looked to have died "for no explicable reason" at the end of their movie. "I agree with you," replied Hayward. "It wasn't written that way. Bette Davis was supposed to die, until she suddenly insisted that she couldn't suicide in less than two pages of dialogue. So we flipped a coin—I lost and won the death scene."

Much later director Edward Dmytryk put in his three cents for *Films Illustrated:* "It was one of those very rare cases of two stars who were jealous of one another, Susan Hayward and Bette Davis. Susan was frightened of Bette who can come on very, very strong if she likes. And much as I like her, Bette didn't help any. As with *The Carpetbaggers,* I knew when I took the film on that the script wasn't right, but with people like that I thought we could look at it a few days before we were due to shoot each scene and rework it. That way, comes the day of shooting we have a new scene that comes to life. Anyway, Bette was always on the set very early, so I would go into her trailer and talk about the day's shooting. And five minutes later, she would come out and say, 'Boys! Everything's changed. We're going to do such and such today.' Of course, everyone assumed *she* was doing it—she had that manner. So Susan got very frightened because she thought Bette was going to do it all her way and walk away with the picture. She went to the front office and said, 'Look, I signed to do that script, and I insist that that is the script we shoot.' They called me in and said, 'She wants to shoot that script and she's got us.' So we shot that script and the film wasn't as good

166

as I know it could have been. But strangely enough the studio liked it very much and I got compliments for that film far more than for *The Carpetbaggers* which, to my mind, was a far better film."

Hayward's next picture was proof that getting good reviews from all the New York dailies is not the insurance for a film that it usually is for a play. A United Artists color comedy released early in 1967, the Italian-made *The Honey Pot*, like *Where Love Has Gone*, also seemed auspicious at first since the literate Joseph L. Mankiewicz both directed and scripted from a soundly sophisticated, long serviceable basic idea, *Volpone*. It concerned "a fabulously wealthy nut," Cecil Fox (Rex Harrison, said to own a large chunk of the film, too), who pretended in his palazzo to be dying so he could watch his three ex-girlfriends claw for his cache. The arriving ladies were Edie Adams, a movie star; Capucine, a princess; and ("Are you sure Cecil sent for those two crows?") Hayward, a Texan millionairess. Called the canniest of the trio, Hayward additionally was the toughest: dumping a roll of nickels from her purse, she fizzed, "Did you know that with one of these in your fist it's like hittin' a man with a hammer?" She was described by a studio story synopsis as "pure vitriol" in a role written expressly for her.

The production, shot mostly in a moldy Venice that was a long paddle from the sunshine of Katherine Hepburn's *Summertime* (not to mention the somnambulist's studio recreation of Hayward's own *The Lost Moment*), was beset by trouble from the start. Her husband, as noted earlier, died while it was filming, as did the cinematographer, Gianni di Venanzo. By opening time much footage had been cut, too, including Herschel Bernardi's entire (and still billed!) part as Adams' agent. Hayward, taking second billing (to Harrison) for the first time in over a decade, and horrendously photographed, managed to enliven the early section as the coarse, drawling Mrs. "Lone Star" Crockett Sheridan ("Hold on to your

167

crown, Highness!"), also a sniffling, pill-popping hypochondriac; but she was murdered too soon.

Recalling their youthful common law liaison, Harrison's foxy slayer could not hide his admiration for "her ambition, her guts, and above all her greed. 'Lone Star' was insatiable. There was never enough of anything—money, possessions, food, sex. Imagine if you can a seventeen-year-old combined Venus and giant squid."

His Mosca-like accomplice for "the charade," Cliff Robertson, was not oblivious to her finer qualities either: "If there ever was a gunfighter with an itchy finger. The fastest draw on the Grand Canal."

She might have turned *Honey Pot* into a minor personal triumph if some of her best moments had not been scissored, particularly a well-publicized dream sequence showing Harrison as a prospector dying in her arms in the desert near thousands of gold coins—"Be ya daid, Ceece?" As the still too long, plotty, conversational imbroglio was edited, mousy Maggie Smith, whose star was rising, got most of the critical attention, as the "specialist in complaining women," Hayward's nurse-companion. But a party close to things has said, "Before the cutting, Susan acted everyone off the screen." For some (like *Motion Picture Herald,* which called her "a master at sarcasm"), even after.

Mankiewicz, who couldn't be stopped from getting off an occasional *bon mot,* might have been wiser to present his money-losing, static revamp (shooting title: *Anyone for Venice?*) of the 1606 Ben Jonson classic as a play, too.

28. VALLEY OF THE DULLS

Hayward also dominated *Valley of the Dolls,* which seeped through later in the year. The source was Jacqueline Susann's bonanza novel whose miserable but sensational people were copped almost proudly from her show business contemporaries. Said Bosley Crowther: "Amid the cheap, shrill, and maudlin histrionics of Patty Duke [as a kind of victim of excess a prime time Hayward might have made work], Sharon Tate, and Barbara Parkins, our old friend Susan Hayward stands out as if she were Katharine Cornell. Her aging musical comedy celebrity is the one remotely plausible character in the film."

As in *Honey Pot,* Hayward had another smallish chore as the cussing ("Tell that son-of-a-bitch to get off his butt and earn his oats!") and cussed ("She'll stab you in the back!") "barracuda" who had played a much more involved role in the book. A great Broadway star who had talented young competition like Patty Duke fired from her shows, she was revealed in her final speech to agent Paul Burke to be a basically lonely woman who had inured herself to "roll with the punches." Whatever else, the lady was "a professional," Burke chastised Duke, now famous herself but addicted to "dolls" (pills) and alcohol and dependable only for some of the most unrestrained screeching fits and barroom downfall scenes ever to embarrass an audience. Patty, the first juvenile actress to win a non-honorary Oscar (in 1962, as Best Supporting Actress, for *The Miracle Worker*), appeared to be playing a game of sick dress-up in *Valley of the Dolls,* probably blowing any chance to ever become Patricia Duke in what could be one of the screen's all-time worst performances. Even some Fox executives at the pre-premiere New York screening I caught gave her the raspberry, which was giving it back to her almost in kind. A particular howl was the scene where Paul Burke (as the character Lyon Burke—imaginative casting?) confronted a hung-over Duke. Grimly holding her pudgy puss up to the camera, he uttered something like, "Look at you. You're 26—and you look 36." Sixteen was still nearer the mark.

Petula Clark had been the first choice for Patty's part of Neely O'Hara, but, in one of her few sage decisions during her *Finian's Rainbow-Goodbye, Mr. Chips* ill fortunes, she turned it down.

The other two main girls, Barbara Parkins as Anne, the TV cosmetics pitchwoman, and Sharon Tate as Jennifer, the skin flick star, came on retarded—but they did keep their voices down. Authoress Susann—her matron's idea of dirty novelizing laundered quite a bit by scenarists Helen Deutsch and Dorothy Kingsley—was typecast in her walk-on as a nosey reporter at a suicide.

Hayward, the "Old Ironsides" whom most agreed was patterned after Ethel Merman, replaced Judy Garland at the last minute, beating out Bette Davis and Jane Wyman. Aided by the voice of Margaret Whiting, she got to belt out the Dory and André Previn tune, "I'll Plant My Own Tree," in the strangely, even hazardously staged production number that had her closely surrounded by large, swaying mobiles. She had to worry not only about putting her song across, but keep from getting an extremity tangled in one of the moving gimcracks.

The highlight, if that's the word, of both color film and book was the ladies' room brawl at a party (shades of *Smash-Up*) between Hayward and Judy Garland plot facsimile Patty Duke. After some malicious give-and-take, Hayward headed for the door, vaunting that she had a man waiting for her. "That's a switch from the fags you're usually stuck with," lashed Duke. "At least I didn't marry one," the older star sallied. A tussle ensued, with Duke pulling off Hayward's red wig to expose a white stubble and then throwing the piece into the toilet. Hayward was allowed to wear the sequined pants suit originally designed for Garland to wear in the role she was unable to play, but which the late Judy did wear in her last concerts.

Even snatched almost bald, Hayward looked at least as fetching as the three squirming starlets in whose pill-polluted valley she was slumming (although Patty called her "Granny"). More to the point, in her spaced-out four scenes she brought a gutsy thrust—even sympathy—

acking everywhere else in a cliché-strewn stinker. Nevertheless, its way paved by the Susann best-seller, the picture was the biggest nonroadshow moneymaking attraction in the history of 20th Century-Fox.

For a real mind-boggler, try this: Susann has said that Garland, glib and competent at preproduction press conferences, was intimidated as things got underway by the youthful, fast-study abilities of Parkins, Duke, and Tate. "Gradually, after the picture started, Judy began to retreat, in a kind of daze. No one knew what she was on, or where she got it. After ten days with still no film on her, she was fired. After all, Judy had been nurtured by the big studios which had accomplished things more slowly. She called me and said she couldn't get anyone on the phone. 'Jackie,' she asked, 'I'm a star, aren't I?' I said yes. She said, 'Well, where did everyone go?' "

When it was announced she would step in for Garland, Hayward expressed her regret at Judy's departure. "She's such a talent, such a fine actress. I guess I don't understand these things, though. I've enjoyed every minute of my career. It isn't art to me, it's work, and darn good work, but it's never been my life. There are other things vastly more important to me."

On the first day of Hayward's first Hollywood part in several years, the set, jammed with well-wishers and news people, froze when Barbara Parkins announced, "Now let me introduce you to one of my co-stars, Miss Susan Hayward." Hayward, a star before Parkins was born, only smiled and answered questions cheerfully. And why not: she was being paid $50,000 for two weeks' work. When director Mark Robson finally asked the set cleared, adding, "Ready, Susan?" she laughed, "I was born ready."

Valley of the Dolls was the first time she took the "special" kind of late-frame billing—"Susan Hayward as Helen Lawson"—that had come to be the lot of many of Hollywood's aging aristocracy, signifying the advent of less than major roles: "Joan Crawford as Amanda Farrow" (*The Best of Everything*); "Barbara Stanwyck as

Jo" (*Walk on the Wild Side*); "Eleanor Parker as the Baroness" (*The Sound of Music*); "Bette Davis as the Countess" (*The Scapegoat*) and—"Ethel Merman as Madame Coco" (*The Art of Love*) and "Judy Garland as Irene Hoffman" (*Judgment at Nuremberg*). Hayward's on-screen *Dolls* billing, though, was in larger lettering than any of her co-players, which was unusual for this sort of thing and maybe unprecedented.

Later, she said, "I did the picture for Mark," her director on the incalculably more tasteful *My Foolish Heart* and who in 1957 had made a respectable movie out of another notorious best-seller, *Peyton Place*.

Before *Valley of the Dolls* came out, Fox presented a thirty-minute product film to its sales personnel and exhibitors. Hayward's rough-cut, harshly lighted extracts from her bathroom battle and song number inadvertently revealed yet another facet of technical expertise in films. Her wig was discernible here, but it was not in the actual movie. By somehow dimming this footage for the feature, studio craftsmen kept Helen Lawson's secret until the final moment of truth in the toilet, heightening the scenes' effectiveness. Richard D. Zanuck, Darryl's son and Executive Vice President in Charge of Production at Fox, narrated the Richard Fleischer-directed short that presented clips from many of the company's other important releases for the 1967–68 season.

The title was *Think 20th*. It was then the studio's slogan and pasted thereabouts everywhere except across the bosom of the lot's latest sex symbol, Raquel Welch—a brunette, indicating as dramatically as anything else how movie times had changed.

29. FROM BROAD TO VIDEO

With due regard for Frank Loesser's song (and her own previous remarks), luck has rarely been a lady to

Hayward. Her success, as seen, was achieved primarily by hard work and, of course, ability. Four years, however, after the unexpected *Valley of the Dolls* she "lucked" into two more jobs, the back-to-back *The Revengers* and the television movie *Heat of Anger*.

Perhaps the serious fire in her Florida haven earlier in '71 had convinced her it was time again to go— *Among the Living?* She had visited Hollywood, made it known that she wanted to work more and had signed with the William Morris Agency's Norman Brokaw, a partner up from the ranks who was the first agent to take Marilyn Monroe around on her initial jobs at $55 a day. Hayward was photographed at West Coast social functions for the first time in ages, once with her press agent, Jay Bernstein, who at least one covering newspaper boo-booed was her new husband. The producers of *Junior Bonner* made some overtures, but when they met her they decided she was too young-looking to play Steve McQueen's mother (and Robert Preston's wife). Ida Lupino, also increasingly a stranger in pictures, got the part.

Shortly, along limped Cinema Center's *The Revengers,* in its preparatory stages a jinxed film that got at least one good break before cameras turned. First, leading man William Holden came down for a time with "jungle fever," picked up around the Mount Kenya Game Ranch and Safari Club, of which he is part-owner. Producer Martin Rackin, a friend of Hayward's for many years, had a mild heart seizure. Co-star Van Heflin suffered a fatal heart attack and was replaced by Ernest Borgnine. Finally, as shooting came nearer, Britain's Mary Ure withdrew from the main feminine role to star on Broadway in Harold Pinter's *Old Times*. Hayward to the rescue again. She inked to team with early fellow Paramount contractee Holden and in the fall of 1971 she left for the Mexico location. From then on, everything went smoothly, productionwise.

The final quality was another matter.

A post-Civil War color "oater" weighted with plot

turns that were tired when not totally incredible, it had Daniel Mann—fresh from that summer's surprise box-office hit, *Willard*—back directing Hayward as an Irish-accented, hard-working nurse solitarily growing old and potatoes in a not so sweet little nest somewhere in the West. She entered briefly to treat and house the critically wounded Holden, whose wife (Lorraine Chanel) and children had been murdered by a band of Comanche horse thieves led by a one-eyed white man (Warren Vanders). During their weeks together, which passed like fifteen minutes, she fell in love with Holden and tried unavailingly to dissuade the healed, revenge-sworn rancher from tracking down the killers. Badly lighted and *sans* the makeup of a respectable corpse, her visage blotchy or freckled (from the recent Florida sun?), she seemed not only essentially irrelevant but unbelievable in the context. Hippocrates aside, why was a still youngish, not too distantly attractive woman with a brogue shriveling up alone in a dreary, sparsely populated Texas border community?

In the Wendell Mayes script as first written, this Elizabeth Reilly was a somewhat more rational romantic padding in her unlikely terrain. She was divorced from a drunkard who probably had dragged her there. This was not brought up in the picture. Before the deviation, her part also was larger. The end that was used found Holden, after instigating the kind of explosive Army post massacre commonplace back in old "cowboys and Injuns" movie days, suddenly humanized and unable finally to kill the now captured Vanders. Riding away, he turned and waved to his bloodied, dumbstruck confederates. The Mayes original, however, had Holden returning to Hayward's little potato patch. As she went off to deliver a baby, she promised she would think over his offer of going back with him to his Colorado home.

Unsurprisingly, *The Revengers* ('72) was director Mann's first Western. Holden, wrinkled beyond his years and otherwise disinterested (even though his son Scott

174

played a wounded young Army officer); Borgnine, as one of Holden's renegade aids whose scruffy, travestied ambivalences looked as if his mother had been frightened by a Wallace Beery movie; and the perhaps mercifully dispensable Hayward have never been seen to worse advantage.

Calling her role "a cameo," the actress alibied, "I did it to get my feet wet again."

A couple of weeks after *The Revengers* was completed, Barbara Stanwyck, who had worked for three days on the TV movie *Heat of Anger* (originally and more pointedly titled *Fitzgerald and Pride*), fell ill and had a kidney removed. The production was to be a pilot for a lady legal eagle series and could not be postponed, so Brokaw, who was also Stanwyck's agent, suggested Hayward replace her as star. Stonehenge Productions and Metromedia Producers Corporation agreed. *Heat of Anger* was wrapped up in seventeen days, the long-absent performer getting even less time to prepare for this than *The Revengers*.

She told *TV Guide:* "Until the first day of shooting on *Heat of Anger,* I felt like a pianist who hadn't touched a piano for years. You wonder if you can still play, and you're terrified, but then you hit the first note and it all comes back to you. It was easier, I guess, because I found myself in the midst of old friends. My co-stars were James Stacy, Lee J. Cobb, and Fritz Weaver; the director was Don Taylor, who played one of my husbands in *I'll Cry Tomorrow;* I knew the executive producer, Dick Berg, and the writer, Fay Kanin, from my days at Paramount and 20th Century-Fox (where much of *Anger* was shot); even many of the electricians and grips were familiar faces from movie productions I'd done. The only thing *un*familiar was the pace. In TV, there's no fooling around and taking it easy. I was frenzied when I had to learn ten pages of dialogue every day, instead of the three pages we used to do in films, but I soon found out I was able to handle it. Fortunately, my brain is in good shape."

Hayward sent the convalescing Stanwyck, whom she greatly admires, three dozen roses with a card that read: "All love from another Brooklyn broad."

She also okayed starring if the project was accepted as a weekly TV series. This was a precarious time for television producers to be thinking about movie names. They had been proving small draws of late on the tube. Shirley MacLaine, Anthony Quinn, Tony Curtis, Rod Taylor, Henry Fonda, Glenn Ford, Gene Kelly, James Stewart Rock Hudson, James Garner, and George Kennedy all had floundering—and, in most cases, failing—series. Obviously, with *Heat of Anger,* both new property and old star looked unusually hearty.

Anger had its first colorcast via "The New CBS Friday Night Movies" ninety-minute showcase on March 3, 1972, and marked what was really Hayward's acting debut for the newer medium. And, as Kay Gardella reported in her New York *Daily News* notice, "the redhaired actress performed in a manner suggesting she never had left a sound stage." Hayward was Jessie Fitzgerald, a wealthy Los Angeles lawyer who took on both the case of a long-time client, contractor Lee J. Cobb, accused of fatally pushing his daughter's wild ironworker boyfriend off a high girder, and a new legal associate, Gus Pride, an "outsider" John Garfield type played by James Stacy with a nicely compatible argumentativeness. They gave her plenty of trouble, but she came out victorious on each count.

The script itself was thin but more literate than most TV movies, holding the interest. And with Hayward's steely steering, it was better-than-average courtroom melodrama. Again, Miss Gardella: "Miss Hayward, still very shapely and attractive, gave a very solid performance, moving around like a little dynamo." She also brought to the small screen something it could sorely use: glamour —even Joe Mankiewicz would have had to approve in this instance. Smartly robed in, say, white ensemble for afternoon legwork, green velvet gown for those pool-playing

176

evenings at home and brown pin-striped suit for, of course, court theatrics, she was in her familiar fashion simultaneously appealing and commanding. While it's impossible to tell exactly how the estimable Stanwyck would have played the role, Hayward couldn't repress a sensuality that the white-haired, older actress seemed an unlikely bet for. To a TV generation raised on endlessly inseparable Kildare-Gillespie youth-age male figures, there was a surprising, even refreshing suggestion of sexual awareness between twenty-year counselor at law Hayward and testy young Stacy that probably wouldn't have surfaced had Stanwyck portrayed this "Portia of the Pacific."

The *Hollywood Reporter*'s Sue Cameron, in her rave, seemed to feel the pilot could be a step forward in women's liberation, at least on TV: "What a joy it is to see an intelligent, warm, vibrant woman character as a series lead in a professional position, played by such a wonderful actress as Susan Hayward. If this doesn't become a series there is no justice . . . one of the lawyers being a woman, portrayed with dignity, strength and femininity, is something new, and it's about time."

The contractor's murder defense was progressing until it was divulged that many years before he had served a term in prison. As "down" as Hayward had *ever* looked, she told Stacy, who had questioned her old friend's accident story from the start, "You said Frank was lying. Funny. It can happen a thousand times and every time . . . you're still surprised."

She had regained faith and composure for her closing argument to the jury. "He [Cobb] hauled himself up and he built himself a good life," she began. The judge had decreed that his early felony not be held against him now, but Hayward knew the jury could not forget it. She suddenly instructed them to close their eyes, adding, "I'd like you to think of anything except a horse, a blue horse. *Do not* think about a blue horse!" When it quickly became obvious that this was impossible for the jury, she explained that it was the same with the information

177

about Cobb's youthful indiscretion. She *wanted* them to take this into consideration—and everything Cobb had proved himself to be since he served his brief prison term.

It was disclosed that the dead lad long had courted death as a life style, and Cobb was acquitted.

Leaving the courthouse, a horde of news people swooped down on them all.

"What's up next?" a TV reporter, seemingly aware of the possibility of a series, asked Hayward.

"A commercial, I'm sure," she quipped.

Right again, counselor.

About a month and a half after *Heat of Anger* aired, Hayward began her second TV feature, another pilot, but this one written for her (by Sandor Stern), entitled *Say Goodbye, Maggie Cole*. It was shown the following September 27 in the ninety-minute "ABC Wednesday Movie of the Week" slot.

Hayward encored a take-charge professional lady, a research doctor who sometime after her husband (Richard Anderson) died returned to general practice in a Chicago slum—"I want to work. I can't hole myself up in that house anymore." The author had been inspired by the star's own story, as was the advertising department: "To a past, and a love, that are gone *Say Goodbye, Maggie Cole*." Hayward's understanding of this still comely contributor thus was complete, fleshing out an already thoughtful dramatic premise. Huskier-voiced (did she have a cold during production?) and talking out of the corner of her mouth a mite more than usual, she was a formidable sidekick for gruff "street doctor" Darren McGavin. When he questioned her capacity to stand up to the clinic's steady flow of crises, she squalled from the door, "When I was seven years old I hated stringbeans. One night my father forced me to eat them. Two hours later I got in his new car and threw up . . . Look, I may stumble a lot, but if you're waiting for me to fall on my face, it's not gonna happen."

178

Dr. Cole's schedule was hectic but her competence irrefutable, and on *her* operating room green looked good. Her manner, though, was immediately almost total detachment from patients.

The physician's life took a calamitous turn once more when she had to fight becoming personally involved with a parentless teen-age leukemia victim (Michele Nichols) where she roomed. "Your husband is *dead*, Maggie, and you haven't even faced up to that!" pleaded a concerned McGavin. "Take a risk. Take your lumps and learn to say goodbye." Her landlady was Jeanette Nolan, cast as the dying girl's severe-looking grandmother who, it came out, had buried her husband, her son, and was now resignedly but at last tearfully preparing for "another funeral." Miss Nolan gave a crash detailed acting lesson, making count brief footage wherein even the inconsequential business of closing a gate behind her hospital-bound granddaughter acquired an unforseen poignance. She created a character more moving than Hayward's.

Unlike most TV medical dramas, then, *Maggie Cole* —an Aaron Spelling-Leonard Goldberg color production directed by Jud Taylor—dealt less with the sick than their loving survivors. In this respect it was, again, a notch above normal video fare; while the work of a pair of Irish-descended thespians named Hayward and Nolan would have done any medium proud.

In the spring of 1972 Hayward, a pink chiffon oasis in a desert of Jean Stapletons and Lily Tomlins, was a presenter on the long-winded twenty-fourth Annual Emmy Awards telecast. Finally escorted on stage near the end by George Peppard, she was introduced by host Johnny Carson as "a truly great star." She and Peppard announced television's Best Actor and Actress in the Single Performance category. As she began to recite the nominated actors' names, their slide likenesses—maybe a second late —didn't flash on the screen fast enough to suit Hayward who tongue-tapped, "I'm waiting."

Her own television career, if it even can be called that, was sporadic and eccentric. In March, 1956, she broke her then "no TV" ruling and was seen quickly as herself in the "live," hour-long *Climax!* dramatization of old friend Louella Parsons' autobiography, *The Gay Illiterate.* Teresa Wright was "Lolly," with an homage-paying guest roster that remains one of the medium's starriest.* That December Hayward darted on again to accept from Dr. Frank Baxter a *Wisdom* magazine award for authoress Pearl S. Buck; and a couple of years later she and her husband, Eaton Chalkley, did *Person to Person.* Early in '59 she graced the Oscarcast to collect her *I Want to Live!* statuette, returning the next year to present Charlton Heston with his award for *Ben-Hur,* and showing up again in 1970 in an Academy telecast film of earlier Oscar winners that showed Hayward's gallop on stage to pick up her gold-plated doorstop.

Jack Paar used an old Hayward clip with particular wit in his satiric late '60s special, *A Funny Thing Happened on the Way to Hollywood.* He intercut Hayward's jilting of Dennis O'Keefe in 1944's *The Fighting Seabees* with Catherine McLeod's of William Elliott in 1947's *The Fabulous Texan*—with each set of players delivering the very same lines.

Also in the '60s, Hayward materialized in on-set candid footage Ken Murray made on the *Tap Roots* location and displayed in his *Hollywood: My Home Town* TV special; was seen in the documentary *Dear Mr. Gable* smilingly lighting the lone candle on Clark's birthday cake on the Fox set of their *Soldier of Fortune;* narrated a tour of Georgia for a *Journey to Adventure* segment; was in-

---

*Others billed: Gracie Allen, Eve Arden, Jean Pierre Aumont, Gene Autry, Joan Bennett, Jack Benny, Charles Boyer, George Burns, Dan Dailey, Howard Duff, Joan Fontaine, Zsa Zsa Gabor, Rock Hudson, Jack Lemmon, William Lundigan, Ida Lupino, Jeanette MacDonald, Fred MacMurray, Robert Mitchum, Kim Novak, Merle Oberon, Ginger Rogers, Gilbert Roland, Red Skelton, Robert Stack, Robert Wagner, and John Wayne.

terviewed by Army Archerd at the *Valley of the Dolls* boat premiere in Miami; appeared in footage from that picture on the early '68 hour-long *Jacqueline Susann and the Valley of the Dolls;* and did the Joey Bishop talk TVer to get her Fort Lauderdale organist friend Jack Frost a shot on same—Bishop asked her to dance on camera "so I can say I danced with Susan Hayward," and she complied for an impromptu whirl.

As mentioned earlier, she had her crack at *Gone with the Wind* shown on the 1969 special *Hollywood: The Selznick Years.* In '72 Selznick's son Daniel and editor Rudy Behlmer used this show's Scarlett montage to help promote their book *Memo from David O. Selznick* on such as the *Today, Midday,* and Mike Douglas programs, giving Hayward's test one of the widest audiences ever for a normally private matter.

She was rumored for TV versions of *Rain* and *The Letter,* but never did them. Soon after her husband's death, she was reported to be interested in her own series as a lady politician. The *Wagon Train* producers once wanted her for a guest star spot, but they refused to meet her salary demands. (Oddly, her 1959 feature *Thunder in the Sun* looked like it could have been a rerouted *Wagon Train* script.) In 1966 a producer who offered her $5,000 a week to star in a Broadway play was told, "You're not even close."

30.   THE MAN IN THE MOON WAS A 'HOOLIGAN'

Two years after, at age 50, Hayward made her professional "legitimate" stage debut as the highest paid *Mame* up to that date in the Ceasar's Palace, Las Vegas, company of the Jerry Herman musical that originally starred Angela Lansbury. Under the tutelage of Oscar-winning choreographer Onna White, she had rehearsed for

181

this marathon singing-dancing zany in New York, and just before the Vegas opening canceled a one-performance benefit run-through at Manhattan's Winter Garden, claiming a cold. A couple of columnists wrote that it had settled in her feet.

A while later, film producer Martin Rackin gave the genesis of Hayward's *Mame:* "After her husband's death, she grieved like an eighteenth century Spanish widow. For several years she couldn't even look at anything she and Eaton had been involved in, including the movie business, with the exception of *Valley of the Dolls,* playing a small part as a favor to a friend. She sold out all his holdings in Georgia, making her very rich indeed. . . . Finally, I had an idea. I was one of the owners of Caesar's Palace then, and I phoned her in Florida. I didn't know how she'd react, so I tried the old-buddy approach. I always had called her 'Hooligan'—with affection, of course—because of her early rough days in Brooklyn. I said, 'Hey, Hooligan, how long are you going to sit there with the old folks in Sun City? How about coming to Vegas to do *Mame* for me?' I wasn't sure she wouldn't tell me to go jump in the river, but she said she'd think it over. A month later she was in Vegas."

The show opened in Las Vegas, two (!) performances a night. Dance director White declared Hayward "a *fantastic* lady, a lady with a lot of guts, a very calm woman even when things are falling apart. I worked with her steadily for the past three months, *everywhere,* from New York to Fort Lauderdale. I found her to be a lady and a very *top* lady. I was really rooting for her with every nerve in my body. With no tryouts, it's quite amazing, really." While Hayward's singing and dancing caused no sensations, her Mame Dennis was applauded by most critics; audiences, as always, loved her and business in the cavernous Palace was great.

However, the rigors of the role which had her swinging on a moon high over the boards proved too much for the novice stage—not to mention musical comedy—star.

182

The *Hollywood Reporter*'s Vegas correspondent Joy Hamann reported: "Susan told me she trained so hard for *Mame* she felt eligible for the Rams team. And watching her propped on her dressing room couch with her right foot encased in an ice pack made her assertion believable, except for her petiteness."

A few months after the December '68, opening, doctors warned that her strained, irritated vocal chords could seriously impair her health unless she quit the show. Tearfully ("I've never backed out on a deal before"), she left and understudy Betty McGuire filled in until Celeste Holm could succeed her. A short time later she said, "Sure, I'll sing again, but right now I'm more interested in straight acting film scripts. A musical is all right if you do it just once a night. No singer can stand up to 14 performances a week—with not a single night's rest in four months." One of the reasons she took the assignment in the first place, she stated, was because it might help her to get the movie of *Mame*.

Evidently, Hayward had not worked on the vocalizing aspect of her performance as purposefully as she had the dancing. Right after signing, she confessed to an acquaintance, "I'm not worried about the singing. My problem is the dancing—I'm such a klutz!"

"I think the reason she had difficulty with her voice was because she didn't have the proper instruction beforehand," Roger Rathburn, who played her nephew, told me early in 1971 when he began his run as the juvenile lead of the hit Broadway revival, *No, No, Nanette*, starring Ruby Keeler. "If she had been trained correctly, Susan wouldn't have had the trouble she did, I'm sure.

"What was she like? One of the greatest ladies I've ever worked with, friendly and conscientious. She had the least vanity of any star I've ever seen. She came to rehearsals without make-up, her hair in curlers and wearing a bandana around her head. There was no formality about Susan. She was nice to everyone. And she was under great strain—it was a tough show to do. The costume changes alone were

183

murder. Mame was always getting into some wild outfit. Because the people weren't supposed to be kept away from the gambling too long, the show was somewhat shortened for Vegas, which gave Susan only half the time Mame usually got to make all her changes. A couple of times she came on stage still fastening things.

"What impressed me most about her? For one thing, she was one of the sexiest women on stage I've ever seen. As an actress, she was tremendously effective in the dramatic scenes, more so than in the comedy parts. I remember that near the end when I sang the reprise of 'My Best Girl' to her, I was often near tears because of the moving way she handled the speech that preceded it. For some reason, at the time I hadn't seen too many of her pictures, but lately I've been catching up with them on television. She certainly came on strong in the ones I've seen—yet she never lost her femininity, did she?"

Two years after she did *Mame,* speculation had her replacing original lead Lauren Bacall in the almost equally demanding long-run Broadway musical, *Applause.* The show was based on Bette Davis' screen apotheosis, *All About Eve*—which right after *I'll Cry Tomorrow* was rumored to have been in the reworks as a movie musical vehicle for the newly discovered Hayward singing talent. The role of the pugnacious, 40-year-old stage star Margo Channing would have found Hayward, in the play's "Welcome to the Theater" song, advising competitive newcomer Eve Harrington, "You'll be a bitch, but they'll know your name."

31. THE ONES THAT GOT AWAY

Writer George Kirgo once joked, "Christine Jorgensen is writing her autobiography. When it's filmed, the title part will be played by Susan Hayward *and* Gregory Peck."

Following initial success portraying real-life personalities, her name began to be mentioned for almost every planned screen biography of a female celebrity, including Aimée Semple McPherson, a part that seemed ideal; Eva Peron; Lillie Langtry; Ruth Etting; Helen Morgan; Diana Barrymore; Helen Keller; Louella Parsons; Carol Tregoff; Candy Mossler; Pilate's wife; pirate Anne Providence; and, as she put it, "a certain nasty female columnist"— meaning Sheilah Graham. In one of her most unfortunate and inexplicable career blunders, she turned down 1957's *The Three Faces of Eve,* which, based on the true incident of a Georgia housewife afflicted with multiple personality, won Joanne Woodward an Oscar. Fox suspended her for nixing 1956's *Hilda Crane,* which brought no honors to Jean Simmons, the story of a disastrously married woman who took an overdose of sleeping pills.

Hayward also has been up for *Gold Diggers in Paris; Three Cheers for the Irish; For Whom the Bell Tolls; Murder, He Says; Duel in the Sun; Forever Amber; Anna Lucasta; Stella* (Ann Sheridan's, not Melina Mercouri's); *Band of Angels; The Painted Veil* (finally called *"The Seventh Sin); The Wayward Bus; Elephant Hill; The Sun Also Rises; Can-Can; The Frog Pond; My Cousin Rachel; Sweet Bird of Youth; Night of the Iguana; The Plot; Hedda Gabler;* and a Ross Hunter-proposed remake of *Stella Dallas,* cancelled when "women's pictures" no longer were boxoffice. Most were made with others; a few are yet to be filmed. She might have had one of her greatest opportunities in an original but eventually abandoned screenplay by Garson Kanin titled *Come What May*—to be directed by George Cukor—that would have cast Hayward as a foundling whose future was given three dramatic, drastically different projections. She was the original choice for Elizabeth Taylor's *Cleopatra,** produced by

---

*On the recent 100th birthday of Adolph Zukor, founder of Paramount Pictures, Toastmaster General George Jessel said Zukor had planned to make *Cleopatra* many years before "with the original Cleopatra, whom he was living with at the time."

Walter Wanger who said that Hayward, while temperamentally right, realized she was physically wrong for the role and turned it down. When Wanger died in 1968 of a heart attack, he was said to have been preparing two pictures for her, one called *The Benefactors* and another women's prison drama.

Although she may never have been in the running for it, Susan ("The Divine Bitch") Hayward and Henry ("The Eternal Ineffectual") Fonda were born to play Martha and George in the movie of *Who's Afraid of Virginia Woolf?* It went instead to a pair of real-life marrieds—hired just for their marquee value—who were able only to masquerade as Edward Albee's tortured, torturing twosome.

Hayward's own former connubial sparring partner, Jess Barker,* is seen occasionally, inconspicuously on TV and in films. Late in 1971, around the time his ex-wife was set for the television movie *Heat of Anger,* he did a small guest role on the *Adam-12* series. He was working mainly in insurance. Barker also has modeled and in the late 1950s was a disc jockey at radio station WCFL in Chicago. In the early '60s a columnist revealed that he was after a franchise to open an Arthur Murray dancing school in a Los Angeles suburb.

May Mann, long-time Hollywood reporter, wrote at the start of 1972 that "in spite of the bitterness when Susan

---

*Jess Barker, one of four sons, was born circa 1914 to a nontheatrical family in Greenville, S.C. He was discovered for pictures in 1942 by Mrs. B. P. Schulberg, wife of the producer, while he was appearing on Broadway in *Magic.* Barker's feature films follow: 1943, *Good Luck, Mr. Yates; Government Girl;* 1944, *Cover Girl; Jam Session; She's a Soldier, Too;* 1945, *Keep Your Powder Dry; Senorita from the West; This Love of Ours; The Daltons Ride Again; Scarlett Street;* 1946, *The Time of Their Lives; Idea Girl;* 1949, *Take One False Step; The Black Book;* 1950, *The Milkman;* 1953, *Marry Me Again;* 1954, *Dragonfly Squadron;* 1955, *Shack Out on 101;* 1956, *Three Bad Sisters; Kentucky Rifle; The Peacemaker;* 1965, *The Night Walker.*

186

Hayward divorced Jess Barker, they're now friends and have dinner together on occasion."

In the mid-1950s she was quoted as being well into the writing of her autobiography, "up to age eleven, so far," but it has never appeared. Someone close to the actress said recently that he didn't know anything about this, but he could say "she has been approached by many writers over the years who wanted to write the story of her life and turned them all down. She doesn't want to dredge up the past."

Hayward threatened to retire for years. "I don't want to go doddering around, making faces in front of a camera until I'm playing grandmother parts," she said in '65, five years before her son Gregory and wife Suzanne had a son, Chris, and made her one for real. (In 1971—the year Timothy married actress Ilse Schenk—Hayward said: "I see my grandson about every six months. After all, he's not my son, he's my son's son, and I try not to be a smotherer. Anyway, with telephones and airplanes, we are never far apart. I can get on a plane and within hours get to wherever Greg and his family are.")

In view of her off-screen and on-screen images, which during her career often have become confused, or intertwined, it was interesting to note during the writing of this book not only how concerned and fond the majority of those checked were of the in-person Hayward, but also, as in the cases of John Gavin and Lee Bowman (both of whom refused to comment unless Hayward personally gave them the go-sign) and Agnes Moorehead, how *protective*. "Thank you so much for your letter requesting information for your project honoring the work of our lovely Susan Hayward," wrote Miss Moorehead. "All I can say is that those films on which we were both engaged [*The Lost Moment, Untamed,* and *The Conqueror*] I enjoyed immensely. I feel this artist has a great deal more to give, so I hope the scripts and roles will be created for her. Please do her justice in your book. Needless to say, I am one of her fans." Needless to say, their apprehensions were groundless.

If I had to choose one film star who has given me the most pleasure over the years, I would choose Hayward. While some waited for Ruby to go into her dance, or Hedy to go into her trance, my palms grew sweaty on the armrest waiting for the little redhead with the carbolic charm to give John Wayne what-for. She was always more *alive* to me than any other actress, despite having begun with an ingénue's none too imposing physical basics (and I am one to whom, in any evaluation of beauty or the interesting countenance, definite looks are important). But the spirit and experience of Hayward, who was born into poverty and a strife which lasted throughout ultimate fame and wealth, took possession early of her very pretty, wholly feminine but not really startling features. In action, Hayward's upturned nose acquires an added precosity . . . her rosebud lips form a mouth of truest grit . . . the petite chin juts out like a Sherman tank . . . hazel eyes flash . . . her cherub-contoured face suddenly, miraculously contracts to a high-cheekboned elegance . . . when tossed, the red, tousled hair becomes a flaming weapon . . . her voice, with a pinch of Brooklyn for flavor, has a rich, "stage" timbre . . . and the small, rather chesty body, slim of hip and limb, walks tall and distinctively.

It is remarkable to observe what, and how, the inner woman overcame. There was something almost majestically gallant about Susan Hayward. A moment comes to mind from *Valley of the Dolls* in which the white-haired veteran star Helen Lawson (Hayward) had her red wig destroyed in a powder room hairpull at a party. Told she could leave via the kitchen, Lawson took a long, hard look at herself in the mirror and, tying her neckerchief around her head, said, "No, I'll go out the way I came in." And she did.

I think Susan Hayward—at last unlike Scarlett O'Hara —would have, too.

SUSAN'S BACK, AND BROADWAY'S HAD HER*
By Bill O'Connell

Boston, Sept. 20

Madame! the Susan Hayward-starred musical based on the life and discoveries of French scientist Madame Curie, has halted previews due to what the producers call "necessary book revisions."

The musical, budgeted at $1,000,000 and receiving its backing solely from the radium industry, marks Miss Hayward's return to the stage after an absence of many years. The previews in Boston had all been sellouts, despite tepid notices from the hub critics.

The book, authored by French scientist LeMere Trotti, is now "almost extinct," according to the producers. "What we didn't realize is that no one could possibly believe Susan in such a role. We are therefore contracting another book writer and changing the locale, while still trying to keep the wonderfully scientific atmosphere created by Mr. Trotti," it was stated.

The new book, by S.U. Hayakawa, has switched the location to China at the turn of the century, and the musical has been retitled *Glow Worm*. It will deal with the discovery of radium by a leading Chinese lady scientist.

---

*This facetious article was first published in a special satirical issue of the Pace College *Push* on Dec. 16, 1970.

The score is being retained, and the hit number, "C'est Moi," will still be sung by Miss Hayward in the new Chinese locale. The composers are now at work trying to fit such new numbers as "Roll That Egg Roll" into the complex score. *Glow Worm* has delayed its New York opening indefinitely.

Detroit, Oct. 14

The producers of the Broadway-bound musical *Glow Worm* have announced that due to internal conflicts the show will close "out of town" this weekend.

Glow Worm, the musical biography of Madame Curie starring Susan Hayward, had been grossing over $90,000 weekly in its tryout at the Colonial in Boston and went on to set a house record the first week in Detroit. The elaborate production, badly received by local critics, had audiences flocking to see Miss Hayward perform such numbers as "Glow, Little Glow Worm" and "If I Had Ten Yen." The original cast recording of the Detroit production, cut last Tuesday, was certified as a million dollar selling gold record today just moments after the Record Industry Association of America had given the producers a gold record for the Boston cast album, cut during rehearsals.

Miss Hayward's only comments at the prospect of her show being closed before it reached Broadway were: "They can twirl on it! Whaddaya think the public wants to see, huh? Well, I'll tell you—it's *me,* that's who the f— they want to see! And they're gonna see me. I'll get this thing to Broadway if I have to build the rest of the sets with my own bleeding fingers. All of you will see! You f—s will see!"

Detroit, Oct. 15

Performances of the Susan Hayward musical *Glow Worm* have continued without interruption due to the intervention of Miss Hayward's personal friend, Darryl F.

Zanuck, who flew in last night at the star's request to assume the duties of producer.

Zanuck has vowed to make the remaining changes in the show and see it through to Broadway "no matter what the cost." This is film mogul Zanuck's first legit venture, and many are eyeing it with extreme interest.

Zanuck brought with him screenwriter Toshiro Monsooni, who is working on a revised book. At Zanuck's request the locale of *Glow Worm* has been changed to Pearl Harbor at the time of the invasion, and the title is now *Glow Worm! Glow Worm! Glow Worm!* Monsooni presents Madame Curie as an exchange scientist from Japan, conducting her experiments in the Pearl Harbor area while carrying on a dalliance with an American G.I. (portrayed by John Gavin, who also accompanied Zanuck to Detroit). Rounding out the supporting cast will be Benson Fong and Hilo Hattie, both appearing as laboratory technicians.

The budget has spiraled to over $3,000,000, due to the extensive laboratory equipment which must be destroyed at each performance during the Pearl Harbor sequence. This section of the show depicts the bombing of Miss Hayward's island laboratory in detail, and the newly written finale number, "Poi for the Hoi Polloi," is being received ecstatically.

New York, Nov. 2

One of the worst disasters in theatrical history took place last night when producer Darryl F. Zanuck presented the Susan Hayward-starred musical *Glow Worm! Glow Worm! Glow Worm!* at the Winter Garden Theater.

Hundreds of opening night patrons were burned to death in a freak accident which occurred during the Pearl Harbor sequence of the show. The massive pyrotechnics and simulated explosions that are employed in the sequence triggered a fire on stage, and the audience sat transfixed while the house curtains and balcony also caught fire. Obviously misled by out-of-town reports concerning the realism of the finale, no member of the audience dared to leave his seat and miss the ending, causing the entire theater to become a human inferno.

Famed screen and stage actress Susan Hayward was among the missing, along with her co-star, John Gavin, and producer Zanuck, who was seated in the front row. Theatrical colleagues already are speculating on the possibility of Miss Hayward receiving a posthumous Best Actress in a Musical award at the Tony ceremonies next year. President Nixon today announced that twin medals will be awarded her twin sons for her "bravery in action."

Sole survivor of the tragedy appears to be *The New York Times* drama critic Clive Barnes, who left the show at intermission.

ADDENDUM

After this book was completed, Susan Hayward, the little fighter from Flatbush, began the toughest battle of her life—*for* her life.

In March, 1973, she was hospitalized in Los Angeles with, the media sirened, a serious illness about which no one would make a clarifying statement. Rumors spread that she had inoperable, cancerous brain tumors: at least one covering periodical even said, "By the time you read this Susan Hayward may be dead." Her son Timothy Barker was forced by her condition to take legal charge of her estate.

There was every indication that she was living a role similar to the one she played in her 1963 film, *Stolen Hours*.

In June, 1973, Dorothy Manners, Louella Parsons' successor, reported Hayward home from the hospital, "the mere fact that she was released from constant care being very good news to her friends and twin sons." Still, only silence on the nature of her illness from those close—ominous in itself. And Hayward went into seclusion, later revealing that she had not wanted to inflict her problem on her friends (including actress-singer Kathryn Grayson and designer Nolan Miller, who nevertheless would occasionally send her bouquets of her favorite flowers, yellow roses).

Her peers were dying all around her. Never had the movie industry's Old Guard been depleted by such a rash of deaths. Betty Grable, Veronica Lake, Joe E. Brown, Robert Ryan, Lon Chaney, Jr., George Macready, Lex Barker, Robert Armstrong, Irene Ryan, Jack Hawkins, and Ernest Truex. Of them all, it was probably hardest to conceive of Susan Hayward succumbing. Backtracking to the words of Lillian Roth at a hairbreadth earlier crisis, "Susan is too vital and eager, too ambitious a girl to want to end her life."

The Hayward faction remained mum, however, and eventually there were widespread stories that she had died. Some newspapers even ran her obituary! This writer, having just authored the only book on the actress, received many phone calls and letters from the concerned from all over the world. Finally, to quell speculation and let her increasingly vocal friends and fans know that reports of her demise were highly exaggerated, Hayward signed up as a presenter on the April 2, 1974, Academy Awards telecast. She was introduced as "a medical miracle" as she walked—none too securely—on stage clutching co-presenter Charlton Heston's arm. Although the camera kept a discreet distance, she looked and sounded surprisingly well yet undeniably not herself.

Confirmation then was made via the media that she had been dangerously ill but had recovered, and that while the initial diagnosis had indeed been cancerous brain tumors, as rumored, she now felt she had been misdiagnosed. She talked of working again.

In an April 7, 1974, *National Tattler* article, writer Toni Holt revealed that at one point earlier Hayward had been given only thirty-six hours to live. "I'm going to lick this," she quoted the actress saying when this grim verdict was handed down. "The Marreners [her maiden name] are not a family of quitters."

But she did not return to work. And before long there were more hospital stays. The optimism that everyone —the star included—first felt began to fade. Again, that ominous silence from her camp.

And again, the prayers of millions.

On March 14, 1975, wondering ceased. Susan Hayward died at her home in Beverly Hills, California. Dr. Lee E. Siegel, who had treated her for more than two years, said, "There was no other case like it, nothing in the medical literature. It was amazing to live that long with this type of lesion. She was one of the great fighters. I've never seen anything like it."

She was buried quietly from the Catholic chapel she had helped to found in Carrollton, Georgia. Her happiest years were spent in the South with second husband Floyd Eaton Chalkley, who died in 1966. She rests at his side in Carrollton's piney woods, a long way from the asphalt jungle of her youth.

FILMOGRAPHY*

1. *Pictorial Short*. Vitaphone, 1936.
2. *Hollywood Hotel*. Warner Brothers, 1937. *Busby Berkeley*. Dick Powell, Rosemary Lane, Lola Lane, Glenda Farrell, Louella Parsons, Hugh Herbert, Mabel Todd, Ted Healy, Frances Langford, Allyn Joslyn, Johnnie Davis, Alan Mowbray, Edgar Kennedy, Jerry Cooper, Carole Landis, Perc Westmore, Grant Mitchell, Fritz Feld, Curt Bois, Eddie Acuff, Sarah Edwards, William B. Davidson, Wally Maher, Paul Irving, Libby Taylor, Joseph Romantini, Jerry Fletcher, Ken Niles, Ronald Reagan, John Ridgely, John Harron, David Newell, Frances Morris, George Offerman, Jr., Rosella Towne, Robert Homans, George O'Hanlon, Bobby Watson, Al Shean, Milton Kibbee, Leonard Carey, Duane Thompson, Georgia Cooper, Billy Wayne, George Guhl, Lester Dorr, Raymond Paige and Orchestra, Benny Goodman and Band (with Harry James, Gene Krupa, Teddy Wilson, Lionel Hampton, Alan Reuss, Ziggy Elman, Vido Musso). 109 minutes.
3. *The Amazing Dr. Clitterhouse*. Warner Brothers, 1938. Edward G. Robinson, Claire Trevor, Humphrey Bogart, Allen Jenkins, Donald Crisp, Gale Page, Henry O'Neill, John Litel, Thurston Hall, Maxie Rosenbloom, Bert Hanlon, Curt Bois, Ward Bond, Vladimir Sokoloff, Billy Wayne, Robert Homans, Irving Bacon, Mary Field, Georgia Caine, William Haade, Thomas Jackson, Ed Gargan, Wade Boteler, Libby Taylor, Edgar Dearing, John Harron, Hall K. Dawson, Sidney Bracy, Earl Dwire, Jack Mower, Frank Reicher, Vera Lewis; the voice of Ronald Reagan. 87 minutes.
4. *The Sisters*. Warner Brothers, 1938. *Anatole Litvak*. Bette Davis, Errol Flynn, Anita Louise, Ian Hunter, Donald Crisp, Beulah Bondi, Jane Bryan, Alan Hale, Dick Foran,

---

*The director's name, whenever available, follows in italics the year of release.

Henry Travers, Patric Knowles, Laura Hope Crews, L.
Patrick, John Warburton, Janet Shaw, Harry Davenpor
Mayo Methot, Irving Bacon, Paul Harvey, Ruth Garlan
Peggy Moran, Arthur Hoyt, Stanley Fields, Vera Lewi
Joseph Crehan, John Harron, Ed Stanley, Russell Simpso
Jack Mower, Frank Puglia, Rosella Towne, Frances Morri
Mildred Gover. 95 minutes.

5. *Comet Over Broadway*. Warner Brothers, 1938. *Busb*
Berkeley. Kay Francis, Ian Hunter, John Litel, Donald Cris
Minna Gombell, Sybil Jason, Ian Keith, Leona Maricle, Ra
Mayer, Chester Clute, Vera Lewis, Clem Bevans, Nat Car
Edward McWade, Melville Cooper, Linda Winters (Doroth
Comingore), Ed Stanley, Emmett Vogan, Raymond Brow
Jimmy Conlin, Janet Shaw, Sidney Bracy, Frank Orth, Ja
Holm, Jack Wise, Jack Mower. 69 minutes.

6. *Campus Cinderella*. Warner Brothers, 1938. *Noel Smit*
Johnnie Davis, Penny Singleton, Anthony Averill, Osca
O'Shea, Wright Kramer, Emmett Vogan, Joe Cunningham
Ferris Taylor, Stuart Holmes, Max Hoffman, Jr., Janet Shaw
Peggy Moran, Sidney Bracy, Rosella Towne, Kay Winter
(Dorothy Comingore), Jan Holm, Sally Gage, Alice Connor
18 minutes.

7. *Girls on Probation*. Warner Brothers, 1938. *Willian*
McGann. Jane Bryan, Ronald Reagan, Henry O'Neill, Eliza
beth Risdon, Esther Dale, Sig Rumann, Sheila Bromley
Joseph Crehan, Anthony Averill, Dorothy Peterson, Larry
Williams, James Nolan, Arthur Hoyt, Lenita Lane, Peggy
Shannon, Janet Shaw, Kate Lawson, Brenda Fowler, Pierr
Watkin, Ed Keane, Dickie Jones, Emory Parnell, Joh
Hamilton, Ed Stanley, Vera Lewis, Max Hoffman, Jr., Ralph
Sanford, Lane Chandler, George Offerman, Jr., Jack Mower
Nat Carr. 63 minutes.

8. *Beau Geste*. Paramount, 1939. *William A. Wellman*
Gary Cooper, Ray Milland, Robert Preston, Brian Donlevy, J.
Carroll Naish, Broderick Crawford, Albert Dekker, Jame
Stephenson, Donald O'Connor, Harold Huber, Ann Gillis
Heather Thatcher, Billy Cook, David Holt, Martin Spellman
Charles Barton, George P. Huntly, Harry Woods, James
Burke, Henry Brandon, George Chandler, Frank Dawson
Duke Green, Harry Worth, George Regas, Barry Macollum
Harvey Stephens, Stanley Andrews, Arthur Aylesworth

Thomas Jackson, Nestor Paiva, Francis McDonald. 120 minutes.

9. *Our Leading Citizen.* Paramount, 1939. *Alfred Santell.* Bob Burns, Joseph Allen, Jr., Elizabeth Patterson, Gene Lockhart, Kathleen Lockhart, Charles Bickford, Clarence Kolb, Paul Guilfoyle, Fay Helm, Otto Hoffman, Kathleen Sheldon, Hattie Noel, Monte Blue, James Kelso, Russell Hicks, Thomas Louden, Olaf Hytten, Frances Morris, Mae Busch, Max Wagner, Gaylor (Steve) Pendleton, Edward LeSaint, Heinie Conklin, Syd Saylor, Ethan Laidlaw. 87 minutes.

10. *$1,000 a Touchdown.* Paramount, 1939. *James Hogan.* Martha Raye, Joe E. Brown, Eric Blore, John Hartley, Syd Saylor, Don Wilson, Joyce Mathews, Tom Dugan, Matt McHugh, Josef Swickard, Hugh Sothern, George McKay, Adrian Morris, Ed Gargan, Dewey Robinson, William Haade, Grace Goodall, Frank M. Thomas, Jimmy Conlin, Emmett Vogan, Jack Perrin, Fritzi Brunette, Phil Dunham, Gertrude Astor, D'Arcy Corrigan, Constantine Romanoff, Charles Middleton, Dot Farley, John Hart, Cheryl Walker, Wanda McKay. 71 minutes.

11. *Among the Living.* Paramount, 1941. *Stuart Heisler.* Albert Dekker, Harry Carey, Frances Farmer, Maude Eburne, Jean Phillips, Gordon Jones, Archie Twitchell, Dorothy Sebastian, Harlan Briggs, Ernest Whitman, Frank M. Thomas, Rod Cameron, Catherine Craig, William Stack, Ella Neal, George Turner, Richard Webb, John Kellogg, Lane Chandler, Clarence Muse. 68 minutes.

12. *Sis Hopkins.* Republic, 1941. *Joseph Santley.* Judy Canova, Charles Butterworth, Bob Crosby and Orchestra with the Bobcats, Katharine Alexander, Jerry Colonna, Elvia Allman, Lynn Merrick, Mary Ainslee, Carol Adams, Charles Coleman, Tim Ryan, Andrew Tombes, Byron Foulger, Charles Lane, Joe Devlin, Hardie Albright, Elliot Sullivan, Hal Price, Anne O'Neal. 97 minutes.

13. *Adam Had Four Sons.* Columbia, 1941, *Gregory Ratoff.* Ingrid Bergman, Warner Baxter, Richard Denning, Fay Wray, Johnny Downs, Helen Westley, June Lockhart, Robert Shaw, Renie Riano, Charles Lind, Steven Muller, Gilbert Emery, Wallace Chadwell, Pietro Sosso, Clarence Muse, Billy Ray, Bobby Walberg. 80 minutes.

14. *Reap the Wild Wind.* Paramount, 1942. *Cecil B. De-*

Mille. Paulette Goddard, Ray Milland, John Wayne, Robert Preston, Raymond Massey, Lynne Overman, Charles Bickford, Louise Beavers, Martha O'Driscoll, Janet Beecher, Elizabeth Risdon, Barbara Britton, Hedda Hopper, Victor Kilian, Walter Hampden, Milburn Stone, Byron Foulger, James Flavin, Julia Faye, Maurice Costello, Gertrude Astor, Hope Landin, Sarah Edwards, Ben Carter, Oscar Polk, Monte Blue, Victor Varconi, William Cabanne, Wee Willie Davis (voice dubbed by Akim Tamiroff), Mildred Harris, Raymond Hatton, Mary Currier, Keith Richards, Lane Chandler, Harry Woods, Davison Clark, Lou Merrill, Frank M. Thomas, Ameda Lambert, J. Farrell MacDonald, Constantine Romanoff, Fred Graham, Eugene Jackson, Forrest Taylor, George Melford, Nestor Paiva, William Haade, Cyril McLaglen, John St. Polis, Stanhope Wheatcroft, Robert Homans, Frank Shannon, Dick Alexander, Emory Parnell, Stanley Andrews, Ottola Nesmith, D'Arcy Miller, Bruce Warren, Buddy Pepper, Leota Lorraine, Claire McDowell, Dorothy Sebastian, Ynez Seabury, Melville Ruick, Jack Luden, Ralph Dunn, Dale Van Sickel, Ethan Laidlaw, Stubby Kruger, Billy Elmer, Christian J. Frank, Max Davidson; narrated by Cecil B. DeMille. 124 minutes.

15. *The Forest Rangers.* Paramount, 1942. *George Marshall.* Fred MacMurray, Paulette Goddard, Albert Dekker, Lynne Overman, Eugene Pallette, Regis Toomey. James Brown, Clem Bevans, Rod Cameron, Chester Clute, Sarah Edwards, Kenneth Griffith, Keith Richards. William Cabanne, Jimmy Conlin, Harry Woods, Wade Boteler, Arthur Loft, George Chandler, Tim Ryan, Monte Blue, Robert Homans, Byron Foulger, Robert Kent, Jack Mulhall, James Millican, George Turner, Bob Kortman, Karin Booth. 87 minutes.

16. *I Married a Witch.* United Artists, 1942. *René Clair.* Fredric March, Veronica Lake, Robert Benchley, Cecil Kellaway, Elizabeth Patterson, Robert Warwick, Mary Field. Eily Malyon, Emma Dunn, Nora Cecil, Robert Greig, Viola Moore, Emory Parnell, Marie Blake, Helen St. Rayner, Aldrich Bowker, Ann Carter, Harry Tyler, Ralph Peters, William Haade, Wade Boteler, Ralph Dunn, Alan Bridge, Jack Luden, Peter Leeds, James Millican, Chester Conklin, Monte Blue, Robert Homans, Billy Bevan, Reed Hadley. 82 minutes.

17. *A Letter from Bataan*. Paramount, 1942. *William H. Pine*. Richard Arlen, Janet Beecher, Jimmy Lydon, Joe Sawyer, Keith Richards, Esther Dale, Will Wright. 15 minutes.

18. *Star Spangled Rhythm*. Paramount, 1942. *George Marshall*. Walter Abel, Eddie (Rochester) Anderson, Irving Bacon, William Bendix, Gladys Blake, Karin Booth, Eddie Bracken, Virginia Brissac, Rod Cameron, Macdonald Carey, Don Castle, Walter Catlett, Chester Clute, Jerry Colonna, Bing Crosby, Gary Crosby, Cass Daley, Barney Dean, Edgar Dearing, Albert Dekker, Cecil B. DeMille, Eddie Dew, Dona Drake, Ellen Drew, Tom Dugan, Katherine Dunham, Frank Faylen, Edward Fielding, Susanna Foster, Eva Gabor, Frances Gifford, Paulette Goddard, the Golden Gate Quartette, Dorothy Granger, William Haade, Sterling Holloway, Maynard Holmes, Bob Hope, Jack Hope, Betty Hutton, Eddie Johnson, Johnnie Johnston, Cecil Kellaway, Alan Ladd, Veronica Lake, Gil Lamb, Dorothy Lamour, Arthur Loft, Richard Loo, Jimmy Lydon, Diana Lynn, Fred MacMurray, Marion Martin, Mary Martin, Matt McHugh, Ray Milland, James Millican, Victor Moore, Ralph Murphy, Lynne Overman, Mabel Paige, Barbara Pepper, Paul Porcasi, Peter Potter, Dick Powell, Robert Preston, Anne Revere, Marjorie Reynolds, Betty Jane Rhodes, Keith Richards, Slim and Slam, Charles Smith. Woody Strode, Preston Sturges, Franchot Tone, Arthur Treacher, Ernest Truex, Vera Zorina, Walter Dare Wahl and Company. 99 minutes.

19. *Hit Parade of 1943*. Republic, 1943. *Albert S. Rogell*. John Carroll, Eve Arden, Gail Patrick, Walter Catlett, Melville Cooper, Mary Treen, Astrid Allwyn, Tim Ryan, Tom Kennedy, Grandon Rhodes, Dorothy Dandridge, Wally Vernon, Warren Ashe, Addison Richards, Ken Niles, Bud Jamison, Paul Newlan, Nicodemus Stewart, Philip Van Zandt, Milton Kibbee, Olaf Hytten, Edwin Mills, Hooper Atchley, Jack Williams, Freddy Martin and Orchestra, Count Basie and Orchestra, Ray McKinley and Orchestra, Pops and Louie (Albert Whitman and Louis Williams), the Three Cheers, Chinita (Marin), the Music Maids, the Golden Gate Quartette, Sunshine Sammy Morrison. 90 minutes.

20. *Young and Willing*. United Artists, 1943. *Edward H. Griffith*. William Holden, Eddie Bracken, Barbara Britton, Robert Benchley, Martha O'Driscoll, Mabel Paige, Florence MacMichael, James Brown, Jay Fassett, Paul Hurst, Olin

Howland, Billy Bevan, Cheryl Walker, Kenneth Griffith, William Cabanne, Fay Helm. 82 minutes.

21. *Jack London*. United Artists, 1943. *Alfred Santell*. Michael O'Shea, Osa Massen, Virginia Mayo, Harry Davenport, Frank Craven, Ralph Morgan, Louise Beavers, Regis Toomey, Hobart Cavanaugh, Morgan Conway, Jonathan Hale, Olin Howland, Paul Hurst, Pierre Watkin, Richard Loo, Sarah Padden, Leonard Strong, Dick Curtis, Albert Van Antwerp, Ernie Adams, John Kelly, Robert Homans, Edward Earle, Arthur Loft, Lumsden Hare, Brooks Benedict, Mei Lee Foo, Robert Katcher, Paul Fung, Charlie Lung, Bruce Wong, Eddie Lee, John Fisher, Jack Roper, Sven Hugo Borg, Sid Dalbrook, Davison Clark, Harold Minjir, Roy Gordon, Torben Meyer, Charlene Newman, Edmund Cobb, Wallis Clark, Charles Miller, Evelyn Finley, Rose Plummer. 92 minutes.

22. *Skirmish on the Home Front*. Paramount, for U. S. Government Office of War Information, 1944. Alan Ladd, Betty Hutton, William Bendix. 13 minutes.

23. *And Now Tomorrow*. Paramount, 1944. *Irving Pichel*. Alan Ladd, Loretta Young, Barry Sullivan, Beulah Bondi, Cecil Kellaway, Grant Mitchell, Helen Mack, Darryl Hickman, Anthony Caruso, Jonathan Hale, Conrad Binyon, Connie Leon, George M. Carleton, Leo Bulgakov, Mary Field, Frank Mayo, Ottola Nesmith, Edwin Stanley, Catherin Craig, James Millican, Minerva Urecal, Betty Farrington, Edith Evanson, Harry Holman, Bobby Barber, Ann Carter, Merrill Rodin, Eleanor Donahue, Constance Purdy, Olin Howland, Byron Foulger, Doodles Weaver, Alec Craig, Bunny Sunshine, Doris Dowling, Mae Clark. 84 minutes.

24. *The Fighting Seabees*. Republic, 1944. *Edward Ludwig*. John Wayne, Dennis O'Keefe, William Frawley, Leonid Kinskey, Grant Withers, J.M. Kerrigan, Paul Fix, Addison Richards, Duncan Renaldo, Ben Welden, William Forrest, Jay Norris, Ernest Golm, Adele Mara, Charles D. Brown, Chief Thundercloud, William Hall, Roy Barcroft, Jean Fenwick, Charles Trowbridge, Nora Lane, Tom London, LeRoy Mason, Herbert Heyes, Forbes Murray, Bud Geary, Terry Frost, Paul Parry, Alex Havier, John James, Crane Whitley, Hal Taliaferro. 100 minutes.

25. *The Hairy Ape*. United Artists, 1944. *Alfred Santell*. William Bendix, John Loder, Dorothy Comingore, Roman

Bohnen, Alan Napier, Tom Fadden, Raphael Storm, Francis Pierlot, Ralph Dunn, Charles Cane, Charles LaTorre, Gisela Werbiseck, Don Zolaya, Dick Baldwin, Mary Zavian, George Sorrel, Paul Weigel, Egon Brecher, Carmen Rachel, Jonathan Lee, William Halligan, Tommy Hughes, Bob Perry, Ruth Robinson, Rod DeMedici, Eddie Kane. 92 minutes.

26. *Deadline at Dawn*. RKO, 1946. *Harold Clurman*. Bill Williams, Paul Lukas, Joseph Calleia, Osa Massen, Lola Lane, Jerome Cowan, Marvin Miller, Roman Bohnen, Joe Sawyer, Constance Worth, Steven Geray, Joseph Crehan, William Challee, Jason Robards, Sr., Emory Parnell, Lee Phelps, Ernie Adams, Myrna Dell, George Tyne, Larry Thompson, Ed Gargan, Dorothy Granger, Eddy Chandler, Al Eben, Phil Warren, John Elliott, Louis Quince, Alan Ward, Dick Elliott, Earle Hodgins, Walter Soderling, Virginia Farmer, Al Bridge, Ralph Dunn, Billy Bletcher, Peter Breck. 83 minutes.

27. *Canyon Passage*. Universal, 1946. *Jacques Tourneur*. Dana Andrews, Brian Donlevy, Hoagy Carmichael, Patricia Roc, Ward Bond, Rose Hobart, Lloyd Bridges, Andy Devine, Tad and Denny Devine, Stanley Ridges, Fay Holden, Victor Cutler, Dorothy Peterson, Onslow Stevens, Halliwell Hobbes, James Cardwell, Peter Whitney, Chester Clute, Harry Shannon, Harlan Briggs, Eddie Dunn, Frank Ferguson, Chief Yowlachie, Dick Alexander, Gene Roth, Ralph Peters, Erville Anderson, Francis McDonald, Virginia Patton, Ray Teal, Mary Newton, Jack Ingram, Rex Lease, Janet Ann Gallow. 90 minutes.

28. *Smash-Up, The Story of a Woman*. Universal-International, 1947. *Stuart Heisler*. Lee Bowman, Eddie Albert, Marsha Hunt, Carl Esmond, Carleton Young, Charles D. Brown, Sharyn Payne, Robert Shayne, Janet Murdoch, Tom Chatterton, George Meeker, Larry Blake, Bess Flowers, George Meader, Ruth Sanderson, Barbara Woodell, Alice Fleming, Virginia Carroll, Nanette Vallon, Dorothy Christy, Al Hill, James Craven, Frances Morris, William Gould, Vivien Oakland, Ernie Adams, Ethel Wales, Noel Neill; the voice of Joan Fulton (Shawlee), the singing voices of Peg LaCentra and Hal Derwin. 113 minutes.

29. *They Won't Believe Me*. RKO, 1947. *Irving Pichel*. Robert Young, Jane Greer, Rita Johnson, Tom Powers, George Tyne, Don Beddoe, Frank Ferguson, Harry Harvey,

Janet Shaw, Anthony Caruso, Milton Parsons, Lillian Bronson, Jack Rice, Robert Scott, Glen Knight, Ellen Corby, Wilton Graff, Byron Foulger, Elena Warren, Dot Farley, Herbert Heywood, Paul Maxey, Frank Pharr, Irene Tedrow, Bert LeBaron, Harry Stang, Lovyss Bradley. 95 minutes.

30. *The Lost Moment*. Universal-International, 1947. *Martin Gabel*. Robert Cummings, Agnes Moorehead, Joan Lorring, John Archer, Minerva Urecal, Eduardo Ciannelli, Frank Puglia, William Edmunds, Martin Garralaga, Eugene Borden, Nicholas Khadarik, Julian Rivero, Lillian Molieri, Chris Drake. 89 minutes.

31. *Tap Roots*. Universal-International, 1948. *George Marshall*. Van Heflin, Ward Bond, Boris Karloff, Julie London, Whitfield Connor, Richard Long, Arthur Shields, Griff Barnett, Sondra Rogers, Ruby Dandridge, Russell Simpson, Gregg Barton, Jonathan Hale, Arthur Space, Kay Medford, William Haade, Harry Cording, George Lewis, Helen Mowery, William Challee, John James, Keith Richards, Hank Worden, Elmo Lincoln. 109 minutes.

32. *The Saxon Charm*. Universal-International, 1948. *Claude Binyon*. Robert Montgomery, John Payne, Audrey Totter, Henry (Harry) Morgan, Harry Von Zell, Heather Angel, Cara Williams, Chill Wills, John Baragrey, Addison Richards, Philip Van Zandt, Maris Wrixon, Barbara Billingsley, Curt Conway, Fay Baker, Martin Garralaga, Eula Guy, Clarence Straight, Bert Davidson, Peter Brocco, Mauritz Hugo, Robert Cabal, Kathleen Freeman, Barbara Challis. 88 minutes.

33. *Tulsa*. Eagle-Lion, 1949. *Stuart Heisler*. Robert Preston, Pedro Armendariz, Chill Wills, Lloyd Gough, Paul E. Burns, Ed Begley, Lola Albright, Harry Shannon, Jimmy Conlin, Roland Jack, Pierre Watkin, Dick Wessel, Tom Dugan, John Dehner, Charles D. Brown, Selmer Jackson, Chief Yowlachie, Lane Chandler, Iron Eyes Cody, Larry Keating, Joseph Crehan, Nolan Leary, Thomas Browne Henry. 88 minutes.

34. *House of Strangers*. 20th Century-Fox, 1949. *Joseph L. Mankiewicz*. Edward G. Robinson, Richard Conte, Luther Adler, Efrem Zimbalist, Jr., Esther Minciotti, Debra Paget, Hope Emerson, Paul Valentine, Diana Douglas, Tito Vuolo, Alberto Morin, Sid Tomack, John Kellogg, Argentina Brunetti, Thomas Browne Henry, David Wolfe, Ann Morrison, Dolores Parker, Mario Siletti, Herb Vigran, Philip Van Zandt,

Frank Jaquet; the singing voice of Lawrence Tibbett. 101 minutes.

35. *My Foolish Heart.* Goldwyn-RKO, 1949. *Mark Robson.* Dana Andrews, Kent Smith, Robert Keith, Jessie Royce Landis, Lois Wheeler, Gigi Perreau, Karin Booth, Martha Mears, Edna Holland, Philip Pine, Barbara Woodell, Marietta Canty, Jerry Paris, Tod Karns, Regina Wallace, Ed Peil, Sr., Kerry O'Day, Ray Hyke, Marcel de la Brosse, Phyllis Coates. 98 minutes.

36. *I'd Climb the Highest Mountain.* 20th Century-Fox, 1951. *Henry King.* William Lundigan, Rory Calhoun, Barbara Bates, Alexander Knox, Lynn Bari, Gene Lockhart, Ruth Donnelly, Jean Lockhart, Ruth Donnelly, Jean Inness, Kathleen Lockhart, Jerry Vandiver, Richard Wilson, Dorothea Carolyn Sims, Thomas Syfan, Grady Starnes, Kay and Fay Fogg. 88 minutes.

37. *Rawhide.* 20th Century-Fox, 1951. *Henry Hathaway.* Tyrone Power, Hugh Marlowe, Dean Jagger, Jack Elam, Edgar Buchanan, George Tobias, Jeff Corey, James Millican, Louis Jean Heydt, Ken Tobey, Edith Evanson, Judy Ann Dunn, William Haade, Si Jenks, Max Terhune, Dan White, Milton R. Corey, Sr., Robert Adler, Howard Negley, Vincent Neptune, Walter Sande, Dick Curtis. 86 minutes.

38. *David and Bathsheba.* 20th Century-Fox, 1951. *Henry King.* Gregory Peck, Raymond Massey, Jayne Meadows, Kieron Moore, James Robertson Justice, John Sutton, Francis X. Bushman, Paula Morgan, Teddy Infuhr, Gwyneth (Gwen) Verdon, Walter Talun, Dennis Hoey, George Zucco, Lumsden Hare, Holmes Herbert, Leo Pessin, Gilbert Barnett, John Burton, Allan Stone, Paul Newlan, Dan White, David Newell, Shepard Menken, John Dodsworth. 153 minutes.

39. *I Can Get It for You Wholesale.* 20th Century-Fox, 1951. *Michael Gordon.* Dan Dailey, George Sanders, Sam Jaffe, Vickie Cummings, Barbara Whiting, Randy Stuart, Mary Phillips, Marvin Kaplan, Harry Von Zell, Richard Lane, Steven Geray, Charles Lane, Marion Marshall, Marjorie Hoshelle, Tamara Shayne, Ross Elliott, Benna Bard, Bess Flowers, Jayne Hazard, Aline Towne, Eda Reis Merin, Ed Max, David Wolfe, Jan Kayne, Shirlee Allard. 91 minutes.

40. *With a Song in My Heart.* 20th Century-Fox, 1952. *Walter Lang.* David Wayne, Rory Calhoun, Thelma Ritter, Robert Wagner, Helen Westcott, Una Merkel, Lyle Talbot,

Max Showalter, Robert Easton, Leif Erickson, Richard Allan, Carlos Molina, Nestor Paiva, Beverly Thompson, Emmett Vogan, Maude Wallace, Eddie Firestone, George Offerman, Stanley Logan, Frank Sully, Billy Daniels, Mary Newton, Dick Winslow, Paul Maxey, Carol Savage, Adele Longmire, John Vosper, Shirley Tegge, Douglas Evans; the singing voice of Jane Froman. 117 minutes.

41. *The Snows of Kilimanjaro*. 20th Century-Fox, 1952. *Henry King*. Gregory Peck, Ava Gardner, Hildegarde Neff, Leo G. Carroll, Torin Thatcher, Ava Norring, Helene Stanley, Marcel Dalio, Richard Allan, Lisa Ferraday, Ivan Lebedeff, Vincente Gomez, Martin Garralaga, Victor Wood, John Dodsworth, Bert Freed, Paul Thompson, Leonard Carey, Charles Bates, Emmett Smith, Agnes Laury, Monique Chantal, Janine Grandel, Maya Van Horn, Julian Rivero, Ernest and Arthur Brunner. 114 minutes.

42. *The Lusty Men*. RKO, 1952. *Nicholas Ray*. Robert Mitchum, Arthur Kennedy, Arthur Hunnicutt, Frank Faylen, Walter Coy, Carol Nugent, Lorna Thayer, Maria Hart, Karen King, Eleanor Todd, Jimmy Dodd, Burt Mustin, Sam Flint, Riley Hill, Robert Bray, Sheb Wooley, Marshall Reed, Paul E. Burns, Dennis Moore, George Wallace, Chuck Roberson, Mike Ragan, Edward McNally, Mike Lally, Dick Crockett, Les Sanborn, Hazel (Sonny) Boyne, Chili Williams, Richard Reeves, Roy Glenn, Emmett Lynn, Glenn Strange, Denver Pyle, Frank Matts, Wally Russell, George Sherwood. 112 minutes.

43. *The President's Lady*. 20th Century-Fox. 1953. *Henry Levin*. Charlton Heston, Fay Bainter, John McIntire, Margaret Wycherly, Carl Betz, Whitfield Connor, Trudy Marshall, Gladys Hurlbut, Nina Varela, Charles Dingle, James Best, Willis Bouchey, Jim Davis, Dayton Lummis, Ruth Attaway, Ralph Dumke, Selmer Jackson, Howard Negley, Robert B. Williams, Harris Brown, Zon Murray, Juanita Evers, George Melford, Ann Morrison, William Walker, Sam McDaniel, Hellen Van Tuyl, Tennessee Jim. 96 minutes.

44. *White Witch Doctor*. 20th Century-Fox, 1953. *Henry Hathaway*. Robert Mitchum, Walter Slezak, Mashood Ajala, Joseph C. Narcisse, Michael Ansara, Timothy Carey, Elzie Emanuel, Otis Greene, Paul Thompson, Myrtle Anderson, Naaman Brown, Charles Gemora, Everett Brown, Dorothy

Hams, Michael Granger, Floyd Shackleford, Louis Polliman Brown, Leo C. Aldridge-Milas. 95 minutes.

45. *Demetrius and the Gladiators*. 20th Century-Fox, 1954. *Delmer Daves*. Victor Mature, Michael Rennie, Debra Paget, Anne Bancroft, Jay Robinson, Richard Egan, Ernest Borgnine, Barry Jones, William Marshall, Charles Evans, Jeff York, Carmen deLavallade, Selmer Jackson, Dayton Lummis, Woody Strode, Paul Richards, Everett Glass, Karl Davis, John Cliff, Fred Graham, George Eldredge, Pete Mamakos, Shepard Menken, Paul Newland, Mickey Simpson, Julie Newmeyer (Newmar); scene clip from *The Robe* showing Richard Burton and Jean Simmons; the voice of Cameron Mitchell. 101 minutes.

46. *Garden of Evil*. 20th Century-Fox, 1954. *Henry Hathaway*. Gary Cooper, Richard Widmark, Hugh Marlowe, Cameron Mitchell, Rita Moreno, Victor Manuel Mendoza, Fernando Wagner, Arturo Soto Rangel, Manuel Donde, Antonio Brihesca, Salvador Tenobra. 100 minutes.

47. *Untamed*. 20th Century-Fox, 1955. *Henry King*. Tyrone Power, Richard Egan, Agnes Moorehead, Rita Moreno, John Justin, Hope Emerson, Brad Dexter, Henry O'Neill, Kevin and Brian Corcoran, Philip Van Zandt, Louis Mercier, Trude Wyler, Charles Evans, Eleanor Audley, Emmett Smith, Alberto Morin, Paul Thompson, Jack Macy, Robert Adler, John Dodsworth, Alexander D. Havemann, John Carlyle, Edward Mundy, Catherine and Christian Pasques, Louis Polliman Brown, Bobby and Gary Diamond, Harry Carter, Walter Flannery, Ken Dibbs, Michael Ross, Leonard Carey, Henry Rowland, Forest Burns. 111 minutes.

48. *Soldier of Fortune*. 20th Century-Fox, 1955. *Edward Dmytryk*. Clark Gable, Gene Barry, Michael Rennie, Anna Sten, Tom Tully, Jack Kruschen, Alex D'Arcy, Russell Collins, Richard Loo, Victor Sen Yung, Mel Welles, Jack Raine, Leo Gordon, Soo Yong, Frank Tang, George Wallace, Robert Burton, Frances Fong, Alex Finlayson, Noel Toy, Grace Chang, Charles Davis, Beal Wong, Robert Quarry, Virginia Lee, Barry Bernard, Ivis Goulding. 96 minutes.

49. *I'll Cry Tomorrow*. MGM, 1955. *Daniel Mann*. Jo Van Fleet, Richard Conte, Eddie Albert, Don Taylor, Margo, Virginia Gregg, Don Barry, Carole Ann Campbell, Ruth Storey (Conte), Peter Leeds, David Kasday, Veda Ann

Borg, Tol Avery, Nora Marlowe, Voltair Perkins, Bob Dix, Peter Brocco, Gail Ganley, Ken Patterson, Harlan Warde, Charles Tannen, Eve McVeagh, Cheerio Meredith, Tim Carey, Jack Daley, George Lloyd, Stanley Farrar, Anthony Jochim, Kay English, Henry Blake, Ralph Edwards. 117 minutes.

50. *The Conqueror*. RKO, 1956. *Dick Powell*. John Wayne, Agnes Moorehead, Pedro Armendariz, Thomas Gomez, John Hoyt, William Conrad, Ted deCorsia, Richard Loo, Lee Van Cleef, Peter Mamakos, Leslie Bradley, Sylvia Lewis, Jarma Lewis, Fred Graham, George E. Stone, Jeanne Gerson, Leo Gordon, Phil Arnold, Torben Meyer, Michael Granger, Pat Tiernan, Ken Terrell, Alberto Morin, Billy Curtis, Gregg Barton, the Chivwit Indian Tribe. 111 minutes.

51. *Top Secret Affair*. Warner Brothers, 1957. *H.C. Potter*. Kirk Douglas, Paul Stewart, Jim Backus, Roland Winters, John Cromwell, Charles Lane, A.E. Gould-Porter, Michael Fox, Frank Gerstle, Edna Holland, James Flavin, Ivan Triesault, Franco Corsaro, Lyn Osborn, Hal Dawson, Jonathan Hole, Charles Meredith, Sid Chatton. 100 minutes.

52. *I Want to Live!* United Artists, 1958. *Robert Wise*. Simon Oakland, Virginia Vincent, Theodore Bikel, Alice Backes, Wesley Lau, Dabbs Greer, Philip Coolidge, Gage Clark, Russell Thorson, James Philbrook, Lou Krugman, Joe DeSantis, Raymond Bailey, Marion (Marshall) Donen, Peter Breck, Brett Halsey, Jack Weston, Evelyn Scott, Olive Blakeney, Lorna Thayer, Hope Summers, Gertrude Flynn, John Marley, George Putnam, Helen Kleeb, Bartlett Robinson, Stafford Repp, Gavin McLeod, Leonard Bell, Bill Stout, Jason Johnson, Rusty Lane, S. John Launer, Dan Sheridan, Wendell Holmes, Gerry Mulligan, Shelly Manne, Art Farmer, Bud Shank, Red Mitchell, Frank Rosolino, Pete Jolly. 120 minutes.

53. *Woman Obsessed*. 20th Century-Fox, 1959. *Henry Hathaway*. Stephen Boyd, Theodore Bikel, Dennis Holmes, Barbara Nichols, Florence MacMichael, Ken Scott, James Philbrook, Arthur Franz, Jack Raine, Mary Carroll, Fred Graham, Mike Lally, Al Austin, Richard Monahan, Dainty Doris, Harry "Duke" Johnson, Tommy Farrell, Freeman Morse, Jimmy Ames. 103 minutes.

54. *Thunder in the Sun*. Paramount, 1959. *Russell Rouse*.

Jeff Chandler, Jacques Bergerac, Blanche Yurka, Carl Esmond, Fortunio Bonanova, Bertrand Castelli, Felix Locher, Veda Ann Borg, Pedro DeCordoba, Jr., Michele Marty, Albert Villasain, June Chalkley (Hayward's stepdaughter). 81 minutes.

55. *The Marriage-Go-Round.* 20th Century-Fox, 1960. *Walter Lang.* James Mason, Julie Newmar, Robert Paige, June Clayworth, Joe Kirkwood, Jr., Trax Colton, Mary Patton, Everett Glass, Ben Astar, John Bryant, Tony Young, Quinn Redeker, Bruce Tegner, Mark Bailey, Ann Benton; title song sung by Tony Bennett. 98 minutes.

56. *Ada.* MGM, 1961. *Daniel Mann.* Dean Martin, Wilfrid Hyde-White, Ralph Meeker, Martin Balsam, Frank Maxwell, Connie Sawyer, Larry Gates, Ford Rainey, Charles Watts, Robert F. Simon, William Zuckert, Richard Benedict, Kathryn Card, Robert Burton, Helen Beverly, Amy Douglass, Helen Kleeb, Peg LaCentra, Ray Teal, Bill Walker, Louise Lorimer, Sherry O'Neil, J. Edward McKinley, Mary Treen, Emory Parnell, Anthony Jochim, Helen Brown, Arthur Lovejoy, John Hart, Gene Roth, Fred Coby, Helen Wallace, Terry Frost, Edgar Dearing, Ken Christy, Gloria Pall, Ed Prentiss, Robert Bice, Harry Stang, Dick Winslow, Wilson Wood, Harry Dunn, Herbert Lytton, Carol Forman. 109 minutes.

57. *Back Street.* Universal-International, 1961. *David Miller.* John Gavin, Vera Miles, Virginia Grey, Reginald Gardiner, Charles Drake, Natalie Schafer, Tammy Marihugh, Robert Eyer, Dick Kallman, Joyce Meadows, Alex Gerry, Hayden Rorke, Doreen McLean, Karen Norris, Hanna Landy, John Holland, Maida Severn, Eddie Foster, Ruthie and Betsy Robinson, Louise Arthur, Doris Fesette, Iphigenie Castiglioni, Jeanne Manet, Mary Lawrence, Albert Carrier, Lilyan Chauvin, Veola Vonn, Joseph Mell, Yale Wexler, Don Dillaway. 107 minutes.

58. *I Thank a Fool.* MGM, 1962. *Robert Stevens.* Peter Finch, Diane Cilento, Cyril Cusack, Kieron Moore, Athene Seyler, Richard Wattis, Laurence Naismith, Brenda deBanzie, J.G. Devlin, Joan Hickson, Yolande Turner, Joan Benham, Miriam Karlin, Clive Morton, Richard Leech, Marguerite Brennan, Judith Furse, Peter Sallis. 100 minutes.

59. *Stolen Hours.* United Artists, 1963. *Daniel Petrie.* Michael Craig, Edward Judd, Diane Baker, Paul Rogers,

Robert Bacon, Joan Newell, Peter Madden, Gwen Nelson, Paul Stassino, Jerry Desmonde, Ellen McIntosh, Chet Baker. 97 minutes.

60. *Where Love Has Gone.* Embassy-Paramount, 1964. *Edward Dmytryk.* Bette Davis, Michael Connors, Joey Heatherton, Jane Greer, Anne Seymour, DeForest Kelley, George Macready, Ann Doran, Willis Bouchey, Anthony Caruso, Whit Bissell, Walter Reed, Bartlett Robinson, Jack Greening, Olga Sutcliffe, Howard Wendell, Colin Kenny; title song sung by Jack Jones. 114 minutes.

61. *The Honey Pot.* United Artists, 1967. *Joseph L. Mankiewicz.* Rex Harrison, Maggie Smith, Cliff Robertson, Edie Adams, Capucine, Adolfo Celi, Luigi Scavran, Hugh Manning, David Dodimead, Herschel Bernardi (cut from final print). 131 minutes.

62. *Think 20th.* 20th Century-Fox, 1967. *Richard Fleischer.* Julie Andrews, Richard Attenborough, Candice Bergen, Olinka Berova, Paul Burke, Michael Caine, Peter Cook, Richard Crenna, Bette Davis, Patty Duke, Judy Geeson, Rosemary Harris, Linda Harrison, Rex Harrison, Charlton Heston, Edward Judd, Deborah Kerry, Steve McQueen, Dudley Moore, Anthony Newley, David Niven, Barbara Parkins, Eric Portman, Giovanna Ralli, Joyce Redman, Beryl Reid, Rachel Roberts, Gena Rowlands, Tony Scotti, Frank Sinatra, Jill St. John, Sharon Tate, Raquel Welch; narrated by Richard D. Zanuck. 30 minutes.

63. *Valley of the Dolls.* 20th Century-Fox, 1967. *Mark Robson.* Barbara Parkins, Patty Duke, Sharon Tate, Paul Burke, Tony Scotti, Lee Grant, Martin Milner, Charles Drake, Alex Davion, Naomi Stevens, Robert H. Harris, Robert Viharo, Richard Angarola, Jeanne Gerson, Corinna Tsopei, Robert Street, Margot Stevenson, Norman Burton, David Arkin, Gil Peterson, Leslie McRae, Marvin Hamlisch, Jason Johnson, Frank Coghlan, Jr., Ernest Harada, Dorothy Neuman, Ted Stanhope, Judith Lowry, Gertrude Flynn, Roy Fitzell, Joey Bishop, George Jessel, Jacqueline Susann; theme song sung by Dionne Warwick. 123 minutes.

64. *Heat of Anger.* New CBS Friday Night Movies/ Stonehenge Productions-Metromedia Producers Corp., 1972. *Don Taylor.* James Stacy, Lee J. Cobb, Fritz Weaver, Bettye Ackerman, Jennifer Penny, Mills Watson, Ray Simms, Tyne

Daly, Lynnette Mettey, Lucille Benson, Arnold Mesches, Noah Keen, Inez Pedroza. 75 minutes.

65. *The Revengers.* Cinema Center, 1972. *Daniel Mann.* William Holden, Ernest Borgnine, Woody Strode, Arthur Hunnicutt, Roger Hanin, Scott Holden, Jorge Luke, Rene Koldehoff, Warren Vanders, Lorraine Chanel, Jorge Martinez de Hoyos, Rosario Granados, Rosa Furman, Raul Prieto, John Kelly, James Daughton, Larry Pennell, Manuel Alvarado, Bob Hall, Charles Fawcett, Ivan Scott, Lance Winston, Jose Espinoza, Phyllis Horney, Myron Levine, Eduardo Noriega, Marco Arzate, Sergio Calderon, Jorge Russek, Jose Chavez Trowe. 110 minutes.

66. *Say Goodbye, Maggie Cole.* ABC Wednesday Movie of the Week/Spelling-Goldberg Production, 1972. *Jud Taylor.* Darren McGavin, Beverly Garland, Dane Clark, Michael Constantine, Jeanette Nolan, Michele Nichols, Madie Norman, Richard Anderson, Frank Puglia, Harry Basch, Leigh Adams, Jan Peters, Robert Cleavers; the singing voice of Dusty Springfield. 75 minutes.

INDEX

Adams, Edie, 167
Adamson, Harold, 51, 76
Adler, Buddy, 123
Adler, Luther, 88, 89
Agee, James, 27, 78
Ager, Cecilia, 30–31
Albert, Eddie, 12, 78, 129
Amfitheatrof, Daniele, 81, 88
Andrews, Dana, 71, 72, 93, 95, 96
Arden, Eve, 52–53, 180
Armendariz, Pedro, 87, 134
Ashland, Jack, 32, 77

Bacall, Lauren, 135, 184
Backus, Jim, 13, 82, 135
Bacon, Robert, 162, 163
Bancroft, Anne, 122, 161
Bari, Lynn, 101, 102
Barker, Gregory, 57, 112, 139, 140, 141, 142, 187, 193
Barker, Jess, 12, 56–60, 110, 126, 132, 152, 186–187
Barker, Timothy, 57, 112, 139, 140, 141, 142, 187, 192, 193
Barry, Donald (Red), 132, 133
Baxter, Anne, 100, 124
Beckley, Paul V., 119, 145
Begley, Ed, 87
Benchley, Robert, 49, 54
Bendix, William, 62, 64, 66
Bennett, Joan, 16, 71, 145, 180
Bergman, Ingrid, 30, 32
Berkeley, Busby, 17, 133
Bernhardt, Sarah, Foreword, 143
Bikel, Theodore, 147, 150
Bogart, Humphrey, 19, 135
Bond, Ward, 73, 84
Booth, Shirley, 114, 131
Borgnine, Ernest, 173, 175
Bowman, Lee, 74, 75, 77, 187
Boyer, Charles, 36, 153, 180
Bracken, Eddie, 50, 51
Brenon, Herbert, 21
Brokaw, Norman, 173, 175

Bronston, Samuel, 54, 55
Brown, Joe E., 23–24, 193
Bryan, Jane, 20
Buchanan, Edgar, 103, 104
Burnett, Carol, 157–158

Cagney, James, 132
Calhoun, Rory, 101, 113–114
Canova, Judy, 28–29
Carmichael, Hoagy, 71, 73
Carroll, John, 52–53, 60
Catlett, Walter, 51, 53
Chalkley, Floyd Eaton, 139–143, 158, 180, 182, 194
Chandler, Jeff, 151, 152
Chandler, Raymond, 62, 133
Checker, Chubby, 162
Cilento, Diane, 159
Clair, René, 47, 48, 49
Clurman, Harold, 69, 70
Cobb, Lee J., 175–178
Colbert, Claudette, 33, 87, 153
Colonna, Jerry, 28–29
Conlin, Jimmy, 87
Connolly, Mike, 126, 142
Connors, Michael, 164
Conte, Richard, 88–91, 129
Cooper, Gary, 21, 72, 123
Cooper, Jackie, 37, 50
Cortez, Stanley, 75, 156
Craig, Michael, 161, 162, 163
Crain, Jeanne, 54, 100, 110
Crawford, Joan, 14, 36, 56, 124, 133, 154, 158, 164, 171
Crowther, Bosley, 41, 63, 69, 87, 143, 152–153, 169
Cukor, George, 15, 16, 64, 149
Cummings, Robert, 80–82
Curtis, Tony, 59, 124, 176

Dailey, Dan, 106–108, 180
Darnell, Linda, 100, 124, 133
Daves, Delmer, 24, 123

210

211

ABOUT THE AUTHOR

Doug McClelland, the author of another book on the movies, *The Unkindest Cuts,* was born in Plainfield, N. J., and raised in Newark. He first observed writers in action during a high school summer vacation as an office boy at the Newark *Star-Ledger.* Later, he became Assistant Theater Editor of the Newark *Evening News,* and, in New York City, Editor of *Music Vendor* and *Record World* magazines. He has had articles published in such periodicals as *After Dark, Films and Filming, Film Fan Monthly, Films in Review, Filmograph, Screen Facts,* and *The Many Worlds of Music,* and had two of his pieces in the anthology, *The Real Stars.* Mr. McClelland also has written the jacket notes for many record albums. Now freelancing, he resides in Bradley Beach, N. J.